VOLUME 443   MAY 1979

THE ANNALS

of The American Academy *of* Political
and Social Science

(ISSN 0002-7162)

RICHARD D. LAMBERT, *Editor*

RALPH B. GINSBERG, *Acting Editor*

ALAN W. HESTON, *Assistant Editor*

RISKS AND ITS TREATMENT: CHANGING SOCIETAL CONSEQUENCES

Special Editor of This Volume

GEORGE E. REJDA

Professor of Economics
University of Nebraska

PHILADELPHIA

Copy Editor

KIM HOLMES, PH.D.

International Standard Book Numbers (ISBN)

ISBN 0-87761-239-0, vol. 443, 1979; paper—$4.50
ISBN 0-87761-238-2, vol. 443, 1979; cloth—$5.50

*Issued bimonthly by The American Academy of Political and Social Science at 3937 Chestnut
St., Philadelphia, Pennsylvania 19104. Cost per year: $18.00 paperbound; $23.00 clothbound.
Add $2.00 to above rates for membership outside U.S.A. Second-class postage paid at Phila-
dephia and at additional mailing offices.*

*Claims for undelivered copies must be made within the month following the regular month
of publication. The publisher will supply missing copies when losses have been sustained in
transit and when the reserve stock will permit.*

Editorial and Business Offices, 3937 Chestnut Street, Philadelphia, Pennsylvania 19104.

CONTENTS

CONTENTS

UNITED STATES

SOCIOLOGY

CONTENTS

PREFACE

Man's quest for economic security is eternal, but the presence of risk in society is a substantial impediment towards attainment of that goal. What is risk? Scholars and risk theoreticians who have rigorously studied its meaning cannot agree on a common definition. Some common definitions of risk include the following:

1. Risk is the uncertainty of loss.
2. Risk is the chance of loss.
3. Risk is the possibility that a sentient entity can incur a loss.
4. Risk is the probability of an outcome which is different from the one expected.
5. Risk is the variation of actual from expected loss.

It is beyond the scope of this volume to evaluate each of the above definitions of risk. Careful analysis, however, reveals that underlying each concept of risk is the idea of potential harm or danger to the individual, to his family, or to his property. That is, certain forces and elements are present in society which, under the proper set of circumstances, can result in serious harm or possibly death to the individual, or loss to or destruction of his property. Moreover, certain new forces are emerging which have potentially severe consequences to society.

In this volume we shall focus attention on the changing impact of certain risks on society and the changing responsibility for the treatment of both new and existing risks.

More specifically, this volume analyzes the effects on society of changes in the nature and treatment of certain risks. The central thrust of the volume centers around the impact on society from shifts in the responsibility for the coverage of specified risks. Three major areas are emphasized: personal risks including premature death and old age, unemployment, poor health, occupational safety and health, and destitution or disability experienced by the victims of violent crimes; property and liability risks, including the automobile liability and no-fault automobile insurance, medical malpractice, products liability, natural disasters, and risks experienced by transnational corporations; and finally, increasing responsibility by government for certain risks. This latter category includes the impact on society from expansion of the Social Security program, and consequences to society from increasing government responsibility in the areas of riots, nuclear energy, crop support and crop insurance programs, federal flood and crime insurance, and the flu vaccination program.

Each author is a nationally recognized scholar in the area of risk and insurance or else is eminently qualified to write on the subject because of intensive research in the area. Robert I. Mehr first analyzes the effects on society from changes in the nature, treatment, and responsibility for the risks of premature death and old age. He points out that individual responsibility for the financial consequences of these risks is diminishing, and the role of government is dramatically increasing. In addition, he argues that the traditional methods for treating the risks of premature death and old age must be improved, and new insurance products are needed. In particular, new insurance products must be developed to meet the problem of inflation, including indexed death protection, death benefits in real terms adjusted for life cycle changes, and a geometrically increasing life annuity for survivors.

C. Arthur Williams, Jr. analyzes the effects on society from changes in the treatment of the risk of unemployment. He examines the changing historical response of society to unemployment, including traditional monetary and fiscal policies, unemployment insurance benefits, and supplemental benefits paid to the unemployed.

Robert Z. Zelten examines the effects on society from changes in the responsibility for the payment of health care costs. Although private health insurance has made enormous progress in meeting the health care problem in the United States, he points out clearly that the present system of financing private health insurance exacerbates the country's health care cost problems. He points out the socially perverse effects that result from the financing of health care costs in the United States today.

Monroe Berkowitz analyzes the effects on society from changes in responsibility for work related accidents and occupational diseases, and the societal consequences of the Occupational Safety and Health Act of 1970. He also examines the effects that workers' compensation laws have on society.

Emil M. Meurer, Jr. analyzes the effects on society from changes in the treatment of destitution or disability experienced by the victims of violent crimes. He points out that the rights of crime victims have been ignored by society, and new approaches for compensating victims of violent crimes are needed. Against this setting, he examines the societal consequences of the relatively new state crime compensation programs that now exist in nineteen states.

Robert J. Myers, former Chief Actuary of the Social Security Administration, examines the effects that the Social Security program have on society. He argues that the program should be maintained at about its present relative level, and should neither be expanded nor contracted. Although many social insurance scholars may disagree with him concerning his position on the future financing of Social Security, he points out clearly some dangers that may result from movement away from the payroll tax for financing the program toward a system of general revenues financing.

In addition, the recent emergence of catastrophe lawsuits in the areas of medical malpractice and defective products has tremendous social implications. Charles P. Hall, Jr. traces the development of the medical malpractice problem, the substantial increase in litigation that precipitated the increase in professional liability premiums, the difficulties of the medical profession in securing liability insurance, solutions to the medical malpractice problem, and the effects on society and the medical profession from changing responsibility in the medical malpractice area. In parallel fashion, Barry B. Schweig analyzes the effects on society from the substantial increase in litigation because of defective products, the difficulties of businessmen in securing products liability insurance at reasonable cost, and the consequences to society from actual and proposed solutions to the problem.

The effects on society from natural disasters are also treated. Howard Kunreuther examines the effects on society from shifts in the responsibility for the payment of losses attributable to natural disasters, including floods, earthquakes, hurricanes, and tornadoes. He attempts to determine why relatively few persons who experience destruction or loss of their property from natural disasters have purchased available insurance protection to cover these risks. He argues that, unless individuals are made graphically aware of the consequences of disasters, typically through past experience, they are unlikely to consider the purchase of insurance protection. Once their interest is stimulated, however, they use informal communication networks, such as friends and neighbors to guide them in their actions. The concluding portion of his paper examines the tradeoffs between using voluntary means of promoting insurance or some form of required coverage.

Transnational corporations operating overseas are also exposed to a wide spectrum of political and economic risks which have potentially severe international consequences. Harold Krogh analyzes the risks faced by transnational corporations in their overseas operations, including credit and political risks, currency deevaluation, kidnapping of key executives, and the expropriation of plants. Several private and public insurance mechanisms are available to meet these problems, and the effects of these approaches on society are examined.

Finally, more than half of the total insurance premiums from public and private insurance programs are now accounted for by federal government insurance programs. Mark R. Greene analyzes the effects on society from increasing government responsibility for certain risks. Six governmental insurance programs are evaluated according to a systematic and rational list of criteria. He concludes that government handling of the flood and swine flu liability risks are justified, but government programs in riot reinsurance, crime insurance, and nuclear energy liability should be terminated. Federal crop insurance is of questionable necessity, since private insurers are better able to insure this risk.

GEORGE E. REJDA

ANNALS, AAPSS, 443, May 1979

Changing Responsibility for Personal Risks and Societal Consequences: Premature Death and Old Age

By ROBERT I. MEHR

ABSTRACT: This paper analyzes the changing responsibility for the risks of premature death and old age of a breadwinner. This responsibility is assumed by three groups: the individual, private industry, and the federal government. The trend appears to be toward an increasingly important role for government in meeting these risks despite the decreasing public support of and confidence in the Social Security system. On the other hand, the role of the individual in providing for his or her financial security is becoming less and less important in providing the needed resources to offset these risks. With regard to new product development for meeting the risks of premature death and old age, indexed death protection, death protection in terms of real dollars adjusted for life cycle changes, indexed income for retirement, and a geometrically increasing life annuity for survivors are essential to deal with these risks under the cloud of inflation which seems to linger.

Robert I. Mehr is Professor of Finance at the University of Illinois at Urbana-Champaign. He has served as a visiting professor at the Leon Recanati Graduate School of Business, Tel-Aviv University, University of Puerto Rico, University of Colorado, University of Hawaii, University of California at Los Angeles and the Graduate School of Business, Stanford University. He is an author of four major textbooks in the fields of insurance and risk management, an author of several research books, monographs, government publications, and numerous articles in refereed scholarly journals. He is currently serving a second three-year term as the editor of The Journal of Risk and Insurance.

WHO IS responsible for the financial security of the survivors of a deceased breadwinner during his or her working life? Who is responsible for the financial security of a worker and his or her dependents when they reach retirement? Traditionally the family was responsible for taking care of its own. This is often referred to as the "American way" by those who either by choice (prejudice) or blindness (ignorance) refuse to recognize societal changes. The American way was changed by the introduction of Social Security legislation and the introduction and growth of life insurance and pensions provided to employees by their employers.

CHANGING RESPONSIBILITY FOR PERSONAL RISKS

Many people, even though a decreasing proportion, still believe that the individual is responsible for his or her own financial problems. For example, the proportion of young people who believe that the individual should be responsible for his or her own financial well being declined from 81 percent in 1970 to 72 percent in 1972.[1] Thus, even as late as the third year of the decade of the 1970's, 72 percent of the population still accepted the idea of the individual's responsibility for his or her financial support. Intuition suggests that no drastic change from this position has occurred since 1972. In fact, one might be led to believe that even greater support exists today for the doctrine of individual responsibility than was present just a few years ago. Witness the spreading tax revolt and the concern over the Social Security system with its increasing cost burden. "An almost equal number of people (three out of every four Americans) are dissatisfied with what they get in return for their federal tax dollars. And nearly three-fourths of those queried would strongly support legislation to put a limit on federal tax increases and an overall lid on government spending."[2]

Other evidence of individual responsibility for financial security is the increasing number of women who have entered the labor force. "The movement of women into the labor force accelerated with World War II, and the percentage of women 16 years and older in the work force had risen to 47.4 percent of all women of working age in 1976 (from 20% of all women of working age in the U.S. in 1900)."[3] As early as the late 1960s, J. F. Oates wrote: "A new phase is being developed in the family cycle. . . . The new life cycle of the family invites the participation of married women in the labor force. This is a relatively new historical phenomenon." Although additional evidence is needed, there are several indications that the earnings of the wife are allocated to the higher education of their children (or their grandchildren) and to plans for retirement.[4]

Changes in social attitudes and values have encouraged women to develop their abilities and talents to the fullest in remunerative work.[5]

1. American Council of Life Insurance, "Youth 1976: Attitudes of Young Americans Fourteen Through Twenty-five Towards Work, Life Insurance, Finances, Family, Marriage, Life Styles, Religion" (New York, 1976), p. 18.

2. *Barron's Magazine*, 6 November 1978, p. 7.

3. Robert I. Mehr, "Working Wife and the Life Insurance Product," Pacific Insurance Conference, 1975, pp. 228–229.

4. James F. Oates, *Business and Social Change: Life Insurance Looks To The Future* (New York: McGraw-Hill, 1968), pp. 72–81.

5. Robert I. Mehr, "Working Wife and the Life Insurance Product," p. 230.

Although financial security is obviously only one among many motives, increased use of income for retirement plans indicates that individuals feel responsible for their own financial security.

Even though public opinion indicates that individuals primarily feel a responsibility for their own financial security, changes in the funding sources for the personal risks of premature death and old age seem to have caused a decrease in this sense of individual responsibility. To an increasing degree, these risks are now being shifted to business and industry through employee benefit plans and to government through the Social Security program. Thus, the responsibility for the risks of premature death and old age currently is divided or diluted among three parties: the individuals themselves, businesses, and government.

Individual responsibility for premature death and old age

Recognition of the importance of personal savings and life insurance purchases gives evidence of individual responsibility for the risks of premature death and old age. A high proportion of young people, more than 9 out of 10, or 90 percent, believe in the importance of saving money. While this 90 percent figure has remained virtually unchanged since 1970, the proportion who believe in the importance of saving *regularly* has declined 6 percentage points.[6]

Life insurance purchases play an important role in dealing with the risks of premature death and old age. "A majority of young people continue to have positive attitudes

about life insurance. . . . Younger respondents and high school students have the most positive attitudes towards life insurance as a great thing.[7] One survey reports that "life insurance is considered to be a necessity by two in three Americans; fewer than one in five disagrees. These attitudes have remained basically the same since 1968."[8] Aside from the recognition by the general public of "life insurance as a necessity," the life insurance industry's share, as one of the major intermediaries, in the accumulation of personal savings appears not only to have stabilized, but to have improved lately."[9]

Another important consideration is people's recognition of the broader role of life insurance compared with other businesses in helping to offset the risks of premature death and old age. "One in four Americans believes that the life insurance business should be more involved than other businesses in trying to solve America's social problems."[10]

The Self-Employment Individual Tax Retirement Act of 1962 (the Keogh Act) and subsequent amendments allow employees of unincorporated businesses and other self-employed persons to be covered under special qualified retirement plans subject to a set of rules and regulations applicable solely to these plans. Individual Retirement Accounts (IRA), established by ERISA, become effective for tax years beginning after December 31,

6. American Council of Life Insurance, "Youth 1976," p. 14.

7. Ibid., p. 21.
8. American Council of Life Insurance, "Map '77 Monitoring Attitudes of the Public," p. 27.
9. John Miller, "Developments of Life Insurance and Pension Programs in the U.S. During the Period 1964–1974," Pacific Insurance Conference, p. 124.
10. American Council of Life Insurance, "Map '77," p. 44.

1974. These plans allow some persons who may be ineligible to participate in qualified pension plans, qualified deferred profit sharing plans or Keogh plans to prepare for retirement through tax deductible contributions to a fund that would grow income-tax free. While these contributions to the fund are income tax deductible and the fund grows income tax-free during the accumulation years, the income tax advantage offered is one of tax deferment rather than tax exemption. When these funds are distributed, the recipient must report the full amount of the distribution as earned income for tax purposes.

The Internal Revenue Code also provides for special treatment of nonqualified annuity plans for employees of Section 501 C(3) organizations, which include nonprofit corporations operated exclusively for religious, charitable, scientific, public safety testing, library or educational purposes, or for the prevention of cruelty to children or animals. Tax-sheltered annuities for 501 C(3) organizations also are available for employees of public schools operated directly by governmental units, even though such schools are not 501 C(3) organizations.

All these legislative enactments have helped individuals assume more responsibility for the risks of premature death and old age. However, even in these cases of individual responsibility, the government plays an important role in financing the preparation for these risks through the use of tax incentives.

Growth of private pensions

Originally private pensions were granted informally on a selected basis as a gratuity and were used primarily to increase employee morale. However, "inflation, tax-ation and wage controls during World War II provided a strong stimulus to the expansion of formal private pension plans. The second significant impetus to private pensions came from the trade unions' post war drive to establish pensions and other supplementary benefits in collective bargaining.[11] The motivation of private pensions as gratuities underwent a major change. Private pensions became an obligation of employers to employees. Employees considered pensions as part of their overall compensation for services rendered. "The belief that employers or unions should be the major providers of retirement income has grown significantly since 1969 and . . . [pensions from these sources are] now at the 43 percent level."[12]

Accompanying the increase in the popularity and growth in private pension plans was the growth of pension funding which produced large and growing assets in recent years. "Private pension plans administered by life insurance companies reached new highs in assets and number of persons covered. Their growth reflects not only the generally improving health of the economy, but also the ever increasing public attitude that employers should bear the major responsibility for providing a worker's retirement income . . . plans funded with life insurance companies had assets . . . of $88,400 million . . . and covered 15.2 million individuals at year-end 1976."[13]

Expanding role of government

For many years the government has assumed responsibility for providing minimum financial security

11. American Council of Life Insurance, *Pension Facts 1977*, p. 9.
12. Ibid., p. 61.
13. Ibid., p. 7.

to dependent survivors of bread-winners and to the aged. The government has not been passive in its attitude toward the risks of premature death and old age. "Government increased its role as a provider of insurance protection and in the regulation of the private sector."[14] However, some people are concerned about the efficiency of government involvement in individual financial planning and believe that private industry, through plans designed to meet the specific needs of employees, can provide more financial security at less cost—both social and individual. In a recent survey, the findings were that "a plurality of respondents (45%) believe that they receive greater value for their money from private industry than from government. Forty percent think they get equal value from both these sectors, while only 14 percent think they get greater value from government."[15]

In spite of adverse public criticism, the government has increased its involvement in recent years in the function of providing financial security to survivors in the event of the breadwinner's death and in providing financial security for old age. The government participates in dealing with these risks through the Social Security program, the Railroad Retirement Act, federal civilian employees retirement systems, and both state and local employees retirement systems. Aside from the direct participation of government in providing some level of individual financial security, the indirect participation of government should not be ignored. Some federal agencies devote their energies

14. John Miller, "Development of Life Insurance Programs," p. 124.
15. American Council of Life Insurance, "Map '77," p. 57.

to making and enforcing laws designed to keep people alive and employed. Federal legislation has been passed to defer mandatory retirement to age 70, effective in 1979. Estate tax law revisions have helped small business estates and farmers in financial planning for death. The Employee Retirement Income Security Act of 1974 (ERISA) has been enacted to enhance the reliability of private pension plans. Other tax sheltered plans have also been enacted to help persons plan their retirement income.

SOME EVIDENCE OF CHANGING RESPONSIBILITY

Table 1 shows the dollar funds available for premature death and old age relief from different sources such as social insurance, private pensions funded through life insurance companies, private pensions funded through agencies other than life insurers, group life insurance, ordinary life insurance, industrial life insurance and payments to policy-holders and annuitants. Table 2 expresses the specific components of these sources as a percentage of their aggregate amount. Social insurance benefits have increased over the time period studied not only in absolute dollar amounts but also relative to other sources included in this study. These observations indicate that, despite the growing belief and concern by some segments of the public about the "inefficiency" of government involvement in dealing with these risks, the government has continued to assume this responsibility in even greater proportions.

Table 2 also shows that the proportion of private pension benefits funded through life insurance companies has decreased sharply until 1965. During the middle 1960s,

TABLE 1

RESOURCES IN TERMS OF CURRENT DOLLARS AVAILABLE TO SURVIVORS AND RETIREES
(1950–1976) (POST DEATH AND POST RETIREMENT)
IN MILLIONS OF DOLLARS

SOURCES OF FUNDS	1950	1955	1960	1965	1970	1973	1974	1975	1976
Social Insurance*	924	4,372	9,896	16,114	27,940	41,297	51,498	56,976	64,401
Private Pensions; Life insurance	1,010	1,835	2,810	720	1,330	1,925	2,230	2,520	2,735
Private Pensions; Other private plans	290	670	1,330	2,800	6,030	9,310	10,740	12,330	13,000
Group Life Insurance	283	591	1,115	1,824	3,027	3,806	4,031	4,256	4,453
Total Pensions	1,583	3,096	5,255	5,344	10,387	15,041	17,001	19,106	20,188
Ordinary Life Insurance	1,090	1,380	1,904	2,604	3,546	4,289	4,382	4,474	4,665
Industrial Life Insurance	217	270	327	404	445	477	472	463	475
Annuities**	1,285	1,885	2,863	3,951	5,659	6,223	6,661	7,072	4,960
Total	2,592	3,535	5,094	6,959	9,650	10,989	11,515	12,009	13,100

* Includes retirement and survivor benefits (adjusted by author to exclude disability benefit).
** Payments to policyholders and annuitants (adjusted by author to exclude disability payment, cash surrender values and dividend).
SOURCE: *Social Security Bulletin*, December 1977 (p. 37). *Life Insurance Fact Book*, 1977 (pp. 46 and 49).

this decline began to taper off. From 1965 to the present, the proportion of private pension plans funded by life insurers became nearly constant with only slight variations. The proportion of private pension benefits funded through other private plans (noninsured or trust fund

TABLE 2

RESOURCES IN TERMS OF PERCENTAGE AVAILABLE TO SURVIVORS AND RETIREES THROUGH SOCIAL
SECURITY, EMPLOYEE BENEFIT PLANS AND INDIVIDUAL LIFE INSURANCE (1950–1976)
(POST DEATH AND POST RETIREMENT) (TOTAL BENEFITS FROM ALL
NAMED SOURCES—100 PERCENT)

SOURCES OF FUNDS	1950	1955	1960	1965	1970	1973	1974	1975	1976
Social Insurance	18	40	49	57	58	61	64	65	66
Private Pensions; Life Insurance	20	17	14	3	3	3	3	3	3
Private Pensions; Other Private Plans	6	6	7	10	13	14	13	14	13
Group Life Insurance	6	5	6	6	6	6	5	5	5
Total Group Plans	32	28	27	19	22	23	21	22	21
Ordinary Life Insurance	21	13	9	9	7	6	5	5	5
Industrial Life Insurance	4	2	2	1	1	1	1	1	0
Annuities	25	17	14	14	12	9	8	8	8
Total Individual Funds	50	32	25	24	20	16	14	14	13

SOURCE: Computed from Table 1.

plans) being a residual naturally increased until 1965. And, as expected, given the experience with private pensions funded through life insurance, the trusteed (non-insured) plans leveled off and became nearly constant after 1965. The declining rate, up to the mid 1960s, of life insurers as funding agencies for private pension plans, coupled with the increasing role of noninsurance funding agencies (banks, trust funds and so on), has caused the position of life insurers as pension funding agencies to deteriorate. Until the early 1960s, life insurers were the leading funding agencies for private pension plans. But since that time life insurers have taken a back seat to trusteed plans so that now private pension plans funded through banks and trust companies exceed those funded through life insurers. The measure in this discussion is not the number of plans, or plan assets but plan disbursements.

Group life insurance is still another source of funds which measure industry's responsibility for financial risks facing individuals. The risk is that of the need for survivorship benefits usually for dependents. These benefits have been nearly stable in terms of the percentage of total benefits (death and retirement). Even though absolute dollar benefits provided by group life insurance and private pensions are increasing, benefits from these sources have declined in relative terms up to 1965, after which time they became nearly stable. An important point to note, however, is that as early as 1950, the responsibility of industry was greater than that of government. Starting in 1955, the pendulum began to swing towards government assumption of the major portion of this responsibility.

The result has been that the government sector has been responsible for benefit payments exceeding not only those of private industry but also, as will be seen, those provided by self-reliant individuals as well.

Group, ordinary, and industrial life insurance benefits have increased steadily over the same time period. However, benefits from these sources in percentage terms have declined over time.

In summary, the responsibility of the government has increased over the time period under study, but the responsibility of the life insurance industry has been nearly stable in recent years. The result has been that the importance of private industry's role stabilized at about one third of the government's role; and the importance of the responsibility of the individual has been stabilized at about one-fourth of the government's role. Overall, the government provides about 66 percent of the benefits under discussion, whereas industry provides about 21 percent, and individuals provide about 13 percent, respectively.

Unfortunately, because of data limitations, financial resources accumulated by individuals reflect only those from life insurance. They do not include important personal savings such as investments in bonds and stocks, savings accounts in banks and other savings institutions, and increases in the equity in homes as mortgage loan payments are made. If it were possible to include the foregoing sources in the study, the results would be dramatically different as well as more realistic. Patently these results would show an increase in the relative importance of individual responsibility in the role of preparation for financial security.

A Survey of Current Business published in the June 1978 Federal

Reserve Bulletin reported that personal savings were 4.8 percent of personal income in 1950, rose to 6.9 percent in 1973, and then declined to 4.8 percent by 1976. Percentages of total income from other sources showed a different pattern: rental income, which began at 3.1 percent in 1950 declined to 2.0 by 1973 and 1.7 in 1976; dividends were 3.9 percent in 1950, dropped to 2.6 percent in 1973 and were at the same level in 1976; personal interest income, on the other hand, rose from 3.9 percent in 1950 to 8.4 percent in 1973 and 9.4 in 1976.

SOME AREAS OF CONCERN

Due to the increasing takeover of the responsibility of premature death and old age by the government, savings and potential capital formation on the part of the general public may be decreasing. "In recent months, editorial and scholarly articles have appeared criticizing the Social Security system for reducing saving and capital formation . . . and the claim (has been) that the Social Security system has reduced savings and as a result the potential for economic growth in this country."[16] In addition, even though the responsibility of the government for the risks of premature death and old age is increasing, public confidence in the support of the Social Security program is diminishing. According to a survey, "despite the fact that perceived knowledgeability of Social Security is low, Americans have become more aware of the difficulties confronting Social Security. . . . Coupled with increased awareness of the problems facing

Social Security, a slight erosion of confidence in the future of the system has occurred.

However, it is important to note that a majority of the public (57%) still expressed confidence in the future of the system in 1976."[17] Another survey found that the public support of the program is decreasing lately. The author concluded: "Public support of the Social Security program is essential for its smooth operation. However, recent evidence indicates that support is diminishing. Major findings are that (1) large numbers of persons are highly skeptical about the program, (2) many respondents preferred lower taxes coupled with lower benefit levels, (3) large amounts of public misunderstanding concerning basic concepts of the program exist, and (4) the Social Security Administration has not been successful in communicating to the public the nature and purpose of Social Security."[18]

A Louis Harris poll reported in early 1979 that, based on a scientific survey, 42 percent of all current employees and more than 50 percent of employees under age 35 have "hardly any" confidence that Social Security will pay them the benefits promised when they retire. In contrast, 68 percent of the pension plan participants expressed confidence that their private pension plans will pay them the benefits to which they are entitled.

Some observers also question the increasing financial burden on the workers to maintain the solvency of Social Security system. "If current fertility rates are maintained,

16. Selig D. Lesnoy and John C. Hambor, "Social Security Savings and Capital Formation," *Social Security Bulletin*, vol. 38, no. 7 (July 1975), p. 3.

17. American Council of Life Insurance, "Current Social Issues: The Public's View," p. 6.
18. Gary W. Eldred, "Does the Public Support the Social Security Program," *The Journal of Risk and Insurance*, vol. 44, no. 2 (June 1977), pp. 179–91.

zero population growth (ZPG) will be attained around 2050. The ratio of aged to active workers will increase sharply, and the real financial burden of supporting the increased proportion of aged persons under the OASDHI program will fall heavily on the active workers. Under ZPG conditions, general revenue financing of the OASDHI program is desirable since the payroll tax burden will fall heavily and unfairly on the working poor; the payroll tax along with the personal income tax will be regressive over a wide income range; and the welfare element in the OASDHI program will increase substantially."[19] The Louis Harris poll reported that 41 percent of current and retired employees have little confidence that future working generations will be willing to pay higher social security taxes. Finally, because of the increasing lack of confidence in Social Security, some groups which are allowed to elect coverage have opted out of the system.[20]

In order to increase public confidence in the Social Security program, the government has pushed the minimum mandatory retirement age (not minimum social security retirement age) to 70, effective in 1979. One editorial writer commented, "Retirement age may have to be pushed back to 68 or even 70 simply to keep the Social Security system solvent. For unless birth rates rise dramatically, the ratio of workers to retired persons will drop from 3 to 1 to 2 to 1 in the not-too-

distant future, putting a heavy financial burden on people who pay social security taxes. There are good reasons for mandatory retirement. One is the need to maintain an efficient, alert work force. Another is to make room for young leadership. But it's beginning to look as though retiring workers at 65 or even younger is a luxury our children and grandchildren may not be able to afford."[21]

NEW PRODUCT DEVELOPMENT FOR MEETING THE RISKS OF PREMATURE DEATH AND OLD AGE

A major concern inherent in product development in recent years is the eroding effect of inflation on the value of fixed dollar retirement incomes and on the fixed dollar amounts of death protection. In general, the result has been that "inflation allows the life insurance marketing organizations to upgrade the amount of the insurance protection as inflation has led to substantial increases in the average family income."[22] Even though an increase of life insurance sales is anticipated, the fear of inflation has caused the general public to change its pattern of insurance purchases. The ratio of term insurance purchases to permanent insurance purchases has been increasing.[23]

Some people contend that "a level premium, increasing term benefit" might be popular, because of the persistent inflation in the near future. However, they emphasize that "even with this type of product . . . there is the problem of paying in

19. George E. Rejda and Richard J. Shepler, "The Impact of Zero Population Growth on the OASDHI Program," *The Journal of Risk and Insurance*, vol. 40, no. 3 (September 1973), pp. 313–25.

20. W. Gary Eldred, "Factors to be Examined in Terminating a Social Security Coverage Agreement," *The Journal of Risk and Insurance*, vol. 42, no. 3 (September 1975), pp. 433–45.

21. *The Cleveland Press*, 10 November 1975, p. A6.

22. John Miller, "Development of Life Insurance Programs," p. 124.

23. Alfred E. Hofflander, "Inflation and the Sales of Life Insurance in the United States—Mixed Results," Pacific Insurance Conference, 1975, p. 201.

dollars for benefits which inevitably will be returnable in more inflated dollars; this will hurt much more than we are accustomed to, with such projected high rates of inflation."[24] Furthermore, they argue that due to the chronic problem of inflation in the foreseeable future, "group life insurance is certain to be increasingly important, and it will increase under higher rates of inflation."[25] However, group insurance does not solve the problem of the reduction of death protection or retirement income caused by inflation. It simply provides insurance protection at lower rates than are charged for individual insurance. Because of its lower costs and potential flexibility, insurance issued on a group basis can be more efficiently adapted to new products designed to cope with the eroding effects of inflation.

The fundamental solution to this problem is to adjust the payment of death protection or retirement income to changes in the purchasing power of the dollar. Thus, a device similar to indexed bonds, which are available in some foreign countries, seems to be needed to solve the problem of the effects of inflation on long-range financial planning. In addition to indexed payment of death protection or of retirement income, some people argue that "the geometrically increasing annuity can be used to provide protection to survivors of a deceased breadwinner. . . . In order to produce a geometric increase of payments after the initial payment, each subsequent payment in the level annuity must be adjusted to provide the approximate amount of increase. The series of payments form a geometric series,

$a, ar, ar^2, ar^3, \ldots ar^n$, where a is the first payment and r is the common ratio. Instead of each payment equaling all other payments, as in the level annuity, each payment of a geometrically increasing annuity is equal to r times the previous payment.[26] This type of product may also be appropriate to smooth the eroding effect of inflation on retirement incomes.

After many years of experiencing inflation, the time has come to express life insurance protection in terms of increasing income payments to dependent survivors rather than in terms of fixed face amounts as is currently the practice. Insurers should write life insurance policies under which they will pay the survivors $X monthly, increasing at a predetermined rate. Life insurance written in terms of a given face amount should be restricted to those exposures where a given capital sum is needed at death to fulfill some predetermined obligation, such as a debt secured by a mortgage or an amount needed to fund a business interest buy-and-sell agreement as in partnerships and close corporations. In the latter case, the face amount of the insurance should be variable in order to reflect changes in the values of a business interest.

"A new product should be developed and offered by life insurers to meet the problem of inflation. This product would operate as follows: During the benefit period, if the experienced inflation rate equals or exceeds the assumed inflation rate, each payment after the first is increased by the assumed inflation rate."[27] Even though this product does not guarantee protection

24. Institute of Life Insurance, "Trend Report Special Issue," September 1974, p. 10.
25. Ibid., p. 10.

26. Terry Lane Rose, *Life Insurance Product Development: Protective Beneficiaries Against Real Income Loss* (Ph.D. diss., University of Illinois, 1977), p. 82.
27. Ibid., p. 81–84.

against an inflation rate higher than that assumed, it does limit the eroding effects of inflation on survivors and retirees.

In summary, new products to deal with the financial risks of old age and premature death include indexed death protection, death protection in terms of real dollars adjusted for life cycle change, indexed retirement income, and a geometrically increasing life annuity. One or more of these products might be appropriate to meet the needs of the general public living under the cloud of inflation.

ANNALS, AAPSS, 443, May 1979

Meeting the Risk of Unemployment: Changing Societal Responses

By C. ARTHUR WILLIAMS, JR.

ABSTRACT: Unemployment is enforced idleness among persons who are willing and able to work. Unemployment was not a serious problem until the Industrial Revolution produced a more complicated, interdependent, impersonal society. Unemployment may be classified according to its cause as aggregate, selective or structural, and personal. Unemployment rates vary greatly according to business conditions; they also vary greatly among different classes of the population. Most unemployment currently lasts less than fifteen weeks. Until the Great Depression society did little to help the unemployed. Friends and relatives were the major outside sources of support, other sources being private charities, public relief, and employer or trade union plans. The Great Depression produced the highest unemployment rates ever experienced and a climate favoring federal intervention. The Social Security Act of 1935 encouraged the formation of state unemployment insurance programs, now only one of several government and private efforts to control unemployment or alleviate its economic consequences. The current principal control measures are: (1) monetary and fiscal policy designed to reduce unemployment, (2) automatic stabilizers, (3) manpower development and training, (4) labor-market information, and (5) public employment. The principal alleviative measures are unemployment insurance, public assistance, and private employee benefit plans, unemployment insurance being clearly the most important.

C. Arthur Williams, Jr. is Professor of Economics and Insurance at the College of Business Administration, University of Minnesota, where he served as Dean of the College of Business Administration between 1970–1978. He earned his A.B., A.M., and Ph.D. degrees at Columbia University. He has also taught at the University of Buffalo and the University of Pennsylvania. He is the coauthor of Economic and Social Security and has authored or coauthored numerous other books and articles.

UNEMPLOYMENT is enforced idleness among persons who are willing and able to work. It was not a serious problem until the development of modern industrialism. Before the Industrial Revolution most people lived in rural areas, their wants were simple, and they satisfied most of these wants directly through their own efforts. They were their own farmers, butchers, bakers, and candlestick makers. Generally they produced little more than they needed for themselves. Some manufacturers and traders hired workers for a wage, but most people who produced goods for others worked for employers in small towns or more frequently in their own homes. These operations tended to provide fairly stable employment; employers tended to develop close relationships with their employees and to be deeply concerned about their continued employment.

The Industrial Revolution produced a more complicated, interdependent, impersonal society that made more persons dependent upon the continuation of a money wage, and made that continuation more uncertain. This paper traces the response of our society to unemployment since the early 1800s when the Industrial Revolution began to change people's lives significantly. Most attention will be paid to the actions taken during and after the Great Depression of the thirties when the United States changed dramatically its view of the nature of unemployment and how it should be handled.

When a worker loses his or her job, income stops but expenses continue. Savings may permit the worker's family to survive, but these savings may have been accumulated for some other objective such as a child's education. A prolonged period of unemployment may also cause the worker's skills to become rusty or outdated, thus increasing the difficulty of securing reemployment.

Fortunately most persons will not in their lifetime experience a period of extended unemployment but almost all persons face the possibility of some unemployment. This threat causes fear and worry which in turn may cause them to make decisions that are not the best for them, their employers, or society.

Society is affected adversely not only by the threat of unemployment but by the actual event. When a person becomes unemployed, society loses the value of the goods and services that the worker's efforts would have produced. Because workers are also consumers, it loses in addition some or all of the unemployed person's consumption expenditures. This loss is particularly troubling if it occurs during a recession and thus further reduces the total demand for goods and services. Unemployment may become a vicious cycle creating more unemployment which in turn creates more unemployment.

Up to this point the discussion has proceeded on the assumption that all unemployment is total. Such is not the case. Many persons work fewer hours a week than they wish. Others are employed unwillingly at jobs for which they are overqualified through training, education or experience. This article deals mainly with visible total unemployment.

TYPES OF UNEMPLOYMENT

Unemployment has several causes. Understanding them is important to understanding unemployment and what to do about it. Three types of unemployment classified according to cause have been identified: aggregate unemployment, selective unemployment, and personal unemployment.[1]

Aggregate unemployment

Aggregate unemployment results from an insufficient demand for labor occasioned by an economic recession. As consumers, businesses, or governments reduce their spending, many workers in a wide variety of industries may be laid off or have their work week shortened. For the nation as a whole, this is the most important type of unemployment.

Selective unemployment

Unemployment may be selective in its impact specifically affecting certain areas, industries, or occupations. For example, most members of an industry or a particular employer may move their principal operations from one area or locality to another, causing workers in the former location to relocate or lose their jobs. A mining community may find its mineral supply exhausted or uneconomical to mine. Changes in the demand for certain products and services such as manually operated calculators may cause an entire industry to adapt to the new environment or to disappear. Workers in certain occupations, such as the operation of a linotype machine, may find their skills outdated. Seasonal unemployment, such as that associated with the construction trades, is a somewhat different type of structural unemployment because of its predictability. Much of the unemployment among disadvantaged groups such as the unskilled, the uneducated, older workers, teenagers, and minorities has also been classified as structural unemployment.[2] Other examples include unemployment caused by a strike, a business failure, or an interruption of business caused by a fire or some similar peril.

Personal unemployment

Personal unemployment is caused by the time lost in securing a first job or a replacement position that is not related to either aggregate unemployment or structural unemployment. Because this unemployment arises out of the time necessary to match job-seekers with available jobs, it is often called frictional unemployment. Ideally there would be no frictional unemployment, but imperfections in the labor market make some of this unemployment inevitable.

THE NUMBER AND COMPOSITION OF THE UNEMPLOYED

How many persons are unemployed? Who are they? The answers to these two questions depend of course upon the time period involved. Unemployment rates dating back to 1890 are presented in Table 1. Unemployment rates tell the number of unemployed as a percent of the civilian labor force. A person is considered unemployed if he or she is not working but is available for work and has made recent efforts to find a job. Also included as unemployed are persons who are not working or seeking employment but who are waiting to be recalled to a job from which they have been laid off, or are waiting

1. J. G. Turnbull, C. A. Williams, Jr., and E. F. Cheit, *Economic and Social Security*, 4th ed. (New York: Ronald Press, 1973), pp. 187–91.

2. George E. Rejda, *Social Insurance and Economic Security* (Englewood Cliffs, NJ: Prentice-Hall, 1976), pp. 325–26.

TABLE 1

UNEMPLOYMENT RATES: 1890 TO 1977

YEAR	RATE	YEAR	RATE
1890	4.0%	1940	14.6
1895	13.7	1945	1.9
1900	5.0	1950	5.3
1905	4.3	1955	4.4
1910	5.9	1960	5.5
1915	8.5	1965	4.5
1920	5.2	1970	4.9
1925	3.2	1975	8.7
1930	8.7	1977	7.0
1935*	20.1		

* The peak rate was 24.9 in 1933.

SOURCE: *Historical Statistics of the United States: Colonial Times to 1970* (Washington, DC: U.S. Department of Commerce Bureau of the Census, 1975), p. 135. *Social Security Bulletins.*

to report to a new job within thirty days. The civilian labor force includes all persons aged sixteen and over (fourteen and over prior to 1947) who are working, who are unemployed, or who are temporarily absent for such reasons as an illness or a strike.

Some weaknesses or limitations in these data should be noted. First, until 1940 data were gathered only in census years and using different definitions than those presented above. On the other hand, the original data have been adjusted to place the rates for 1890–1940 on as comparable a basis as possible to the present rates. Second, current rates are based on a sample of about 47,000 households conducted once each month. The results, therefore, are subject to sampling errors. Third, the annual rates are the average of the twelve monthly rates. Consequently they do not tell how many persons were unemployed in a year. To the extent that some of the unemployed in February, say, were not among the unemployed in January, the number of persons unemployed sometime during the year is larger

than the annual rate indicates. Fourth, the rates reveal only total unemployment—not partial or disguised unemployment. They also ignore unemployment among those unemployed who have become discouraged and dropped out of the labor force.

In spite of these limitations, however, Table 1 tells an important story. Unemployment is always present, there is no strong upward or downward trend, and economic recessions have, at least on two occasions, pushed unemployment rates for several years over 10 percent.

Who are the unemployed is as important as their number. Table 2 classifies for a recent year the proportion of the unemployed who had lost their last job, who had voluntarily left their last job, who had reentered the labor force, or who were looking for their first job. Only about 41 percent were unemployed because they had lost their last job. Because unemployment insurance programs, to be explained later, pay benefits only to workers with recent past earnings or employment experience, Table 2 explains why a large proportion of the unemployed do not receive unemployment insurance benefits.

Table 3 shows that unemployment

TABLE 2

UNEMPLOYED PERSONS BY REASON FOR UNEMPLOYMENT JUNE, 1978

CLASS	PERCENT OF TOTAL
Lost their last job	40.6%
Voluntarily left their last job	14.7
Reentered labor force	30.6
Looking for first job	14.1
	100.0%

SOURCE: *Monthly Labor Review*, CI, No. 8 (August 1978), 67.

rates vary among different classes of the population. Teenagers, non-whites, women heading a family, especially if no husband were present, part-time workers, and blue collar workers have much higher unemployment rates than the national average.

The duration of the unemployment is also an important consideration in evaluating the seriousness of the problem. Table 4 shows that in 1977 over 70 percent of the unemployed were without a job for less than fifteen weeks, but for almost 15 percent the duration was more than twenty-six weeks.

SOCIETY'S RESPONSE PRIOR TO 1935

Until the Great Depression individuals were generally forced to bear the economic consequences of unemployment themselves. Indeed the prevailing public attitude was that, except during serious depressions, it was the worker's fault if he or she became unemployed. If the worker's resources were not sufficient for support during the period of unemployment, he or she could in most cases turn only to friends or relatives for support. Other sources

TABLE 3

UNEMPLOYMENT RATES AMONG SELECTED CLASSES OF THE POPULATION 1977

CLASS	RATE
Total	7.0%
Teenagers	17.7
Non-white	13.1
Non-white teenagers	38.3
Married men, spouse present	3.6
Married women, spouse present	6.5
Women who head families	9.3
Full-time workers	6.5
Part-time workers	9.8
Blue collar workers	8.1

SOURCE: Monthly Labor Review, CI, No. 8 (August 1978), 66.

TABLE 4

UNEMPLOYMENT DURATION 1977

DURATION*	PERCENT OF TOTAL
Under 5 weeks	41.7%
5–14 weeks	30.5
15–26 weeks	13.1
Over 26 weeks	14.8
	100.0%

* Average duration was 14.3 weeks.
SOURCE: Monthly Labor Review, CI, No. 8 (August 1978), 67.

that aided some of the unemployed were private charities, local public relief, and private employee-benefit plans. Public unemployment insurance did not become effective at either the state or federal level until 1934. The subject, however, was discussed in the United States as early as 1907, and an unemployment insurance bill was introduced in the Massachusetts legislature in 1916.[3]

European interest and action came much earlier. Great Britain, acting on trade union experience dating back at least seventy years, passed its original limited act in 1911. The coverage and benefit provisions were substantially liberalized in 1920 and further amended substantially in 1934. By 1930 at least 13 other nations had compulsory unemployment insurance plans.[4]

During the depression of 1920–21, unemployment insurance bills were introduced in several states including New York and Wisconsin. The Wisconsin bill, sponsored by Senator Huber and developed by Professor John R. Commons, a renowned University of Wisconsin labor econ-

3. William Haber and Merrill G. Murray, Unemployment Insurance in the American Economy (Homewood, IL: Richard D. Irwin, 1966), pp. 65–75.
4. Ibid., Chapt. 4.

omist, attracted the most attention. None of the bills passed but the Huber bill and others were reintroduced or introduced throughout the twenties. In 1932, to become effective in 1934, the Wisconsin legislature passed the Huber bill, now sponsored in a revised form by Senator Graves. Only four states other than Wisconsin passed laws prior to the Social Security Act of 1935. Of these four laws only that of New York became effective.[5]

At the federal level, in 1916 a U.S. Commission on Industrial Relations recommended the investigation and preparation of unemployment insurance plans. Not until shortly before the Great Depression, however, did the federal government pay much attention to unemployment insurance. In 1934 Senator Wagner and Congressman Lewis introduced a bill imposing a federal tax against which employers could receive a 100 percent credit for contributions to a state plan meeting prescribed benefit standards. Although President Roosevelt originally supported this bill, he later decided to appoint a Committee on Economic Security which would study unemployment insurance in the context of the general problem of economic security. In response to the report of this committee Congress passed the Social Security Act of 1935 which dealt with unemployment as well as other economic insecurities.

SOCIETY'S RESPONSE 1935–PRESENT

The Social Security Act of 1935 marked the beginning of a new era.

5. For a detailed discussion of this history see Harry Malisoff, "The Emergence of Unemployment Compensation," *Political Science Quarterly* 54 nos. 2, 3, 4 (June, September, December, 1939): 237–58, 391–420, and 577–99, respectively.

The unemployment insurance program it introduced is now only one of several government and private programs designed to control unemployment or alleviate its economic consequences. The principal control measures are: monetary and fiscal policy designed to reduce unemployment; automatic stabilizers; manpower development and training; labor-market information; and public employment. The principal alleviative measures are unemployment insurance, public assistance, and private employee benefit plans.

Monetary and fiscal policy

The 1936 publication of John Maynard Keynes' *General Theory of Employment, Interest, and Money* provided a theoretical basis for those who advocated more federal intervention in stimulating employment. The Employment Act of 1946 committed the federal government to take whatever steps were necessary to achieve "full" employment. Because it is impossible to eliminate all unemployment, the goal was an unemployment rate of about 4 percent. Many economists believe that because of changes in the composition of the labor force and the increasing uncertainties of life, full employment today would be consistent with a somewhat higher unemployment rate. Nonetheless, in 1978 Congress passed the Humphrey-Hawkins bill which sets twin goals of 4 percent unemployment and 3 percent inflation by 1983 (0 percent inflation by 1988). Steps taken to reduce inflation, however, are not supposed to impede achievement of the unemployment goal.

The two major tools used to expand the aggregate demand for labor and thus reduce aggregate unemployment are monetary policy and fiscal policy. Monetary policy is determined by the Federal Reserve Board. If the Board wishes to stimulate demand, it can expand the money supply through an easy money policy. The Board can reduce the reserves that banks must maintain in Federal Reserve Banks or in cash in their own vaults to support a given volume of loans; it can reduce the rate banks must pay to borrow money from the Federal Reserve banks, and it can buy government bonds in the open market thus raising their prices and lowering interest rates.

Fiscal policy is determined by Congress acting often on recommendations from the President. To stimulate the economy Congress can reduce taxes, thus encouraging more private consumption and investment, and increase government spending even though this may create a deficit in the federal budget. Some economists favor monetary policy; others favor fiscal policy. Both policies have worked at times, but both have their limitations. For example, most economists believe that expansionary policies are almost certain to raise prices, and that to achieve full employment today, the inflation rate has to be higher than it was in the past.[6]

Automatic stabilizers

Since 1935 a number of automatic stabilizers have been built into the economy that tend to increase the spendable incomes of families and businesses during a recession. Like monetary and fiscal policy, automatic stabilizers reduce primarily aggregate unemployment. Examples are the federal income tax and unemployment insurance.

6. In other words the so-called Phillips curve relating unemployment rates and annual price increases has shifted over time. See Rejda, *Social Insurance*, pp. 349–50.

As important as these stabilizers have been, they do not replace all of the purchasing power lost. Unemployment insurance benefits, moreover, may eventually be exhausted. Furthermore, in the same way that automatic stabilizers tend to check rising unemployment rates, they also retard the rate of recovery.

Manpower development and training

Unlike the first two loss control measures, manpower development and training programs are designed to reduce structural unemployment. Their objective is to increase the employability of individuals through basic and vocational education and on-the-job training. Illustrative are some of the programs established under the Comprehensive Employment and Training Act of 1973.

Evaluations of these programs have been mixed. Although admitting there have been some notable exceptions, critics complain that the reduction in unemployment relative to the cost has been low. They also claim that many persons do not complete their program or are trained for the wrong jobs—jobs that are not available or jobs for which they have no skills or interest. Finally, they point to gaps and overlaps in the programs and the need for more coordination.

Labor market information

To better match workers with jobs, the Employment Service has expanded its services greatly since it was created in 1933 by the Wagner-Peyser Act. The Employment Service performs three major functions: matching workers and jobs through local offices, registering for work recipients of unemployment insurance, and providing counseling and testing services and conducting labor market surveys.[7] Despite its accomplishments the Employment Service has not yet achieved its potential. The labor market is still far from perfect, even allowing for practical limitations.

Private placement firms also provide valuable labor-market information and help workers find jobs for a fee. Colleges and universities have placement offices for their students and sometimes their alumni.

Public employment

Although not nearly as important as during the Great Depression, public employment remains one of the ways to reduce unemployment. For example, the Comprehensive Employment and Training Act of 1973 provides temporary public service employment for certain unemployed persons. Public works projects such as dam construction also employ some workers. Finally, public jobs have been used in connection with public assistance programs. For example, under the Work Incentive Program, established in 1967 and strengthened in 1971, public service employers are encouraged through a subsidy to provide jobs for recipients of Aid to Families with Dependent Children. Some states require public assistance recipients who are able to work but cannot find any job to work for the community.

Although some persons believe that public-service jobs can both reduce unemployment greatly, especially among the disadvantaged, and meet some important community needs, others see severe limitations. The cost is high if wages are adequate, the wages may be too attrac-

tive relative to some wages paid in the private sector, advance planning is necessary if the work is to be efficient, public needs often cannot remain unsatisfied until people need public-service work, and the opportunities provided are often dead-end jobs for the recipients.

UNEMPLOYMENT INSURANCE

The discussion turns now from loss control measures to the principal alleviative measure—public unemployment insurance. The Social Security Act of 1935 levied a 3 percent payroll tax (limited starting in 1939 to the first $3,000 of an employee's wages) on employers in all states which provided monies to pay the administrative expenses incurred by states operating unemployment insurance programs. Employers in states with unemployment insurance programs were permitted to deduct from the federal tax the state unemployment tax up to 90 percent of the federal tax. Given this incentive, it is not surprising that shortly all states had unemployment compensation programs. Although the details have changed, the same principle holds today. Currently the federal government levies a 3.4 percent tax on employers on the first $6,000 of an employee's wages. The offset for state taxes is still limited to 2.7 percent. The 3.4 percent rate will be reduced to 3.2 percent in years when the federal trust fund has repaid loans it received from the U.S. Treasury to finance part of its share of the extended benefits described later.

Federal standards

The federal government sets few standards for the state programs. The states of course have an incentive to include all employers subject to the

7. Turnbull, Williams, and Cheit, *Economic and Social Security*, p. 199.

federal tax. At first this tax applied only to employers of eight or more workers. Since the Employment Security Amendments of 1970, except for a few types of employment, there has been no size limitation. The federal law originally excluded agricultural workers, family workers, domestic workers, services provided for nonprofit organizations, government employees, and the self-employed. Today, most of these excluded employments are covered, though they may be subject to special size requirements.

Each state must deposit the unemployment insurance taxes they collect in a separate account in a federal unemployment trust fund. It must not deny benefits to any worker refusing to accept a job if the position is available because of a labor dispute, if the working conditions are substantially substandard, or if he or she would have to join a company union or not join a non-company union.

If a state bases an employer's tax on the firm's individual experience, any reduction below the standard rate does not reduce the offset against the federal tax. Although the federal agency in charge of this program has developed model coverage and benefit standards, these standards are simply advisory. The states are free to set their own coverage, benefit, and financing provisions.

State unemployment insurance laws

All states plus the District of Columbia and Puerto Rico have unemployment insurance laws. The major provisions are summarized in the following paragraphs.

All states cover at least the employees covered under the federal law. To be eligible for benefits the unemployed person must first demonstrate a past attachment to the labor force. In most states this is accomplished through qualifying wages or employment during the worker's base period. The base period is usually the first four of the last five completed quarters prior to filing a claim. For example, if the person files a claim on April 1, the base period is the preceding calendar year. Usually the law requires base period compensation equal to some multiple such as 1½ of the high quarter wage. The objective is to require wages in more than one quarter during the base period. Most other states require at least a flat dollar amount of wages or a specified number of weeks of employment.

The claimant must also be willing and able to work, though a few pay a worker who is temporarily disabled. All states require registration with the Employment Service; most states require in addition that the claimant be actively seeking work.

Voluntary separation, misconduct, refusal of suitable work, or involvement in a labor dispute may cause the claimant to lose some or all of the benefits or to postpone the starting date. The most severe penalty is to cancel all the wage credits during the base period.

All but a few states have a waiting period of one week before benefits begin. When the worker files a claim, a benefit year starts which is the 52-week period starting that date. The worker need satisfy only one waiting period during a benefit year and can receive benefits during that year only for the maximum duration to be discussed later. Usually the weekly benefit is some percentage, such as ¹⁄₂₆, of the high quarter wages subject to a maximum amount. The ¹⁄₂₆ produces a benefit equal to half the average wage during the high quarter. Some states use a lower fraction to allow for weeks of unemployment during the high quarter. Some use a lower fraction for lower wages. Other approaches base the benefit on the annual wage or the average weekly wage. In most states the maximum amount is adjusted automatically each year as the state-wide average weekly wage increases.

In about one-fifth of the states the weekly benefit amount is increased if the worker has dependents. Some states pay benefits for the duration of unemployment up to a stated maximum, usually 26 weeks. Most, however, limit the maximum dollar payments to a fraction such as one-third of the base period wages. In these variable duration states the maximum payment period is also usually 26 weeks. In periods of high unemployment, however, the maximum duration may be extended under a federal-state program established by the Employment Security Amendments of 1970. This program extends the benefit duration to the lesser of either one-half the total amount of regular benefits or thirteen times the weekly benefit. The maximum duration under both the regular and extended programs is thirty-nine weeks.[8] Four states have separate extended benefit programs that will pay additional benefits under conditions or terms not covered by the federal-state program.

The state programs are financed through: payroll taxes paid by employers (and in three states by employees), federal grants that pay administrative costs, and federal

8. Under a 1975–77 emergency extended benefit program, the triggering conditions for the permanent extended benefit program were somewhat relaxed and the maximum duration for regular and extended benefits combined was increased to sixty-five weeks. The federal government financed this emergency extension completely.

grants that pay one-half the cost of the extended benefit program. In addition, states may and have borrowed monies from the federal trust fund. The standard payroll tax rate is 2.7 percent, sometimes higher, in order to take full advantage of the offset provision in the federal law. The wage base is the federal wage base of $6,000, sometimes higher, for the same reason. Few employers, however, actually pay 2.7 percent. All states have experience rating plans which in effect causes employers whose firms experience high unemployment rates to pay more than employers who experience low unemployment rates.[9] The schedule of rates varies depending upon the state balance in the federal trust fund. Rates are lower when the state balance is high and higher when the state balance is low. Under the most favorable schedules, in thirteen states the minimum rate is 0 percent; in eight states the maximum rate is only 2.7 percent. Under the least favorable schedules, in seventeen states the minimum rate is 1 percent or less; in 31 states the maximum rate is 4 percent or more.

Table 5 shows how the insured rate of unemployment has varied during selected years since 1940, the average weekly benefit paid during those years, and the funds available for benefits at the end of the period. Note especially that unemployment rates among insured people are substantially less than the total unemployment rates presented in Table 1, and that the funds available for benefits in recent years are much less despite a substantial increase in benefits paid. In 1940 the funds available were about 3.5

9. Puerto Rico and the Virgin Islands do not use experience rating.

TABLE 5

UNEMPLOYMENT INSURANCE: SELECTED DATA
1940–1977

YEAR	INSURED UN-EMPLOYMENT RATE	AVERAGE WEEKLY BENEFIT	FUNDS AVAILABLE, END OF PERIOD IN $ BILLION
1940	5.6%	$10.56	$ 1.8
1945	2.1	18.77	6.9
1950	4.6	20.76	7.0
1955	3.5	25.04	8.3
1960	4.8	32.87	6.6
1965	3.0	37.19	8.4
1970	3.4	50.34	11.9
1975	6.0	70.23	4.5
1977	3.9	78.77	4.4

SOURCE: Social Security Bulletins.

times the benefits paid; in 1977 available funds were about half the benefits paid. Many states are in debt to the federal trust fund.

Some critics of unemployment insurance would liberalize the system by covering all types of jobs, increasing the proportion of lost wages that the system is designed to replace, raising the maximum weekly benefits so that a much smaller number of workers would be affected by this maximum, reducing disqualification penalties, setting uniform maximum durations for all workers, and increasing the wage base which would transfer more of the responsibility to employers paying higher wages.[10] They would liberalize the eligibility requirements by using a shorter, more recent base period and by reducing the amount of work experience required. Many would also eliminate or modify experience rating on the grounds that it encourages employers to fight claims and is logically deficient because it assumes individual employers have complete control over their claims experience.

An opposing view has been most ably articulated by Professor Martin Feldstein of Harvard University.[11] He maintains that unemployment insurance was designed to handle mass unemployment of primary breadwinners at a time when workers paid much less taxes on their incomes. In today's climate, he maintains, the system is overly generous for most workers, provides inadequate aid for those with the longest unemployment or the least income, and creates disincentives for both employers and employees that raise unemployment rates. For a wide variety of unemployed men, he argues, the system replaces more than 60 percent of the income lost after taxes; unemployed women typically recover close to 80 percent. In the more generous states, these two percentages are over 80 percent for men and over 100 percent for women. Employers are protected against the instability they create through limits on experience rating and the use of cumulative experience. To achieve equity and reduce disincentives, he would tax unemployment compensation benefits. To stabilize employment he would make experience rating more responsive to individual employer experience. To reduce costs and increase incentives, he would replace unemployment insurance with an unemployment loan-insurance system.

In A New Job Security System for Michigan, Saul J. Blaustein of the W. E. Upjohn Institute for Employment Research has suggested

10. For a careful analysis of those proposals see William Papier, "Standards for Improving Maximum Unemployment Insurance Benefits," Industrial and Labor Relations Review, vol. 27, no. 3 (April 1974): 376–90.

11. Martin S. Feldstein, "Unemployment Insurance: Time for Reform," Harvard Business Review, vol. 53, no. 2 (March-April 1975), 51–61.

that unemployment insurance be restructured into three tiers of thirteen weeks each to provide benefits for short-, medium-, and long-term employment.[12] Eligibility requirements would become stiffer for each tier. More emphasis would be placed on helping the worker become reemployed. A new unemployment public assistance program would also be created for those who exhaust or do not qualify for unemployment insurance.

In 1976 Congress established a National Unemployment Compensation Commission which is currently reviewing the existing system in depth.

Public assistance

Public assistance is not nearly as important a source of income for the unemployed as unemployment insurance. The major sources are Aid to Families with Dependent Children, food stamps, and general assistance. AFDC, a state program supported by federal grants, helps unemployed mothers with dependent children who are poor because the father has died, become mentally or physically disabled, or is continually absent from the home because he has divorced his wife or deserted his family. The federal government will also contribute to but does not require payments to families in which the father is unemployed. Only about half the states make such payments. The federal food stamp program provides poor families with coupons that can be

exchanged at retail stores for groceries. General assistance programs, supported by state and local governments, are the public assistance programs of last resort. In many of these states, the able unemployed are not eligible; in many of the others, only emergency or short duration aid is available.

Private employee-benefit plans

In addition to attempting to stabilize employment over time through product diversification, production planning, marketing efforts, and other devices, employers may provide some income replacement or work guarantees. The newest approach is privately administered and financed Supplemental Unemployment Benefit plans which pay unemployed workers the difference between some objective, such as 80 percent of gross wages, less the state unemployment insurance benefit. Less than three million employees are covered under these plans which were initiated by unions and are concentrated in a few industries such as automobiles, glass, rubber, and steel.

EFFECT ON SOCIETY

The changing response of society to the threat of unemployment has affected society itself. Society is more secure because workers have better protection against unemployment.[13] The loss control tools that have been introduced and improved reduce the likelihood of unemployment and its duration; new alleviative tools reduce the economic consequences. Workers can worry less

12. The Upjohn Institute has recently completed a comprehensive study of unemployment insurance. See especially *Strengthening Unemployment Insurance: Program Improvements* (Kalamazoo, MI: The W. E. Upjohn Institute for Employment Research, 1975).

13. For a thoughtful comparison see J. G. Turnbull, *The Changing Faces of Economic Insecurity* (Minneapolis: The University of Minnesota Press, 1966), pp. 66–93.

about being unemployed or suffering serious economic consequences if they become unemployed. The cushioning of the blow suffered by those who become unemployed is clearly helpful to them and beneficial to society as a whole. On the other hand, efforts to handle the threat of unemployment have been less successful than those aimed at premature death, old age, or poor health. The problem is more complex and less amenable to certain approaches such as private insurance. The protection is far from complete in its coverage; many workers receive inadequate protection; and the protection is uneven among workers and sectors of the economy. In some cases the protection actually creates or prolongs unemployment. Future efforts must be devoted to correcting these deficiencies and exploring new approaches.

Consequences of Increased Third-Party Payments for Health Care Services

By ROBERT A. ZELTEN

ABSTRACT: The growth of third-party programs to pay the costs of health care has occurred in an unplanned manner. As a result, the country presently is faced with a number of uncoordinated payment programs that sometimes work against each other. While the expansion of health insurance programs has provided the financing necessary to keep our health care system up-to-date, and while such programs doubtlessly have reduced the financial barriers to seeking health care for some population segments, health insurance also has produced some problems. Generally, the contribution of health insurance to these problems is subtle and cannot be quantified. Yet, policymakers increasingly are recognizing that there are factors at work in our health care system that, if continued unabated, will exacerbate the country's health care cost problem. Many of these factors owe their existence to the socially unacceptable incentives provided by most health insurance programs. This article focuses on some of the adverse consequences of health insurance programs and indicates that the future of private health insurance depends upon how these problems are addressed.

Robert Zelten is Associate Professor of Insurance and Health Care Systems at the Wharton School, University of Pennsylvania. He received his Ph.D. from the University of Pennsylvania.

HEALTH insurance and liability insurance stand out as two forms of insurance that have had remarkable social ramifications. Many commentators on the "liability problem" and the "health care problem" place much of the blame on the existence of third-party protection against the risks of legal liability and medical expenses. Yet, these two risks are very different. Legal liability is a risk that can be altered by law or contract. The risk of poor health cannot be dealt with so directly. Moreover, most liability protection is purchased on an individual basis, whereas the majority of those covered by health insurance are covered on a group basis, and such protection is recognized as a basic component of the employee compensation package. While these characteristics of the health risk and health insurance make unemotional discussions of this product difficult, this article will attempt to highlight the major social consequences of health insurance.

EVOLUTION OF PAYMENT FOR PERSONAL HEALTH CARE SERVICES

Pre 1930's

Prior to the development of any major third-party payment programs, services and the payment for those services followed the same path. Physicians related to their patients both medically and financially and were very conscious of the financial impact of the services ordered or provided because the patient paid for this care almost totally out-of-pocket. Hospitals too received most of their revenues directly from patients. Total per capita health care expenditures were $29.16 in 1929,

and nearly all of the 87 percent derived from private sources[1] came directly out of the pockets of patients. During this period, price played an important role as an allocator of health care resources.

1930s and early 1940s

The development of Blue Cross and Blue Shield programs in the 1930s paved the way for the wide-spread growth of private, third-party payment programs.[2] Early Blue Cross and Blue Shield benefits were not sold on a group insurance basis as that phrase is technically employed, but were marketed door-to-door individually, or at the place of employment where a selected employee collected the premiums, or where the employer agreed to remit (but did not contribute) required premiums through payroll deduction.

Blue Cross programs, which cover hospital services, were often sponsored and controlled by participating hospitals. The sponsoring hospitals signed participation contracts with Blue Cross which specified the reimbursement arrangement and, in many cases, set forth the nature of

1. Robert M. Gibson and Charles R. Fisher, "National Health Expenditures, Fiscal Year 1977," *Social Security Bulletin*, vol. 41, no. 7 (July 1978), p. 5.
2. The first Blue Cross plan was organized in Texas in 1929. The initial motivation for Blue Cross was the need for a mechanism to solve the financial plight of hospitals. The first modern Blue Shield plan is traced to the organization of the California Physicians' Service by the California Medical Association in reaction to a proposed state insurance program. The Blues have consistently avoided characterizing their operations as "insurance." See Robert D. Eilers, *Regulation of Blue Cross and Blue Shield* (Homewood, IL: Richard D. Irwin, 1963) Chapt. II.

the risk accepted by the hospitals in the event of Blue Cross insolvency. Subscribers of the first Blue Cross plans were required to receive covered services only from participating hospitals. The plans became "community-wide," however, at the urging of the American Hospital Association (AHA). Until recently the AHA owned the Blue Cross symbol and approved Blue Cross plans. Most Blue Cross plans are no longer provider controlled.

Blue Shield plans, which cover physician services, were often sponsored and controlled by medical societies. All physicians in the plan's area were eligible to participate in Blue Shield. Physician payment usually was based on a fee schedule, and the fee schedule allowances served as payment in full only for subscribers whose income was below a specified level. Currently, fee schedule programs have given way to "prevailing fee" or "usual, customary and reasonable" (UCR) payment programs. Provider control of Blue Shield has not faded to the extent it has in Blue Cross plans.

From a health care financing standpoint, the development of these early third-party payment programs had significance in two ways. First, it divorced the payment for health care services from the actual receipt of those services for those covered by the plans. Price began to lose its significance as a rationing device both as regards the demand for and supply of health services. Second, to the extent that these plans negotiated reimbursement arrangements with providers that differed from existing pricing structures, dual prices resulted. This gave rise to certain system subsidies and some competitive advantages for the Blues in the health insurance market.

Mid-1940s to early 1960s

An increase in the development of private third-party payment programs indicated that health care benefits were increasingly being provided as an employee fringe benefit. Commercial health insurance companies[3] began to compete aggressively with the Blues. Commercial health insurers typically cover hospital services *and* physician services. They do not contract with providers of health care and do not confine their operations to a restricted geographic area as do the Blues.

The expansion of third-party payment programs forced health care providers to adapt to a multiplicity of reimbursement arrangements. Providers also derived a decreasing proportion of their revenues directly from patients. In 1950, direct out-of-pocket payments accounted for slightly over 70 percent of national personal health expenditures. In 1965, fifteen years later, this had dropped to 52 percent. These percentages were lower for services extensively covered by insurance (hospital services) and higher for services less extensively covered.

Early 1960s

In 1959 Congress enacted the Federal Employees Health Benefits Program (FEHBP). This legislation resulted in the federal government entering the system as an employer providing a fringe benefit to its

3. Commercial health insurance refers to coverage sold by companies regulated under the state insurance laws. Actually, health insurance is not the primary line of business for very many commercial insurers. Most commercial health insurance is sold by life insurance companies.

FIGURE 1

PAYMENT FOR HEALTH CARE SERVICES (MID-1960'S TO PRESENT)

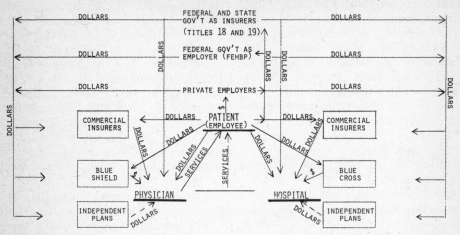

employees.[4] In spite of the fact that it represented the largest group insurance case in the country (currently covering about 8.5 million employees, annuitants and dependents), the program chose to rely on existing third-party payers rather than choosing to exercise its considerable financial clout by negotiating directly with health care providers.

Federal employees select one of several optional coverages each providing somewhat different benefits at a different price. If the employee chooses the indemnity program, the premium is paid to a commercial insurer. If the service benefit program is selected the premium goes to Blue Cross/Blue Shield. In addition to the aforementioned traditional third-party payment programs, federal employees were also provided an opportunity to enroll in various "independent plans" depending upon the availability of

such plans in an employee's geographic locale.

At the end of 1978, 81 independent plans were offered. Thirteen of them are employee organization plans that are available only to persons who belong to the employee organization (usually Postal Employee Plans). The remaining 68 independent plans are referred to as comprehensive plans and are generally known as health maintenance organizations (HMOs). While HMOs are not discussed extensively in this article, it should be noted that the favorable experience with HMOs under FEHBP contributed significantly to the federal HMO support which began with the enactment of the HMO Act of 1973 (P.L. 93-222).

Current status of health care financing

The highly fragmented system of paying for personal health care services that now prevails is shown in Figure 1. The figure indicates how complex our present system is com-

4. The federal government pays about 60 percent of the cost of the program, and Federal employees contribute the remainder through payroll deduction.

pared to the simple payment for services characterization of the patient-physician relationship pre-1930. It incorporates the Medicare and Medicaid programs (Titles 18 and 19 of the Social Security Act) wherein government has entered the health care payment system as an insurer. The figure shows payments to providers of Title 18 and Title 19 care flowing through fiscal intermediaries and directly from governmental agencies (particularly the states under Medicaid). The sources of funds for these programs include payroll taxes (levied on employees and employers), general revenues, and premiums (for Medicare, Part B). A recognition of the growing complexity of the "system" of paying for personal health care services helps to reveal the difficulty of developing a national policy that might be able to control the escalation of health care costs.

DIMENSIONS OF CURRENT HEALTH CARE EXPENDITURES

The size of the bill

For the fiscal year ended September 30, 1977, *total* national health expenditures were $162.6 billion. Table 1 indicates that $142.6 billion was spent for *personal* health care services. The total figure represented 8.8 percent of 1977's gross national product. The respective percent of GNP figures for the years 1970, 1960, 1950 and 1940 are 7.2, 5.2, 4.5, and 4.1. In the past 35 years, health care has more than doubled its share of GNP. Total expenditures in fiscal 1977 were 12.1 percent above 1976

TABLE 1

NATIONAL HEALTH EXPENDITURES—TYPE OF EXPENDITURE AND SOURCE OF FUNDS FISCAL 1977

Type of expenditure	Total	Source of funds					
		Private			Public		
		Total	Consumers	Other [1]	Total	Federal	State and local
				1977 [2]			
Total	$162,627	$94,185	$87,807	$6,378	$68,442	$46,563	$21,879
Health services and supplies	153,887	91,294	87,807	3,487	62,594	42,542	20,051
Personal health care	142,586	85,465	82,574	2,891	57,121	39,823	17,299
Hospital care	65,627	29,427	27,887	1,540	36,199	25,715	10,484
Physicians' services	32,184	24,360	24,318	42	7,824	5,808	2,016
Dentists' services	10,020	9,520	9,520	0	500	310	190
Other professional services	3,212	2,288	2,175	113	924	683	241
Drugs and drug sundries	12,516	11,373	11,373	0	1,143	614	529
Eyeglasses and appliances	2,086	1,956	1,956	0	130	66	64
Nursing-home care	12,618	5,434	5,343	91	7,184	4,204	2,980
Other health services	4,322	1,105		1,105	3,217	2,424	793
Expenses for prepayment and administration	7,572	5,829	5,233	596	1,743	1,430	313
Government public health activities	3,729	....	....	....	3,729	1,289	2,440
Research and medical-facilities construction	8,739	2,891	....	2,891	5,848	4,020	1,828
Research [3]	3,684	284	....	284	3,400	3,139	261
Construction	5,055	2,607	....	2,607	2,448	881	1,567

[1] Includes spending by philanthropic organizations and for industrial in-plant health services.
[2] Preliminary estimates.
[3] Research and development expenditures of drug companies and other manufacturers and providers of medical equipment and supplies excluded from "research expenditures" but included in the expenditure class in which the product falls.
SOURCE: U.S. Dept. of HEW, *Social Security Bulletin*, July 1978, p. 6.

TABLE 2

PERCENTAGE DISTRIBUTION OF NATIONAL HEALTH EXPENDITURES FOR SELECTED YEARS

Type of expenditure	Years ending June—							Year ending September 1977[2]
	1929	1940	1950	1960	1965	1970	1975[1]	
	Percentage distribution							
Total	100.0	100.0	100.0	100.0	100.0	100.0	100.0	100.0
Health services and supplies	94.2	96.0	93.0	93.4	91.7	92.6	93.9	94.6
Personal health care expense	88.2	87.9	86.5	87.9	86.1	86.9	86.8	87.7
Hospital care	18.1	25.0	30.7	32.9	33.8	37.4	39.1	40.4
Physicians' services	27.7	24.4	22.4	21.6	21.6	19.4	19.3	19.8
Dentists' services	13.3	10.4	7.8	7.5	7.0	6.5	6.4	6.2
Other professional services	6.9	4.5	3.2	3.3	2.5	2.0	1.9	2.0
Drugs and drug sundries	16.7	16.0	13.7	13.9	11.9	10.3	8.4	7.7
Eyeglasses and appliances	3.7	4.6	3.9	2.9	3.0	2.6	1.4	1.3
Nursing-home care		.7	1.5	1.9	3.3	5.5	7.6	7.8
Other health services	1.8	2.4	3.3	4.0	3.0	3.2	2.8	2.7
Expense for prepayment and administration	3.6	4.1	3.6	3.9	3.8	3.6	4.7	4.7
Government public health activities	2.5	4.0	2.9	1.6	1.7	2.1	2.4	2.3
Research and medical-facilities construction	5.8	3.5	7.0	6.6	8.3	7.4	6.1	5.4
Research		.1	.9	2.3	3.6	2.7	2.4	2.3
Construction	5.8	3.4	6.1	4.3	4.7	4.8	3.7	3.1

[1] Revised estimates.
[2] Preliminary estimates.
SOURCE: U.S. Dept. of HEW, *Social Security Bulletin*, July 1978, p. 15.

expenditures which were 13.5 percent above 1975 expenditures.

Where the money goes

Table 1 shows the importance of various services in terms of dollar expenditures. Hospital services account for the largest single share of the total pie. The $65.6 billion hospital care figure does not include amounts billed separately by physicians for services performed by them for their hospitalized patients. Thus, more health care expenses are incurred in the hospital setting than reflected in the amount paid for hospital care.

Table 2 may be more meaningful from the standpoint of the impact of insurance programs. It shows the trend in the relative share of expenditures for various services. For example, in 1977 twice as much was paid to hospitals as to physicians even though physicians received a larger share of the total pie until 1940. Those services which have

increased their share tend to be those most extensively covered by insurance programs.

Who uses the services

Per capita health care spending in fiscal 1977 was $737 based on *total* expenditures or $646 based on *personal* health care expenditures. Per capita expenditures, of course, are not uniform across all ages. For example, the population segment between the ages of 19 and 64 incurs per capita costs near the average while those under 19 incur per capita costs about 45 percent of the average. Those 65 and over incur per capita costs almost three times the average. Stated another way, while those 65 and over constitute about 10.5 percent of the population they account for about 29 percent of all personal health care expenditures. Those under 19 represent 33 percent of the population but only 15 percent of the costs. Further differences are observable

TABLE 3

PERCENTAGE DISTRIBUTION OF PERSONAL HEALTH CARE EXPENDITURES BY TYPE OF EXPENDITURE AND SOURCE OF PAYMENT—FISCAL 1977

Source of payment	Total	Hospital care	Physicians' services	Dentists' services	Other professional services	Drugs and drug sundries	Eyeglasses and appliances	Nursing-home care	Other health services
Total	100.0	100.0	100.0	100.0	100.0	100.0	100.0	100.0	100.0
Direct payments	30.3	5.9	38.8	79.5	43.5	83.1	91.9	41.4	
Third-party payments	69.7	94.1	61.2	20.5	56.5	16.9	8.1	58.6	100.0
Private health insurance	27.6	36.6	36.7	15.5	24.2	7.8	1.9	.9	
Philanthropy and industrial inplant	2.0	2.3	.1		3.5			.7	25.6
Government	40.1	55.2	24.3	5.0	28.8	9.1	6.2	56.9	74.4
Federal	27.9	39.2	18.0	3.1	21.3	4.9	3.2	33.3	56.1
Medicare	14.6	23.6	13.8		14.2			2.9	
Medicaid	6.4	5.1	3.2	2.2	5.7	4.6		28.6	4.5
Other	6.9	10.4	1.1	.8	1.3	.3	3.2	1.9	51.6
State and local	12.1	16.0	6.3	1.9	7.5	4.2	3.1	23.6	18.3
Medicaid	5.0	4.0	2.5	1.7	4.4	3.5		22.0	3.5
Other	7.2	12.0	3.8	.2	3.1	.7	3.1	1.6	14.9

SOURCE: U.S. Dept. of HEW, *Social Security Bulletin*, July 1978, p. 7.

when per capita expenditures for particular services are analyzed.

Who pays the bill

In the end, the entire population pays the total health care bill in the form of out-of-pocket payments, higher taxes, and higher prices for goods and services. What is presented here, however, is a portrayal of the "proximate" bill-payers. In the most aggregate sense, payers can be divided into private payers and public payers. Table 1 indicates that about 42 percent of *total* expenditures come from public sources and 58 percent from private ones. Public sources pay 40 percent of the bill for personal health care services.

Table 3 is a more pertinent portrayal for the current analysis. It shows that currently 70 percent of all personal health care expenditures come from third-party payment programs. The 70 percent is made up of 40 percent from public third-party programs and 30 percent from private health insurance and a small amount of philanthropy and industrial medicine. Third parties provide 94 percent of the dollars paid to hospitals.

CONSEQUENCES OF GROWTH OF THIRD-PARTY PROGRAMS

The growth of private and public health insurance programs has contributed significantly to the growth of the health care sector of the economy. Health insurance has impacted society positively and negatively. Without the widespread existence of third-party payment programs, national expenditures for health care would not be as high as $162.6 billion. There would not be as many physicians or other health care resources as currently exist and the mix of resources employed in the health care sector would be different.

Unfortunately, it is impossible to isolate the impact of health insurance. Many other changes were occurring while third-party payment programs were developing. Improved technology, better medical education, and growing consumer expectations played a significant role in shaping the country's health care system. In addition, some arguments are circular. Does better and more expensive technology give rise to more insurance or does the existence of insurance coverage encourage the development and use of sophisticated technology? Also, if there is too much first dollar coverage in group insurance programs is it the fault of insurance program designers or the tax laws which provide significant incentives to provide such fringe benefits?

There follows some of the consequences that appear to have resulted, at least in part, from the growth of health insurance programs. The items discussed have been selected largely because of their impact on health care costs—a major national concern. Some of the consequences noted are not attributable so much to the existence of insurance as to the mechanics of the programs. Hospital reimbursement based upon costs incurred and physician reimbursement based upon usual, customary and reasonable fees, for example, impact differently than alternative reimbursement methodologies.

Physician-patient relationship

With the exception of an initial physician visit, physicians are the "traffic cops" in the health care system. They determine who gets what and when they get it. In a nontechnical sense, physicians act as agents for their patients. This relationship has always been acceptable from a quality of care standpoint, and before the widespread existence of health insurance was also acceptable from a financial standpoint. When services provided were paid for directly by the patient, physicians tended to weigh the need for a service against the cost of that service to the patient.

As third-party payment programs became more prevalent, however, physician fiscal accountability lessened. As fewer services were paid for directly by the patient, it became easier to provide the marginal or completely unnecessary items of service in the name of "quality." The health care transaction became less personal from a financial standpoint. Costs tend to be viewed as less significant when paid by an insurance company or governmental agency than if paid by the patient directly. Providers appears to be willing to incur substantial costs to improve the reliability of a diagnosis or chance of recovery only minimally. Predictably, there has been growing disenchantment with the way physicians act as agents.

In no other area of insurance is the size of the covered loss in as much control of the recipient of insurance proceeds as in health care. Physicians are the demanders and suppliers of services, and fee-for-service reimbursement encourages providers to do more rather than less. One of the most attractive aspects of HMOs is the way it alters these incentives. In the HMO setting a sum of money is made available to provide the health care needs of a defined population and is not affected by the quantity of services provided or the mode of delivery. On the bottom line, the HMO form of health care delivery and financing represents an attempt to force physicians to be sensitive once again to the financial consequences of the services provided.

Conversely, it can be argued that health insurance has freed physicians to do what is best for their patients by separating the cost issue from the quality issue. Should any patient be deprived a potentially beneficial service because of inability to pay? This is a difficult question but one which is being increasingly answered in the affirmative—at least in an aggregate sense. Until it can be demonstrated that the increasing sums spent for personal health care services are generating equal improvements in health status, there will be continued pressure to contain the dollars flowing to health care.

Health care resources

Table 3 indicates that physicians receive about 39 percent of their practice revenue in the form of direct patient payments. This is an average figure across all specialties and if one were to examine each specialty separately a large amount of variation would be observed. For example, surgeons probably receive much less than 39 percent of their revenues from patients directly whereas the primary care specialties, like family practice and pediatrics, receive a higher percentage from patients directly. Because of patient collection problems and the relative certainty of third-party payments, it could be argued that insurance has introduced a bias in favor of nonprimary care specialties since it tends to cover the services provided by physicians in these specialties more extensively. It is clear that recognition of a category of health professionals by third-party payers is important to the financial viability of that professional group. There are repeated attempts by professionals to have legislation enacted that would require third-party payers to pay for services performed by them, or to mandate that every insurance policy sold cover the services performed by members of their profession.

There is growing agreement that the country is not suffering from too few physicians overall. However, there is unanimous agreement that there exists a maldistribution of physicians geographically and by specialty. Specifically, there is a shortage of primary care physicians.

These are the physicians who guide the patient through the complicated health care system. They are the initial contact. Physicians who fill this role represent a decreasing percentage of all physicians in private practice. In 1931, approximately 75 percent of all practicing physicians were primary care physicians. Now, fewer than 40 percent are in primary care specialties. Also, the number of primary care physicians per 100,000 of population has dropped about 25 percent over this time period.[5] There is little to indicate that this decrease in supply is a response to a decrease in consumer demand for primary care.

Many consumers are unable either to identify or locate an appropriate entry point into the system, and a substantial amount of improper self-referral occurs. Primary care physicians have lost control of the health care dollar. Overspecialization results in more expensive services through high specialist fees, more hospitalization, more ancillary services, and a tendency to treat symptoms within the narrow context of a single specialty. Finally, in third-party payment programs with substantial physician control (such as Blue Shield), it is the specialty physicians who often have the strongest voice in policy matters.

The preceding discussion is not meant to imply that the growth of health insurance has created the specialty distortion all by itself. The nature of the coverage in most contracts and the levels of reimbursement provided, however, have been a major contributing influence. Even the geographic maldistribution of

5. U.S. Dept. of H.E.W., *A White Paper*, "Towards a Comprehensive Health Policy for the 1970's" (Washington, DC, USGPO, May, 1971), p. 9.

physicians may be contributed to by third-party payment programs. Many physician reimbursement programs vary payment based on the geographic area of practice. It just so happens that the higher fee allowances tend to exist in areas with surplus physicians and lower allowances in areas suffering a physician shortage.

Vast resources have been committed to hospital construction since the mid-1940s. New-bed construction has outpaced the growth in population to the extent that there now exists an oversupply of hospital beds. Nationally, there are 4.4 hospital beds per 1000 population and the industry operates at about a 75 percent occupancy rate. One goal of current health planning is to reduce the excess supply of hospital beds. The existing oversupply leads to unnecessary hospital use in the form of needless hospital admissions and longer stays than medically necessary. More controlled health care delivery systems are able to get by with substantially fewer hospital beds. The Kaiser-Permanente Medical Care Program, for example, operates with about 1.6 beds per 1000 members. While Kaiser has fewer over age 65 members than the population in general, even on an age-adjusted basis, the Kaiser system uses far less hospital days than the traditional health care delivery system.

The rapid expansion of hospital care is reflected in the figures displayed in Table 2. Since 1929 hospitals have increased their share of expenditures from 18 to 40 percent. Insurance has been an important contributor to this in three ways.

First, the design of insurance benefit programs traditionally has encouraged hospitalization by providing better coverage for inpatient than outpatient services. In fact, third-party coverage for hospital care has grown so widespread that in 1977 less than $.06 out of every dollar received by hospitals was derived directly from patients (see Table 3). In real out-of-pocket dollars, a day of hospital care is no more expensive now than it was 50 years ago even though the product has been substantially improved.

At one time a substantial portion of hospital capital expenditures was financed with grants and philanthropy. As these sources have become unavailable, hospitals have come to rely on long-term bonds to finance their construction needs. Hospitals have had to compete for dollars in the capital markets along with other demanders of long-term funds. Health insurance has assisted hospitals in securing capital. Lenders now look more favorably upon hospitals because increased third-party payment for hospital services makes hospitals better credit risks due to more limited exposure to patient bad debts.

Perhaps most important is the reimbursement methodology employed by many third-party payers. Table 3 shows that governmental programs pay 55 percent of the hospital bill. These programs pay hospitals on the basis of the costs incurred in treating beneficiaries of governmental programs. Many Blue Cross plans pay hospitals in the same fashion. Hence, it is not uncommon for a hospital to derive 70 percent of its total revenues through cost-based reimbursement. Generally, any costs related to patient care, including debt service, are reimbursed. This payment method adds another degree of certainty to hospital lenders. Also, it is difficult for a hospital to refrain from adding new technology or new services when cost-based reimbursement virtually assures that such additions can be supported financially. It is generally recognized that cost-based reimbursement does little to promote hospital efficiency.

An additional point must be made relative to the consequences of cost-based hospital reimbursement. This method of payment minimizes the aggregate cost saving potential of alternatives to hospital care. For example, if a service that costs $1,000 to provide an inpatient is rendered instead on an outpatient basis for $200, it is incorrect to conclude that aggregate health care costs will decline by $800 due to this substitution. The aggregate savings, if any, will depend on how much of the $1,000 inpatient cost is eliminated by transferring the service. The portion that remains, basically the fixed portion will still be recovered through cost-based reimbursement. Hence, changes in patterns of utilization that appear financially attractive when viewed in isolation, lose much of their cost-saving lustre when viewed more globally.

Consumer demand

Third-party coverage of health care costs is not complete. While estimates vary, approximately ten percent of the population does not possess any form of health insurance. Secondly, many insurance programs do not provide complete protection for all covered services. Finally, many health care items are not covered at all in traditional insurance programs. These gaps exist in both public and private programs.

In spite of coverage deficiencies, third-party payment programs cover 70 percent of personal health care expenditures (see Table 3). This is up from 65 percent in 1972 and 32 percent in 1950.[6] The Committee for Economic Development said the following about the growth of third-party coverage.

. . . . where there is coverage, it modifies significantly the behavior of the patient and provider in the health-care marketplace. The amount paid by the patient at point of care is a residue after the insurance or government payment. These payments reduce the price paid by the consumer relative to the price charged by the provider; this tends to increase demand for services, particularly those paid for by third parties. (This reduction is the largest in the case of hospital and surgical care and almost nonexistent for preventive care.)[7]

For some services the out-of-pocket price to the consumer is near zero at point of service. This has led to the unnecessary consumption of services. Now proposals are heard that would increase the cost to consumers by inserting a variety of patient cost-sharing provisions into existing public and private health insurance programs.

Much of the demand for health care created by the expansion of health insurance is good. Prior to enactment of Medicare and Medicaid, for example, the poor of all ages had fewer physician visits than the nonpoor. By 1974, however, the poor were seeing physicians at a somewhat higher rate than the rest of the population.[8]

Health care prices

Total expenditures for health care are a function of two items—price

6. Committee for Economic Development, *Building a National Health Care System* (New York: April, 1973), p. 9.

7. Ibid., p. 40.

8. U.S. Dept. of H.E.W., Public Health Service, *Forward Plan for Health* (FY1978-82) (Washington, DC: USGPO, August, 1976), p. 18.

of services consumed and quantity of services consumed. The preceding sections have focused primarily on the impact of insurance on the quantity of services consumed. Insurance programs, however, have also had an impact on the price of services (that is, inflation). The mechanics of some widely used reimbursement methods provide a strong incentive for providers to increase their fee levels. It is well documented that physician fee increases have outpaced the increase in the consumer price index generally.

Early insurance programs covering the cost of physician services provided "fee schedule" reimbursement. When a patient received covered services, the physician would receive the fee schedule allowance from the insurer, and the patient would be responsible for the amount that the physician's actual charge exceeded the insurer payment.[9] Some private insurance programs and some Medicaid programs still employ fee schedules. However, many private insurance programs, some Medicaid programs, and Medicare have changed to "prevailing fee" or "usual, customary and reasonable" physician reimbursement. The demand for these new programs arose both from patients and from physicians. Patients were finding themselves responsible for more physician charges as physicians increased their fees while fee schedule allowances remained unchanged. Physicians, some of whom accepted the fee schedule allowance as pay-

ment in full even when not required to do so, became increasingly dissatisfied with the perceived inadequacy of the fee schedule allowances.

Under UCR reimbursement arrangements a physician is paid his or her *usual* fee for a particular procedure as long as that fee does not exceed what is considered to be the *customary* fee for that procedure. Generally, the customary fee is that fee that would fully reimburse 90 percent of the physicians performing that procedure in a designated geographical area. A higher payment could be made if *reasonable* in view of any unusual features of the particular case. Physicians agree to accept the insurer's UCR payment as full payment if the patient is covered by Blue Shield and the physician is a participating Blue Shield physician, or if the patient is covered by Medicare and the physician has accepted assignment for the case.[10]

A UCR program may be viewed as one where an insurer maintains a fee schedule for *each* physician and automatically updates that fee schedule periodically. The fee schedule is made up of a physician's usual charges and is often referred to as the physician's "profile." The maximum fee paid for any particular procedure, that is, the customary fee, is also automatically updated periodically. Under such programs, physicians have an incentive to increase their usual fees to the maximum, that is, to move up to the customary limit. Many programs limit the frequency of profile updates, but some permit instantaneous increases. Few programs place limits on the magnitude of permissible increases. What one finds after these programs operate

9. Most fee schedule programs contain "income limits." Under these programs, those persons with income below the income limit are covered in full by the fee schedule payment. Specifically, participating physicians agree to accept the fee schedule payment as full payment for their low income patients.

10. The actual mechanics of UCR reimbursement varies among programs. This discussion should be viewed only as an overview.

for a period of time is that the average fee gets closer to the maximum as physicians begin to "bunch" near the top of the customary range.

As a result of the growth of these payment programs, physician charges are difficult to evaluate. Often, physicians will inflate their charges over what they actually expect (or even want) to collect because they know that today's fees will establish next year's profile since there often is a lag in the data used to update profiles. Unfortunately, those not covered by a UCR program may be faced with an inflated bill which they feel obligated to pay in full.

The inflationary tendencies of UCR reimbursement increasingly are being recognized. More than a little interest exists in returning to fee schedule programs, or placing more control on allowable UCR payments.

Reduced financial accountability

The fact that health insurance has minimized the importance of price as a resource allocator in health care already has been noted. Providers, particularly hospitals, are under little pressure to be price conscious. But what if a hospital, or other provider, decided it wanted to attract more patients by lowering its prices? Would it be a useful endeavor? Probably not. First of all, patients use a hospital's services because they are directed to do so by a physician. It is doubtful that more physicians would be attracted to a hospital's staff or that the existing staff would use the hospital more because of lower prices. Moreover, insurance would preclude the hospital from passing on the full benefit of its lower prices to the purchasers of its services. This is so because its prices are reflected in insurance

premiums. The insurance mechanism pools hospitals and derives essentially what is an average price for hospital care. As such the low cost hospital benefits the high cost hospital by reducing the average price for hospital care. Hence, the hospital has its low prices diluted through the pooling mechanism.

Health care providers are insulated further from the pressures of consumers and premium payers by the manner in which most health insurance plans are administered. The vast majority of all health insurance is purchased on a group basis wherein an employer, for example, holds a master contract with an insurer that provides protection for that employer's employees and dependents. Under these arrangements, claims are normally submitted directly to the insurer who reviews and pays them. Periodically, summaries of claim payments are reported to the employer. For the most part, the summaries are of little use to the employer. Third-party payers shield providers from criticism because providers are never identified by name. Hence, employers are unable to exercise any influence over inefficient or high-priced providers. It is not clear, of course, that all employers desire provider-specific utilization and cost information, or, that they would use it if they had it. There is no question though that more of them are asking for such data. It is interesting to note that many insurers are not enthusiastic about providing such information even though an employer would have it if it self-administered its health benefits program.

Inequities

A variety of subsidies and inequities arise from third party payment programs. They stem not from insurance per se but from the mechanisms employed in various programs to reimburse providers. A few examples will be described briefly. They are limited to the hospital setting.

Subsidies across programs

Hospitals receive their revenues primarily from five classes of payers: self-pay patients, commercial insurers, Blue Cross, Medicare, and Medicaid. The first two classes and some Blue Cross plans pay hospitals on the basis of billed charges. Most Blue Cross plans and the two governmental programs pay costs, that is, the costs incurred by the hospital in treating beneficiaries of these programs regardless of what the hospital charges for these services. If all hospital "costs" were recognized as allowable by the cost-based payers *and* a hospital set its charges just sufficient to cover its costs, charges and costs would tend to be equal. Since neither condition obtains, charges and costs are not equal.

Suppose, for example, that a hospital administrator estimates that to meet all the financial needs of the hospital in a given year $10 million will be required. Assume further that 30 percent of the hospital's activity in the year involves treating Medicare patients. Medicare agrees then to reimburse 30 percent of the hospital's cost as their share of the financial burden. However, Medicare typically will not recognize the full $10 million as allowable costs.[11] Hence, if Medicare only

reimburses 30 percent of, say $9.5 million, or $2.85 million, it will mean that 30 percent of those cared for by the hospital only contribute 28.5 percent of the hospital's financial needs. Since this same payment methodology applies to other cost-based payers, a hospital may find, for example, 70 percent of its patients contributing 65 percent of its financial requirements. In order to meet its financial needs, the hospital will be forced to collect the other 35 percent of its revenues from the remaining 30 percent of the patients who have no control over what they must pay. Thus, it is often alleged that the public programs are being subsidized by private payers of hospital care. The higher premiums that result represent a hidden tax.

Inequities across hospitals

The situation described above also creates problems in attempting to assess relative hospital efficiency by examining a hospital's charge (price) structure. As an illustration, assume that Hospitals A and B provide identical services and have identical operating budgets. If the fiscal objective of each hospital is to generate revenues equal to full financial requirements and prices are cost-related, both would have identical price structures if all patients paid charges. However, if Hospital A serves more patients covered by cost-based reimbursement programs than Hospital B (and costs are not defined to include full financial requirements), Hospital A will be forced to implement a higher charge (price) schedule than Hospital B if it is to recoup its full financial requirements.[12] As a result, A's

11. A variety of items may account for the differences between allowable costs for reimbursement purposes and an administrator's view of full financial requirements. A few examples would be the difference between historical cost depreciation and price-level depreciation, the cost of charity and bad debt care, research support costs and unrecovered cafeteria costs.

12. Another way to state this result is as follows: Assume that the full financial requirements of each hospital is $1.00. Assume further that 70 percent of Hospital A's serv-

prices would compare unfavorably to B's due solely to its source of payment and not to its relative efficiency. This result could influence management to discriminate in the clientele it treats based solely on the nature of the clients' source of payment.

Inequities across patients within a hospital

In addition to the inequities resulting between A and B noted above, inequities may also result among the patients treated within each of the hospitals. This results from the fact that those patients not covered by the cost-based reimbursement programs must contribute more than their proportionate share of the hospital's financial needs. Hence, two patients using identical hospital services would pay the hospital (or, have paid on their behalf) different amounts based upon their insurance status.

Current reimbursement programs also contribute to wide discrepancies between the price of specific hospital services and the cost of those services. Because third-party payers represent a more certain source of funds to hospitals than do direct patient payments, hospital administrators have had a tendency to mark up covered services more than those not as extensively covered. For example, commercial insurance programs often limit coverage for room

and board charges to a stated dollar amount while ancillary services are covered more fully. This has resulted in hospital room and board charges not adequate to cover underlying costs while ancillary services have been priced to provide substantial margins. Hence, certain users of hospital services, those requiring extensive ancillary services, subsidize other users, those needing less intensive care.

CONCLUSION

This article has focused on some of the negative consequences of the expansion of third-party payment programs covering the costs of health care services. It has attempted to point out the role played by insurance in the tremendous expansion of national health care expenditures. The points discussed are not as widely known as most of the positive contributions of health insurance to society. The discussion was not meant to diminish these positive contributions.

Yet, it is the growing awareness of the points discussed herein that appears to be shaping the country's current policy with regard to health. Early proposals for national health insurance were often based upon the gaps in available coverages. Comprehensiveness and universality were often the primary descriptors of these proposals. Now, however, some believe that the country's health care cost problem is due to too much insurance coverage and that, absent some concomitant alteration in the health care economy, more coverage will simply exacerbate the cost problem.

Thus, policymakers have shifted their attention to health care cost containment. Most cost containment proposals recognize the perverse economic incentives operating in

---

ices and 10 percent of Hospital B's services are rendered to those covered by cost-based programs that define allowable costs in a manner that includes only 90 percent of their proportionate share of full financial requirements. As a result, A will have to recover 37 percent of its revenues from 30 percent of its patients while B needs to generate 91 percent of its revenues from 90 percent of its patients. A will be forced to charge higher prices than B.

health care which tend to drive up costs. Most of those incentives owe their existence to health insurance. Justice Department and Federal Trade Commission activities are aimed at increasing competition in health care thereby promoting more efficiency. Health Maintenance Organizations are being encouraged largely because they reorient the financial incentives and disincentives providers have to be efficient. Experimental reimbursement methods also are being incorporated in existing insurance programs to alter provider behavior. The real future of third-party payment programs for health care services depends on their ability to address the consequences noted herein.

Occupational Safety and Health

By MONROE BERKOWITZ

ABSTRACT: Work accidents became a matter of societal concern in the Progressive era of Woodrow Wilson. When other contingencies of modern life were brought under social security in the New Deal reforms of the 1930s, work accident legislation remained separate. One possible reason was that work accidents can be controlled within industrial and chance limits. But control does not imply elimination since a risk-free environment would paralyze production. In spite of imperfections caused by low benefits and imperfect insurance arrangements, the workers' compensation legislation does help internalize the costs of accidents, but internalization of costs is only one remedy. Regulation and a much broader community responsibility are others. It is argued that regulation poses greater problems and that broader community responsibility may evade the issues involved in choosing the appropriate tradeoff point between production and health which will maximize social welfare.

Monroe Berkowitz is Professor of Economics at Rutgers University, New Brunswick, New Jersey. His research interests center around workers' compensation and disability economics. He spent the last six months of 1978 as Visiting Professor at Victoria University, Wellington, New Zealand, where he completed a study on the economics of work accidents in New Zealand. He is collaborating with John F. Burton, Jr. on a nationwide study of permanent partial benefits under workers' compensation, financed by a grant from the National Science Foundation.

WORK accidents and occupational illnesses are different from accidents and illnesses that arise outside the work relationship. The work environment is different from the home or the highway. Workers perform their activities under the direction of management; in a sense accidents are a by-product of the production process. What is intriguing is that the same motivations that bring both management and labor to the workplace might be used to decrease the number of these unwanted events.

Society's responsibility for work accidents was recognized long before risks from other causes became a matter of community concern. It took the depression and the reforms of the New Deal to alter societal perceptions as to the treatment of the risks of unemployment, disability, old age, and premature death. But the workplace has been the subject of regulation since the mid-nineteenth century, and modern workers' compensation statutes date back to 1911. Since work accident legislation came earlier in time, it has a different character than the later legislation. Workers' compensation partakes of the atmosphere, delineated in Woodrow Wilson's Progressive era, of the mutual responsibilities shared by the individual and society.

Protection from the risks of unemployment, old age, and general disability borrows from Franklin Roosevelt's New Deal era when we were confident that the state could solve these pressing social problems. What is interesting is that in spite of the newer social security legislation, work-related accidents remain the province of special state programs administered quite separately from the federal acts.

In this paper, we look at the nature of risks of modern life in general, particularly those at the workplace, and concentrate on how the workplace might be different. We note that societal assumption of risks has meant not only the payment of benefits but has extended concern to ways and means to optimize the number of accidents. Unless safety is a consideration, there would seem to be no good reason to separate out work-related accidents from the other risks of modern life. One could pay accident benefits as part of a general social security scheme. The only reason to separate them would be if there were some way to control these events to a degree that is not feasible in the event of old age and death, unemployment, and nonwork accidents.

RISKS OF PERSONAL INJURY

All of us are at risk. We run the danger of crossing the street and being struck by an automobile, being injured in an earthquake, an elephant stampede, or falling down the stairs in our homes. Yet, we still cross streets, live in San Francisco, visit game parks in Africa, and build two-story homes.

Some people are more risk averse than others. They would just as soon not get involved, even if somebody offered a fair gambling bet where the odds have been scientifically chosen. Such risk averse people cross the streets at intersections, live in earthquake-proof homes if they are located near the San Andreas fault, stay in vehicles in game parks in Africa, and take care to see that handrails are installed on stairs. Others show a higher preference for risk. If the odds are pretty good, they would just as soon take a chance. These people delight in hanggliding on weekends, climbing mountains, and driving at 70 miles an hour on country roads.

Is it fair to say that if we fall into the risk preference category, we value the thrills of the sport or the savings in time more than we fear the increased risk of personal injury? At any rate it seems quite obvious that the chances of being injured depend on exposure to risk and that the chances can be reduced by avoidance of that risk, or by making modifications in the environment. Whether we avoid the activity or modify the environment, obviously, will be influenced by the cost of avoidance or modification as contrasted to the benefits derived from the activity.

In dealing with accidents, however, we must recognize that chance is an important variable. Running through the thread of countless definitions of what is meant by the term "accident" is the notion of an unplanned, uncontrolled and unexpected event.[1] I may avoid hanggliding and sit at home by the television set and be electrocuted by a faulty home-wired connection. Alternatively, I may indulge in hanggliding or even Russian roulette and emerge safe and unscathed. Chance is important. Accidents which result in personal injuries are random events and, it should be said, comparatively rare events in the work environment. Fortunately, we know something about the distribution that mere chance can bring about, and in that sense, we can take account of these ran-

dom chance variations. What gives cause for worry is when the number of accidents that occur under particularly defined circumstances is greater than is expected by pure chance variations.

The opportunity we have to do something about work accidents is based on the notion that we can calculate the number of expected accidents and determine whether the number of observed accidents is different than the number that is expected.

Occupational safety and health legislation, workers' compensation legislation, or any other type of employer liability arrangements are not going to do very much to alter the laws of chance. What we hope to do by effective regulation or other type of legislation designed to stimulate management to adopt safe and healthful work conditions is reduce the averages of the distributions which chance brings about. But it is always a reduction from what might be *expected*, given the type of industry activity and the type of people that are involved. In order to take a look at this more closely, we note the basic regularities that we find in the data relating to accidents in general and to work accidents in particular.

REGULARITIES IN THE DATA

Trends in deaths and serious injuries

No matter which country's data we look at we find a long-term decline in accidental deaths and serious injuries in the work environment. Where we have such data, as in the coal mines of Great Britain, the trends are most easily discernible, although similar patterns are found in the United States. In the 1850s

1. An excellent survey of various definitions of an accident can be found in *Review of Industrial Accident Literature* (London: National Institute of Industrial Psychology, 1972), published as one of the research papers prepared for the Committee on Safety and Health at Work in Great Britain, Lord Robens, Chairman.

fatal injuries in the coal mines in Great Britain were running at a rate of nearly four per thousand employees each year. By 1970 they had declined to less than one per thousand employees. Serious reportable nonfatal injuries per thousand employees declined more than 50 percent over the three-quarters of a century since 1908. What is true of coal mining is also true of industry in general. The Robens Committee in Great Britain found that in the decade 1961 to 1970, the fatality rate in factories (the annual rate of fatal accidents per 100,000 employees averaged over a 10 year period) was 4.5, whereas the comparable figure for the first decade of the century was 17.5.

At the same time we must note that there is no such comforting trend in less serious injuries. Trends in less serious injuries are influenced by the type of reporting system and the compensation system in effect.[2] The tendency is not to report less serious injuries unless there are benefits to be claimed. The higher the compensation benefits, the greater the incentive to claim these benefits and hence to report the injuries.

Home versus work

Safety people argue about the comparative safety of home versus work, and in part the argument is about what exposure base ought to be used. It is clear, however, that motor vehicles come first as a major cause of accidental deaths. Nonfatal injuries, however, are different. Although possibly one-third of them occur at work, two-thirds of them do not. Home injuries account for approximately one third of the total and if we add to the home injuries

those caused by defective and faulty goods and services we account for more than half of the injuries. The workplace is certainly by no means the most dangerous place to be.[3]

Young versus old

Another regularity in the data has to do with the age of employees. It is the propensity of the young, and particularly young males to injure themselves by accidents. Unfortunately, the same holds true of fatal accidents. A high percentage of industrial accidents occur among male workers under 21 years of age.

Business cycles

There is some evidence to indicate that accident frequency rates are susceptible to business cycle influences. In periods of prosperity, rates tend to increase whereas in a recession they tend to decline. The reasons for this are fairly obvious. In periods of prosperity the increased press of work brings additional stress but, just as important, it brings younger more inexperienced workers into the work force. Accident rates tend to fluctuate not only with age of workers, but with time and experience on the job.

Industry rankings

We have unambiguous data relating to the relative stability of industry rankings of accident frequency rates. Certain industries consistently rank at the top as accident producers and others are usually found at the

2. *Safety and Health at Work*, Report of the Committee, 1970–1972, Chairman Lord Robens (London: HMSO), p. 3.

3. An interesting comparative survey of these types of injuries in Great Britain can be found in the *Report of the Royal Commission on Civil Liabilities, and Compensation for Personal Injury*, Chairman Lord Pearson (London: HMSO, 1978); the survey of comparative accidents is in Volume II, "Statistics and Costings," Part III.

bottom. Within manufacturing, for example, timber and wood products, fabricated metal products, rubber and plastic products will rank near the top with the highest frequency rates and apparel and textile near the bottom. When we look at all industrial subdivisions, finance, insurance, real estate, and other largely clerical occupations have relatively few accidents whereas the meat packing, logging, timbering, and coal mining have a great many. Such consistent differences stem from the varying innate or inherent risks in each of the industries.[4]

The same consistency in rankings is true of minor subdivisions within an industry. Within the construction industry, the heavy construction, or tunneling divisions consistently have higher accident rates than say the painting and decorating sections of the industry. These consistencies in rankings show that something more than chance is at work. It suggests that accidents are based on something more than random occurrences.[5]

Size of plant

Accident rates are not independent of the size of the plant. The largest size and the smallest plants have the lowest accident frequency rates as compared to the mid-size firms.[6]

Whether this is due to personal relationships in the smaller plants or the existence of organized safety in the larger size plants cannot be proven, but such an explanation is intuitively plausible.

CONCLUSIONS ABOUT THE STABILITY OF DATA

It is reassuring to note these regularities in accident data. We see a decline over time in serious disabling injuries and fatalities, but note the sensitivity of the trends in less serious accidents to reporting requirements and amounts of benefits available. These are long term trends. We cannot discern these declines in the shorter term such as over the period of the last decade or so. Industry rankings in terms of measures of accidents remain surprisingly stable from year to year. That would indicate that factors other than mere chance are at work, and gives some underpinning to the notion of the efficacy of accident prevention efforts. Something more than chance is at work.

INTERVENTION IN THE WORK ACCIDENT AREA

If we wish to analyze the effects on society of changes in responsibility for work-related accidents and occupational diseases, we have to note that these first changes took place long ago, in the latter part of the nineteenth century, with the passage of employer liability laws. Society's objectives were rather narrow and designed to change aspects of the common law governing the master servant relationships. Under the common law, the worker was compelled to negotiate with his employer to recover damages as a result of an industrial accident, and

4. U.S. Bureau of the Census, *Statistical Abstract of the United States*, 98th ed. (Washington, DC: USGPO, 1977), Table 687, "Occupational Injury and Illness Incidence Rates by Industry, 1973–1975," p. 423.

5. C. L. Wong and H. J. Hilaski, "The Safety and Health Record in the Construction Industry," *Monthly Labor Review* vol. 101, no. 3 (1978), p. 5.

6. U.S. Bureau of the Census, *Statistical Abstract of the United States*, 98th Edition (Washington, DC: USGPO, 1977), Table 686, "Occupational Injury Rates in Private Industry by Employee Size, Class, Industry Group, 1974 and 1975," p. 422.

if he could not receive a satisfactory adjustment, then his only recourse was to sue in a court of law. The employer had the advantages that accrued to him by reason of his position, and in addition was aided by several judicial interpretations of common law doctrines. The negligence of a fellow servant or the employee himself could interfere with his recovery. In addition, if it could be shown that the employee knew about the job dangers and, therefore, could be said to have assumed the risks of the occupation, that might defeat his claim.[7]

We can only guess about the developments that may have taken place had the common law been allowed to evolve into the twentieth century with this social outlook. Suffice it to say that the employer liability laws passed by several states did soften these defenses and did allow the employee to recover damages without having to overcome what was thought then to be these rather unfair defenses.

As we look about us today and see what is happening to court judgments in the area of medical malpractice and recoveries for personal injury due to motor vehicle accidents, we might speculate the same liberalizing trends would have occurred in the area of industrial accidents. But as noted above, such developments never matured. Beginning in 1911, New Jersey, Wisconsin, and a number of other states passed workers' compensation statutes. These statutes were modeled generally after those prevailing in England, whose Parliament in turn had copied from the pioneering efforts of Bismarck

in Germany. In effect, these statutes abolished the notion of negligence and fault in the area of industrial accidents. Any employee involved in an accident that arose "out of and in the course of" employment, was entitled to benefits.

Neither the courts nor the newly established administrative tribunals under the workers' compensation acts were to inquire into fault or negligence. These recoveries were not to be in the nature of payment for damages but rather payment of compensation based upon wage loss. Since all accidents were to be compensated regardless of fault, the theory was that the compensation should be at a percentage of wages paid, usually two-thirds of the normal weekly wage. In addition, payments were to be made in the event of permanent disability or death, but no recovery was to be had for pain or suffering or other psychic consequences.

Financing the liability

The obligation to pay these specified amounts were set forth in the statute. Certain states, principally in the far West, set up exclusive state agencies to finance the new program, and other states, New York and California, for example, set up competitive state funds to write insurance. However, most states required the employer to secure his liability by purchasing insurance from a private carrier, or in the event the employer could show financial responsibility, he might be allowed to self-insure.[8]

The employer paid an insurance premium based on his industrial

---

7. Harry Weiss, "Employers' Liability and Workmen's Compensation," Chapter VI, Section III, in John R. Commons, *History of Labor in the United States 1896–1932* (New York: Macmillan, 1935), vol. 3, pp. 565–69.

8. National Commission on State Workmen's Compensation Laws, *Compendium on Workmen's Compensation*, "Security Requirements and Arrangements" (Washington, DC: USGPO, 1973), pp. 243–65.

classification and if he were large enough he might be experience rated. If his experience proved better than expected, he would receive a lower rate, and if worse than expected, he would receive a higher rate than the average for his industrial classification. Thus, some safety incentives were built into the program from the outset. The employer paid a classification rate based upon the average expected number of accidents for employers who were similarly situated. Thus the meat packing industry would pay one rate, the logging industry, another. If the business employed largely clerical workers, it would pay a much lower rate than if it were engaged in metal fabrication where the inherent hazards were higher. Even within those classifications, however, provided the employer was large enough so that his experience was credible, he could receive a differential rate based upon his tested accident experience during the current period.

It is worthwhile to note that this type of intervention on the part of the government was not far-reaching or intrusive. It is fair to say that it was designed to remedy what many perceived to be an obvious evil. Under the common law procedures, some workers received fairly large settlements by reason of their industrial accidents, others nothing, and how much a worker received depended on circumstances that many felt were extraneous to the main problem. Employees involved in industrial injuries suffered losses. The workers' compensation statutes set forth a particular method of sharing these losses. Workers involved in accidents received some continuing stream of income for some period of time. The amounts may not have been as much as they would receive had they been successful at common law, but there was the assurance that they would receive something regardless of fault.

As the laws developed, they did not lose sight of the notion that the employer's activities could influence the number of accidents within limits defined by chance and the innate hazards associated with his industry. It was acknowledged that the employer was able to modify his environment and thereby reduce the number of accidents. In order to provide incentive for him to undertake such activities, he was subject to both classification and experience rating.

Possibly one reason why this contingency was not brought into the social security fold was the conviction that accidents can be controlled in both number and type. The system of workers' compensation, with its private insurance financing and experience rating, presumably was designed to give these incentives to employers to provide safe and healthful working conditions.

Safety technology

Assuming that there exists some sort of safety technology which is effective in controlling accidents, that it costs the firm money and presumably that it affects the level of safety, the question then becomes how much of this safety technology should be adopted? If a slower speed of production will reduce accidents, the slower the speed, the fewer the number of accidents. But slower speed means less production and probably a higher cost for each item. If the firm is rational (interested in its profit picture at the end of the year), then it may find it wise to invest in safety technology until the last dollar spent results in a dollar saved in accident costs.

Granted that these accident costs are shared and that motivations are blunted by insurance and the pooling of risks, yet some type of classification and insurance system at least points in the direction of imposing costs of these accidents on management. Imposition of these costs should influence management to adopt a type and level of safety technology so as to reduce these charges. Increases in the amount spent for safety should result in lower accidents and consequently lower insurance rates.

Benefit levels

Although theory demands imposition of full costs upon management, the laws always provided for some cost sharing; yet, over the years the laws became outmoded. Benefits fell behind increases in costs of living and wages. The results were inequitable from the workers' point of view and since full costs were not met by management, the safety incentives were dulled. The villain in the piece was largely the weekly maximum rate written into the law which made a mockery out of the requirement that two-thirds of wages be paid in compensation benefits.

Fortunately, many of the states have now modernized their laws, largely under the impact of the recommendations of the National Commission on State Workmen's Compensation Laws. The Commission recommended that benefits be two-thirds of wages and that the weekly maximum be set so that the worker who makes at least the average wage would receive the statutory benefits.[9] Unhappily, not all states have responded to the challenge thus

making federal intervention in the area of minimum standards a possibility.[10]

Is social security disability legislation the road for workers' compensation legislation to travel? Would it be simpler to have the federal government administer the entire program and pay benefits to workers in accordance with some uniform national standard and to finance the costs out of general taxation?

The answer has to be affirmative if one is willing to give up whatever advantages accrue to society by reason of incentives that workers' compensation gives firms to minimize the number of accidents.

COMMUNITY RESPONSIBILITY

It may be, however, that a different analysis ought to be applied to this situation. In one sense, accidents are caused by individuals working in particular environments, some of which can be made safer than others. However, if we look at the philosophy of a man such as Sir Owen Woodhouse, author of New Zealand's Royal Commission report, which produced its comprehensive accident compensation statute:

It is society itself that has built up and encouraged the heavily risk laden activities that exact a known and expected cost of life and limb. I speak of the use that we all make of motor transport on the one hand and the essential nature of industrial production on the other.[11]

9. National Commission on State Workmen's Compensation Laws, *Report of the*

National Commission on State Workmen's Compensation Laws (Washington, DC: USGPO, 1972), pp. 56–57.

10. Statement of John F. Burton, Jr., on S.3060, the "National Workers' Compensation Standards Act of 1978," Before the Labor Subcommittee of the Senate Committee on Human Resources, 22 September 1978.

11. Sir Owen Woodhouse, "National Compensation and the Insurance Industry," an address delivered, Panang, 19 August 1977, mimeo.

Woodhouse speaks of "statistically inevitable" victims of accidents and the heavy responsibility upon the community to share in some way the burden that falls upon those that become the random casualties. In his view, once society as a whole has accepted the need to support certain groups of injured persons, it cannot be right to exclude others with equal problems who, like their fellow citizens, have been contributing to the general funds. "The notion of community responsibility carries with it as a natural collinear the principle of comprehensive entitlement."[12]

Underlying the whole of the Woodhouse report is the notion of benefits and entitlement as a matter of right, and community responsibility as the key to the development of a modern system of social welfare. Woodhouse argues that the private insurance industry is bound to face problems with escalating costs and increasing claims. He sees complete disengagement as the only sensible commercial course for the industry to pursue. Escalating requirements for premium income will cause the system to break down under its own weight, precipitated no doubt by rebellion on behalf of those who are expected to provide the premiums. In his view, despite the evident problems of transition, the future destiny of the insurance industry is surely not in the field of social welfare.

SOCIETAL RESPONSIBILITY AND THE MARKET

Conceding the indictment that has been made and the problems which have been identified, the question is whether a public enterprise would be better prepared to deal with them. Should an increasing portion of the

tax dollar go for these particular benefits? The identification of very real unanswered problems in the private sector does not necessarily mean that solutions will be forthcoming quite magically once the state assumes responsibility. Difficult questions of social choice are involved in any accident compensation scheme and they may be by-passed but not solved by the recommendation that the state assume full responsibility.

The questions remain: How many accidents is society prepared to absorb? How many resources should go into safety and prevention? As Gaskin notes, at one time it was thought that the state could supply the answer, but because of the difficulties many academic writers began to feel that the market is ideally suited to answer these questions. He believes that perhaps now the circle has turned again as a number of doubts are being raised about market solutions and economic approaches.[13]

What seems to be ignored in these analyses which contrast market responsibility and state responsibility are the inherent differences between the workplace and the highway or the home. There is no readily available way to bring market forces to bear on the number of accidents on the highway or in the home. On the other hand we do have a chance to allow market tactics to function in the work environment. We have a chance of internalizing the costs of the accidents to the employer and thereby at least approaching an answer as to how many accidents to have and how many of the nation's

12. Ibid., p. 5.

13. Richard Gaskin, "The Option in Tort Law Reform: A Survey," in Jane C. Kronick, project director, *Community Responsibility: The New Zealand Accident Compensation Act as a Value of Response to Technological Development*, U.S. National Science Foundation Report, 20 January 1978, pp. 21–29.

resources ought to be devoted to preventing them.

The evidence of the variability in accident frequency rates among firms within an industry, as well as the evidence of stability in differentials between industries, argue that such a safety technology is available. It could be utilized, provided the appropriate incentives were given to firms to make decisions which will be optimal from their point of view. It also depends on costs being internalized so that the individual firms' decisions are optimal from the point of view of society as a whole.

THE SENSITIVITY OF CLAIMS TO THE BENEFIT LEVELS

Old age is a matter of chronology as far as the social welfare system is concerned. Retirement may come at age 65, or before, and obviously the number and type of these retirements will be sensitive to the benefits that are paid. Death, of course, is a contingency which comes to us all and, problems of suicide aside, poses few problems in the way of moral hazard.

The number of work accidents, however, are subject to the effects of safety technology on one hand and quite sensitive to benefit levels on the other. The latter sensitivity cannot be understood as a matter of malingering or dishonesty on the part of the workers. It is simply confirmation of the fact that the number of claims that will be filed for less serious injuries is not independent of the rate of compensation benefits for those injuries. If workers suffer little monetary loss by being off work, one should expect to see an increase in the number of claims that are filed. In part, this stems from the difficulties of defining a state of disability and, in part, from the fact that in the case of some minor injuries, the worker could or could not continue working depending upon his subjective evaluation of the severity of the injury, and his evaluation of his alternatives.

Administrative problems

In short, there is a real need for competent administration of these claims for benefits. The effects on society arising from the assumption of the responsibility for work injuries cannot be discussed independently of the nature of the administration of whatever benefit program is set up. It so happens that work accident legislation is a rather difficult program to administer. The early state laws were fairly clever (realistic) in this respect in that they did not expect state administrators to do very much in the way of administration. Administration was left largely in the hands of the private insurance carriers and the assumption was that a type of adversary relationship might aid in the administration of these claims.[14]

According to investigators of the program, things may have gone too far. The assumption of a self administering system bumped into the difficulties involved in evaluating the nature and extent of permanent disabilities, and obviously there is room for a great deal of reform in this area. Whether privately administered or administered by a federal agency, the problem is the same. No one has yet discovered the ideal way to relate a physical impairment or a state of disability to a finite sum of money. At least the present system in the United States workers' compensation systems has the advantage of

14. Monroe Berkowitz, "The Processing of Workmen's Compensation Cases," Department of Labor, Bureau of Labor Standards, Bulletin 310 (1967), p. 4.

pluralism with some 50 odd different solutions. But we may be paying too high a price in terms of the inequalities suffered by workers in terms of differences in benefits for identical injuries in the several states.

Another unsolved problem has to do with occupational illnesses. Newspapers carry daily reminders of the deadly effect of industrial carcinogens. We do not yet have an adequate data base to evaluate the long term effects of working with various toxic substances. Yet it becomes increasingly evident that the effects of working with asbestos or lead can be debilitating even though the diseases may not manifest themselves until 10 or 20 years after initial exposure. There are grave doubts that a private system of workers' compensation, with its characteristic of assigning responsibility to a particular employer's experience of a particular year, can accommodate to the phenomena of slowly developing occupational illnesses. Given the long latency periods and the confusion as to etiology, a system which depends upon fixing responsibility on a particular employer's account may not survive. Yet solutions are not immediately obvious. To change to a system of benefits paid under a philosophy of broad community responsibility will not solve the problems of causation. If causation is deemed to be irrelevant, then of course we are into an entirely different area where we must face the issue not only of a general health insurance but income benefits to those who are ill due to nonoccupational as well as occupational causes.

Regulation

At this point the worker can be excused for impatience if he feels that the world is being made too complicated. Why should any indus-

try be allowed to use toxic materials which shorten the life of those exposed to them? Why should any machine go unguarded? Why should not all the safety technology that engineers can dream of be installed forthwith?

The matter can be pushed too far. Obviously, the safest work environment may not be productive enough to survive. Regardless of how the matter is stated (trade unions tend to talk about cannibalizing the worker and management people about benefit-cost margins), all recognize that some tradeoffs are involved.

It is not only possible but quite usual and traditional for the state to regulate safety and health at the workplace. Massachusetts enacted a law requiring the safeguarding of machinery, hoists and elevators as early as 1877, with New York passing similar legislation a decade later. When the seventh annual conference of the International Association of Factory Inspectors was held in Chicago in 1893, there were 14 states and provinces with factory laws and 110 inspectors.[15]

HEALTH

The maintenance of health as well as safety became a matter of state government concern quite early. The first report on occupational health hazards appears to have been written in 1837, and by 1910 the American Association for Labor Legislation called the First National Conference on Industrial Disease.[16]

Those of us who follow the controversies about lack of enforcement of standards promulgated by the administrators of the 1970 Occupa-

15. Don D. Lescohier, "The Campaign for Health and Safety in Industry," Chap. 19, in *History of Labor in the United States 1896–1932*, pp. 359–70.
16. Ibid., p. 361.

tional Safety and Health Act (OSHA) can be forgiven for believing that industrial hazards are a new concern at the federal level. But President Taft recommended use of the federal taxing mechanism to outlaw, in effect, the production of phosphorous matches after their deleterious effects were dramatized in a report by John Andrews.[17]

It would be foolish to contend that direct regulation has no role to play in safety and health at the workplace. But we must also recognize the problems and the limits of such regulation. OSHA was ushered in with high hopes that federal intervention would solve many of the pressing problems and bring a safe and healthful workplace into being. But the problems proved formidable.

Each employer is required to comply with standards promulgated by the Occupational Safety and Health Administration and has a general duty to furnish employees a job "free from recognized hazards that are causing or likely to cause death or serious harm." The type of standards to be set has plagued the administrators who have been criticized for being too stringent at times and too lenient at other times.

The bulk of OSHA's safety rules were adopted in 1971, a few months after the agency was created. For the most part these were based on the voluntary job safety standards adopted by industry known as consensus standards. OSHA now admits many of these were unsuited for governmental administration and were slated for discard. Newer standards are to be based on eliminating "real causes" of accidents; they are

to be simpler and easier to understand, administer and meet.[18]

No one can quarrel with these objectives and only the future can tell the extent to which they can be met. The problems are technical and difficult. They involve tension among groups with widely different attitudes; they involve tension between creating some ideal environment and what is feasible from an engineering point of view (relatively non-controversial); and also what is desirable from an economic viewpoint (very controversial).

The Industrial Union Department of the AFL-CIO criticizes an economics approach. "Since it is generally cheaper to let easily replaceable workers die than to reduce risk below unnecessary levels, when methods of cost-benefit analysis are used, the worker's life is sacrificed. . . ."[19]

Yet the IUD admits that there is no such thing as a "risk-free environment" and when OSHA determines a standard it must somehow arrive at specific levels of substances that satisfy both sides, that allow industry to operate and products to be produced at price levels which consumers find attractive.

Under the OSHA 1978 lead standards, industries are given from one to three years to reach an interim standard of 100 microgram level of lead per cubic meter of air, averaged over an eight-hour day and from one to ten years to reach 50 micrograms. The new standard provides for examinations of exposed workers to determine blood lead levels and for the removal—without

17. U.S. Bureau of Labor, *Phosphorus Poisoning in the Match Industry in the United States*, Bulletin No. 86 (January 1910), pp. 31-144.

18. Eula Bingham, "OSHA Wants Your Ideas," in *IUD Spotlight on Health and Safety*, Fourth Quarter (1978), vol. 7, no. 4, p. 3.

19. *IUD Spotlight on Health and Safety*, Fourth Quarter (1978), vol. 7, no. 4, p. 2.

loss of seniority, status or pay—of workers with elevated blood levels.

The controversial nature of such standards is illustrated by the fact that the Lead Industries Association and the United Steelworkers union rushed to be the first to contest the standards in the courts. The Association protested the stringency of the standards and the union filed suit to tighten them.

But controversy is to be expected and is not in and of itself undesirable. The real vice may be inherent in any standard-setting approach, which is necessarily rather rigid, applicable to all firms regardless of position and dependent upon a sophisticated inspection effort which most regulatory agencies do not seem capable of sustaining for long periods of time. Robert Stewart Smith argues that government should seek to provide that amount of safety and health which workers would provide for themselves if they did not have an employer standing between them and what we have called the safety technology.[20]

A CONCLUDING NOTE

Societal systems for dealing with work accidents and illnesses remain quite separate from the general social security mechanism. One reason for separate treatment is that economic motivations can be used to control

20. Robert Stewart Smith, *The Occupational Safety and Health Act: Its Goals and Achievements* (Washington, DC: American Enterprise Institute for Public Policy Research, 1976), p. 3.

the number and type of accidents which occur at the workplace.

If we can choose, within limits, the number of accidents we wish to experience, then any system, public or private, cannot evade the difficult matter of choosing the trade-off point between production and safety. Maintaining a separate work accident system keeps alive the possibility that economic motivations, implicit in our industrial organization, can be used to make such claims.

Of course there are alternatives in the form of increased regulation or broader community responsibility. We have traveled far down the road of regulation. OSHA standards, of necessity, are controversial, rigid, difficult, and expensive to enforce. The mood of the nation in the 1980s may not be conducive to more regulation, and that may reemphasize the benefits to be gained by making work accidents and illnesses expensive enough to the employer so that he chooses to have fewer of them.

The problems of choosing the tradeoff point between production and health will not disappear by waving the magic wand of regulation or legislation. The politicians may have to learn to say publicly what all parties concede privately. We cannot live in a risk-free environment and continue to enjoy the fruits of a dynamic economy. We must take advantage of the systems now in place which are capable of maximizing social welfare by deciding on the optimal amounts of resources which should be devoted to safeguarding the working environment.

Violent Crime Losses:
Their Impact on the Victim and Society

By EMIL M. MEURER, JR.

ABSTRACT: Crimes of violence have increased rapidly since 1950. In the face of increasing crime, the rights of the criminal have been protected and increased. At the same time, the rights of the victim of crime have remained relatively unchanged. The traditional rights of the victim have proven largely ineffective in providing compensation for losses suffered as a result of violent crimes. Against this setting, a number of states have seen fit to enact victim compensation programs. The existing state programs indemnify only losses which result from medical expenses and loss of earnings. They do not cover intangible personal losses or property losses. While far from a perfect solution, these laws emphasize the changing attitude of society toward the victims of violent crime.

Emil Meurer received his Masters Degree from Mankato State University and his PhD from the University of Nebraska—Lincoln in 1972. He is currently an Associate Professor of Finance at the University of New Orleans. Over the past five years, he has published several articles on the topic of compensation for victims of violent crime. He has also presented papers on the subject before several professional societies, and offered testimony on behalf of a state program in Texas.

ACCORDING to recent Gallup and Harris polls dealing with domestic problems, citizens rank crime second only to inflation as the most pressing problem facing the society. This section will examine trends in crime, the profile of the criminal and the victim, and the financial impact of crime given the traditional methods of recovery in our society.

TRENDS IN CRIME RATES

The most comprehensive figures dealing with both violent and non-violent crime are compiled by the Federal Bureau of Investigation and are reported annually in the publication, *Crime in the United States, Uniform Crime Reports*. According to this source, violent crime rose over 120 percent in the decade 1966 to 1975.[1] The two most recent years for which data are available, 1976 and 1977, show a decrease in the rate of growth but an increase in the absolute number of violent crimes.

Violent crimes included in the FBI reports are murder, forcible rape, robbery, and aggravated assault—certainly not an exhaustive list of violent crimes. Furthermore, substantial understatement of violent crime was suggested by the Commission on Law Enforcement and the Administration of Justice in its 1967 report, *Crime and Its Impact*.[2] The commission estimated the true number of major violent crimes was roughly twice the reported rate. This conclusion was based on three rea-

sons: failure of the victim to report the crime to police authorities, failure of local police to report accurately the crimes occurring in their jurisdictions, and the relatively small number of violent crimes actually included in the FBI reports (four).

PROFILE OF THE CRIME VICTIM

The crime victim tends to live in a large metropolitan area and is most often victimized in the economically depressed areas of the city. Furthermore, the victimization rate is highest among males (rape excepted), younger people, lower income groups, and minorities. Robbery is an exception. Here the victim is often an older, white person of lower middle income status. Since homicide, aggravated assault, and rape appear to be crimes of passion, the victim is often closely acquainted or related to the criminal. This is generally not true of the robbery victim.

Based on the above profile of the victim of a violent crime the following conclusions seem appropriate. By far the largest percentage of violent crimes are concentrated among those least able to absorb the financial burden of crime. For many, their existence is already cloaked in poverty or near poverty. As the number of violent crimes has increased, the increase has hit harder at those who can least afford to bear the burden of such crime.

EXISTING MEANS OF REDRESS

Given the scenario of the basically impoverished victim, what means of indemnification are available? How effective are these mean in meeting the needs of the victim? What changes are occurring? At the present time, the victims of violent crimes may receive some financial relief

1. Federal Bureau of Investigation, *Crime in the United States, Uniform Crime Reports 1975 and 1977* (Washington, DC: USGPO, 1976 and 1978).
2. Task Force on Assessment, the President's Commission on Law Enforcement and Administration of Justice, *Crime and Its Impact* (Washington, DC: USGPO, 1967).

from their losses through restitution, private insurance, public assistance, social insurance, and state sponsored victim compensation programs.

Restitution

It would seem logical that the perpetrator should be made to bear the financial burden of his act. While simple justice may dictate this solution, its application is often impractical or impossible. The criminal must be identified and apprehended. Based on FBI data, more than half of all crimes go unsolved. When the criminal is apprehended, the state provides for his criminal prosecution, but the victim must resort to the civil court for reimbursement of his damages. Merely conducting a successful civil suit is no guarantee that the victim will be indemnified. Often the criminal is judgment proof since he has no resources which can be used to satisfy the judgment. Although due process is served the victim is financially no better off.

Private Insurance

While over 85 percent of society has some form of medical expense coverage, the lower income segment of society rarely has adequate insurance benefits to cover their losses for hospitalization and other related medical expenses. Disability income insurance for replacement of lost earnings is almost nonexistent among the lower income members of society. The outcome is obvious; victims of violent crime are not being compensated for their losses through private insurance coverage. One study indicated that only nine percent of the victims received any indemnification for loss from private insurance sources.[3]

3. Herbert S. Denenberg, "Compensation

Social Insurance

Several social insurance programs may benefit crime victims. The most important of these is the Old Age, Survivors, Disability, Health Insurance provisions of the Social Security Act. Under this law, disability benefits and medical coverage may be provided to the injured victim, and survivorship benefits to the deceased victim's dependents. However, many victims are not covered since they do not fulfill the eligibility requirements established under the law. Typically, victims are young, unemployed males from racial minorities. They have not worked a sufficient number of quarters to meet the coverage provisions of the law. Lack of coverage also makes compensation available under Workers' Compensation Laws inappropriate. In addition, only a small number of violent crimes arise out of a condition of employment. Temporary disability benefits in six states may offer a partial solution.

Public assistance

In some instances public assistance does provide aid to violent crime victims. This is true if the victim is currently receiving public assistance, or is cast into poverty as the result of the crime. In such cases dependents may also be aided. However, the results of the crime may prevent the victim from becoming productive in the future. For other victims, their losses may reduce their standard of living but still leave them ineligible for either social insurance benefits or public assistance. Finally, the stigma of welfare may dissuade victims from seeking aid.

for the Victims of Crime: Justice for the Victim as Well as the Criminal," *The Insurance Law Journal* 574 (November, 1970).

Victim compensation plans

In 1966 the states of California and New York enacted the first state laws designed specifically to aid crime victims and their dependents. Through 1977 an additional seventeen states have established some form of victim compensation program.

The Crime Victim and Society

The victim is often the forgotten member of the criminal-state-victim triangle. Most studies which show an interest in the victim are conducted by criminologists who are primarily concerned with the victim as a tool, in their quest for a fuller understanding of the criminal.

Historical review

Stephen Schafer devotes the first chapter of his book, *The Victim and His Criminal*,[4] to a discussion of the history of the victim. He points out that until the rise of the manorial system in the Middle Ages, it was difficult to draw a distinction between criminal and civil law. Most societies placed emphasis on the punishment of the criminal as a method of exacting compensation for the victim. This concern for the victim waned during the Middle Ages.

It was chiefly owing to the violent greed of feudal barons and medieval ecclesiastical powers that the rights of the injured party were gradually infringed upon, and finally to a large extent, appropriated by these authorities, who exacted a double vengeance, indeed upon the offender, by forfeiting his property to themselves instead of the victim, and then punishing him by the dungeon, the torture, the stake or the gibbet. But the original victim of the wrong was practically ignored.[5]

This attitude still prevails in many societies today. Schafer contends that the renewed interest in plans to compensate the victim shows a reawakening of the society's concern for the victim of violent crimes.

Economic condition of the victim

It is unfortunate that while the importance of the victim has been recognized for nearly a century, very little research has been undertaken in the area. Commenting on the matter, the President's Commission on Law Enforcement and Administration of Justice observed: "One of the most neglected subjects in the study of crime is its victims; the persons, households, and businesses that bear the brunt of crime in the United States."[6]

Based on limited empirical studies, it seems reasonable to conclude that in many instances the victims of violent crimes are left in an even more seriously deprived economic state after the offense than was their original lot. It is difficult to estimate the number of individuals actually left destitute due to violent crime. Many of the victims and their dependents probably live in poverty both before and after the crime. While more empirical research in this area is needed, it seems apparent that violent crime weighs more heavily on the low income members of society—those who have a real need for financial assistance.

Cost of crime to society

Some estimates of the cost of crime to society have been made. A recent

4. Stephen Schafer, *The Victim and His Criminal* (New York: Random House, 1968).
5. William Tallack, *Reparation to the Injured, and the Rights of the Victim of Crime to Compensation* (London: London Press, 1900).
6. President's Commission on Law Enforcement.

estimate by the FBI placed the total cost of crime at $80 billion dollars annually.[7] However, as Morris and Hawkins point out in *The Honest Politician's Guide to Crime Control*,[8] it is absurd to attempt to aggregate all types of cost and produce one figure as the total cost of crime. In many instances, property crime results in an illegal transfer of property but no appreciable loss in value. In other instances, the nonfinancial costs are substantial but unestimated. Based on an estimate of loss as the result of additional medical expenses and loss of income due to violent crimes, a figure in excess of $7 billion dollars for 1978 seems reasonable. This amount was determined by taking a 1967 estimate of the President's Commission and adjusting for the increase in the number of crimes and the increase in the price level. This figure makes no attempt to value the intangible losses associated with violent crime. Whatever the true figure, there can be little doubt that it is measured in terms of billions of dollars annually.

VICTIM COMPENSATION PROGRAMS

It is against this background that some nineteen states have enacted legislation to aid victims of violent crime. In addition, four states have limited statutes for this purpose. State laws vary widely in their coverage of loss and in specific provisions.

Right vs. need — a philosophical question

Two basic arguments emerge in support of crime compensation. The first centers about the duty of the

7. Federal Bureau of Investigation, *Crime in the United States*.
8. Norval Morris and Gordon Hawkins, *The Honest Politician's Guide to Crime Control* (Chicago: University of Chicago Press, 1970).

state to provide police protection to its citizenry. When it fails to fulfil this obligation, the state should compensate the injured party if no other effective method of recovery is available. As noted earlier, most victims have no viable alternative. Since civil liability, restitution, and private and social insurance are not effective avenues so far as the typical victim is concerned, the state must fulfill its obligation to indemnify the victim. This approach established the *right* of the victim to compensation.

The second major argument in support of crime compensation laws is founded on a welfare concept. People made needy by an act outside of their control are entitled to public aid from the state. This argument denies an obligation on the part of the state to indemnify victims of crime unless they are made needy as a result of the crime. It requires that all other methods of potential recovery have been ineffective and only then provides compensation as a "last line of defense" against economic insecurity. This approach establishes the *need* of the victim for compensation.

Major provisions

Given the basic philosophical approaches to the existing state laws, it is worthwhile to review some major provisions of laws already enacted. Table 1 summarizes some of the features of these existing laws.

All existing state laws provide compensation to the victim; both medical expenses and loss of income are included in determining the loss. (Virginia covers only medical expenses.) Only a few states allow any compensation for pain and suffering, mental anguish, or other intangible losses. Generally, property losses are not covered by any of the states.

TABLE 1

STATES WITH CRIME VICTIMS COMPENSATION PROGRAMS

	Compensation to Victims			Compensation to Survivors			Must Be State Resident	Limitations	
	Medical Expenses	Lost Earnings	Lost Property	Burial Expenses	Pension	Lump Sum		Overall Benefits Not to Exceed	Time Limit to File Claim
Alaska	yes	yes	no	yes	no	yes	no	$25,000 (medical) $40,000 (lost earnings)	2 years
California	yes	yes	no	yes	no	yes	yes	$23,000	1 year
Delaware	yes	yes	no	yes	yes	yes	no	$10,000	1 year
Hawaii	yes	yes	no	yes	no	yes	no	$10,000	18 mos
Illinois	yes	yes	no	yes	no	no	no	$10,000	2 years (6 mos. intent)
Kentucky	yes	yes	no	yes	yes	no	yes	$15,000	90 days (can be extended to one year)
Maryland	yes	yes	no	yes	yes	yes	no	$45,000	2 years
Massachusetts	yes	yes	no	yes	no	yes	no	$10,000	1 year
Michigan	yes	yes	no	yes	yes	yes	no	$15,000	30 days (extended to 1 year for cause)
Minnesota	yes	yes	no	yes	yes	yes	no	$10,000	1 year
New Jersey	yes	yes	no	yes	yes	yes	no	$10,000	1 year
New York	yes	yes	no	yes	no	yes	no	no limit	2 years
North Dakota	yes	yes	no	yes	no	no	no	$25,000	1 year
Ohio	yes	yes	no	yes	when justified	when justified	no	$50,000	1 year
Pennsylvania	yes	yes	no	yes	yes	yes	yes	$25,000	1 year
Tennessee	yes	yes	no	yes	no	no	yes	$10,000	not determined yet
Virginia	yes	no	no	yes	no	when justified	yes	$10,000	6 mos. (can be extended to 2 years)
Washington	yes	yes	no	yes	yes	yes	yes	no limit	6 mos.
Wisconsin	yes	yes	no	yes	yes	yes	no	$10,000	2 years

Some exceptions to this rule do exist. For instance, in California a property loss may be indemnified if the victim is assisting a police officer or attempting to apprehend a felonious criminal. But the general intent of the laws is to cover only medical expenses and loss of income. In the case of the death of the victim, burial expenses are included with medical expenses and therefore are allowed in all states.

The benefits available to the dependent survivors of the victim vary considerably from state to state. Most states require a close relationship of the survivor to the victim and a strong demonstration of financial dependency. Once these requirements are satisfied the survivors may be entitled to a pension (1 state), a lump sum benefit (6 states), or both (9 states). Only Illinois, North Dakota, and Tennessee make no arrangement for payment to the survivors of the victim.

Certain limitations are imposed on the victim under all of the existing laws. Generally these limitations deal with residency requirements, maximum dollar awards, the time in which a claim must be filed, the time in which the crime must be reported to proper police authorities, and the duty of the victim to cooperate with law enforcement authorities after the crime has been reported. Six states require the claimant to be a resident of the state, while the other 13 do not impose this condition. In terms of maximum awards, only three states allow total compensation to exceed $25,000. Alaska has the highest limit, $25,000 for medical expenses and $40,000 for lost earnings, with Ohio allowing a total of $50,000 and Maryland, $45,000. The New York and Washington laws impose no limit, but the majority of states (9) have a $10,000 maximum award.

The time limit for filing a claim ranges from 30 days in Michigan to two years in five states. In several states the limit can be extended if circumstances indicate that the time limit imposes an unreasonable hardship on the victim. Most of the states also require that the crime giving rise to the claim be reported to the proper authorities within 24 hours, 48 hours, or some other short period. As in the case of filing claims, the time limit may be extended if conditions warrant an extension. Finally, a large majority of the laws require the victim to cooperate fully with law enforcement authorities in the apprehension and conviction of the criminal.

The laws deny any compensation to the victim or dependents if the victim was responsible for, or might have anticipated the damages which resulted from the crime. This provision is applied within the discretion of the commission charged with the administration of the law. The relationship of the victim to the offender is significant in determining eligibility for awards. All states limit in some respect, the amount that may be awarded if the victim is related to the criminal. Generally a relative, a member of the family, a member of the household, or one maintaining sexual relations with the criminal or offender is denied any recovery.

Empirical results

It is impossible to offer a comprehensive analysis of the operating experience of the state plans. Many have been enacted in the last two or three years and have little history. New York, Hawaii, and California offer experience based on approximately ten years of operation. In each of these states, the number of claims filed and allowed has increased at a faster rate than the rate of crime in the state. This is probably due to an increased awareness on the part of victims of the compensation plans and benefits available. In fiscal 1968 total payments of $425,426 were were made to 200 claimants in the state of New York. In fiscal 1977 this had increased to $3,228,667 paid to 1510 claimants. Increases in other states have not always been as rapid, but in every case they have been substantial.

In most states the number of claims has increased faster than the ability of the administrative process to cope with them. This had led to a substantial backlog of claims in many states. Delays in obtaining necessary information to verify claims has also presented some problems. In spite of these problems, the existing laws have benefited many crime victims and appear to offer a partial solution to the problems faced by the victim.

Federal legislation

At the present time, no federal crime victim compensation program exists. Attempts to enact such legislation date back to 1965 when Senator Yarborough of Texas sponsored legislation designed to aid victims of violent crime. Every session since has seen one or more bills introduced. Committee hearings have been held and on September 18, 1972, Senate Bill S. 750, sponsored by Senator Mansfield, was passed by the Senate by a vote of sixty-one to seven. To date this is the only bill to have passed either House.

While variations exist between the various federal bills which have been introduced, the majority of these bills would provide federal funding to states which voluntarily enact a state law to compensate victims of violent crime. States which have enacted legislation are actively supporting the passage of federal legislation, but the immediate future of a federal crime victim compensation program appears dim.

VICTIM COMPENSATION AND SOCIETY

The last ten years have witnessed a change in the attitude of society toward the victims of violent crime. The trend toward new methods of aiding the crime victim seems clearly established. A recent Gallup poll conducted nationally on the compensation of crime victims indicated that 62 percent of the respondents favored the establishment of such a program.

Benefits to society

The enactment of crime victim compensation will provide a number of benefits to society. One such benefit is the reduction in lost output due to insecurity, unemployment, and social disruption caused by uncompensated losses. On the surface, the victim presently sustains the full burden of medical expenses, lost wages, and related expenses. Ultimately society suffers in terms of lost jobs, productivity, and purchasing power. Reimbursement through victim compensation would allow the victim to secure the necessary medical attention needed for rehabilitation after the crime and once more become a productive member of society.

A second social value to be gained from crime victim compensation is the reduction of crime. Victims of violent crime would be required to notify promptly and to cooperate with authorities. This would help law enforcement officials increase the rate of apprehension and reduce crime by removing criminals from society who would otherwise remain at large to commit further crimes. Prompt reporting of crimes and cooperation with authorities would also allow for the compilation of more accurate statistical data. This would help to identify criminal characteristics and trends in crime. This information could be used not only to increase apprehension of criminals but also to reduce the incidence of crime in certain areas, thereby reducing the overall cost of crime to society.

Social value may accrue to society through the creation of public awareness of the cost of violent crime. At the present time, the cost of crime is a relatively unknown factor. Crime compensation programs will furnish an indication of the cost of violent crimes borne by the victims and ultimately by society as a whole. This recognition of cost will add emphasis to the need for a more effective program of crime prevention and perhaps spur the society to action. Finally, society may benefit from the increased prosecution and conviction of criminals. When the victim is fairly treated by society, he is more willing to cooperate with law enforcement officials.

Benefits to the crime victim

The most obvious benefit of a crime compensation program to the victim is that all or a portion of the financial loss he and his dependents have suffered will be reimbursed. To the extent that benefits are adequate to provide an acceptable standard of living for the victim, he will be freed from the burden of financial worry that often retards recovery from injury. Furthermore, the victim and his dependents will be able to maintain their status in the community. Assuming the plan is based on benefits as a matter of right, no stigma will attach to the receipt of benefits. This is not true of public assistance benefits.

CONCLUSION

Violent crime is a problem which faces the entire society; however, its physical and financial hardships fall more heavily on some segments of the society than on others. Several sources of indemnification for losses do exist, but they have proven to be largely ineffective. For this reason a number of states have seen fit to enact legislation designed to ease the financial burden encountered by victims of violent crime. While far from a perfect solution to the problem, it has resulted in some shifting of the cost from the individual victim and his dependents to the society as a whole.

ANNALS, AAPSS, 443, May 1979

Expansion or Contraction of Social Security: Serious Side Effects

By ROBERT J. MYERS

ABSTRACT: During its first three decades of operation, the Social Security program was almost unanimously approved of by the populace and the press. The benefits were many times as large as actuarially purchasable from the contributions paid. The administration was efficient and prompt. However, in the 1970s, the situation considerably changed: financial problems arose—both over the short range and the long range—and the administration deteriorated. The press became critical and cried "crisis." Many feared that the program was bankrupt and that benefit promises would not be kept. Accordingly, proposals were made to contract the system, despite considerable expansionist pressure for increasing benefits. Good and compelling reasons exist to maintain the program at about its present relative level, neither to expand or contract it. Further, its financing should continue to be solely through direct, visible payroll taxes, and not, as many propose, by designated, but unrelated, taxes or from general revenues. Financing the program indirectly is deceptive at best, because the American public would then believe that somebody other than themselves would be paying for a substantial portion of the cost. The simple facts of economic life are that all taxes are paid by people and that, although different taxes might appear to have different incidences, it is impossible to determine whether this is actually so.

Robert J. Myers is a professor of actuarial science at Temple University. He received his Bachelors Degree at Lehigh University and his Masters Degree at the University of Iowa. He also received honorary Doctor of Laws Degrees from Muhlenberg College and Lehigh University. During 1934–70, he served in various actuarial positions with the Social Security Administration and was its Chief Actuary during 1947–70. He is a Fellow of the Society of Actuaries, and was its President in 1971–72. Currently, he is a member of the National Commission on Social Security, established by the Social Security Amendments of 1977.

THE SOCIAL Security program has been in operation for only about four decades, but in this time it has grown to be one of the most important components of our society in the responsibility for treatment of personal risks. This paper will examine the various possible side effects of either an expansion or a contraction of the program. Considered here as Social Security will be only the program of cash benefits— Old-Age, Survivors, and Disability Insurance—and not the health-care benefits provided under the related Medicare program.

THE FIRST THREE DECADES

In 1937 the Social Security program began operations by collecting contributions from specified covered workers. The payment of monthly benefits began in 1940. For approximately three decades, the Social Security system enjoyed its "golden days." Everything about it seemed to be perfect, and it had high acceptance by almost all the populace and the public media.

For many years the tax rates were relatively low, although they were scheduled to increase over future years in order to provide adequate long-range financing, and the benefits were "actuarial bargains" for those receiving them. Although there was a significant amount of public dissatisfaction with what appeared to be low benefits, many people recognized that they far exceeded the amounts actuarially purchasable from the contributions paid.

In the course of three decades, the benefit level was increased a number of times, but generally at only about the same rate as the moderate increases in the price level that were occurring. These changes were quite popular politically, be-cause it was possible to vote benefit increases without sharp boosts in the tax rates. This "magic" was achieved primarily because wages were rising so much more rapidly than prices, and this meant sufficient income to finance the higher benefit costs (especially because the maximum taxable earnings base was increased correspondingly).

Another factor in the political popularity and acceptance of Social Security in its first three decades was its outstanding administrative success. The Social Security Administration was widely acclaimed for its operating efficiency. Claims were handled speedily and accurately. As in any new enterprise, the staff was enthusiastic about the program and anxious to make it work well.

Still another factor of great importance was the rapid development of record-keeping equipment during this period. When the Social Security Act was enacted in 1935, serious concern prevailed among the top officials as to whether the vast amounts of lifetime earnings records could be efficiently and accurately maintained. The development of punch-card methods, and then the advent of electronic data processing equipment, readily handled the situation, especially as the coverage of the Social Security program approached universality.

At the same time, during these first three decades of operation, Social Security experienced no serious financial problems. As in any pension plan in its early years of operation, the system had significant excesses of income over outgo, despite the fact that the financing of the program was arranged on the basis of a schedule of increasing tax rates, so that large funds were not expected to be accumulated. As a result, the general public had little concern about the Social Security program from a fiscal standpoint. The tax rates were relatively low, and yet what appeared to be sizable funds accumulated. At times, it may be noted, significant increases in the tax rates occurred—for example, rises of at least ½ percent for both the employer and the employee took place in 1950, 1954, 1960, and 1966. Relatively little public complaint occurred on each of these instances (contrast that with the current situation, when much smaller increases are causing significant public outcries!).

PROBLEMS OF THE FOURTH DECADE

The Social Security program began to experience serious difficulties in its fourth decade of operation. The inauguration of the Medicare program, which is much more difficult to administer than the periodic cash benefits, began to make the administrative machinery creak. Administrative delays and backlogs arose. The personnel of district offices were gradually losing much of their initial zeal to provide services to the beneficiaries.

In 1970, Congress decided to provide the so-called black-lung benefits for miners suffering from pneumoconiosis. The question then arose as to what agency should administer this program. The Social Security Administration was selected on the basis of its great reputation for administrative skill. Unfortunately, this additional burden tended to worsen further the administrative operations of the Social Security Administration, especially in the disability-benefits area.

Then, in 1974, the public assistance programs for the three adult categories (aged, blind, and disabled), which had formerly been administered by the several states, was nationalized, to be administered by the Social Security Administration. Once again, this agency had been selected because of its past reputation for administrative efficiency. The result was far less than successful. Serious administrative bottlenecks arose, and large amounts of funds were incorrectly paid. It had not been realized that payments based on needs, and therefore frequently varying from month to month, were considerably different to administer than "insurance" benefits determined from purely arithmetical computations on the basis of maintained earnings records.

Also, in this fourth decade, serious financing problems arose. Over the short range, these were caused by unfavorable economic conditions (prices at times rising more rapidly than earnings and high unemployment), political over-expansion of the benefit level as a result of competition between the legislative and executive branches, and unfavorable disability experience. Over the long run, however, even more serious problems arose, partially as a result of a technical flaw in the automatic-adjustment provisions enacted in 1972, and partially from what would apparently be the vastly changed demographic situation resulting from sharply reduced fertility rates.

RELATIVE CURRENT STATUS OF SOCIAL SECURITY PROGRAM

Let us next examine the question as to whether the Social Security program has been greatly expanded over the years. Simplistically, some people would say that such expansion is obvious. After all, the maximum annual tax for both employers and employees was only $30 until

1950, whereas in 1979 it is $1,404. The average monthly benefit for a retired worker was less than $25 in 1940, whereas in early 1979 it was about $263. Similarly, both the employer and employee tax rate was only 1 percent on the first $3,000 of annual wages, whereas in 1979 it is 6.13 percent on the first $22,900.

In this real economic world, such a comparison of merely dollar figures is not valid. Also considered must be such other factors as changes in prices and wages, and changes in the scope of the benefit protection provided. As contrasted with the late 1930s, the wage level is now about nine times as high, while the price level is almost four times as high.

It should also be kept in mind that the financing basis of the original Social Security program was such that the tax rates would gradually increase over the years, trebling in about a decade, and thus building up a rather substantial fund whose interest earnings would help finance the costs of the program. Instead of such a rapid increase in the tax rates, they were held low for quite a number of years. As a result, all other factors being equal, higher rates would eventually have been required.

Although the current maximum taxable earnings base of $22,900 in 1979 is more than seven times as large as the initial base of $3,000, there has, in relative terms, been a contraction rather than an expansion. To be comparable with the $3,000 of the late 1930s, the current base would have to be $29,400. The two ad hoc increases in the earnings base in 1980–81 will move quite close to relative comparability with the initial base of $3,000, although it will still be somewhat lower—in 1981, the actual base of $29,700 versus the projection of the original base being $33,900. In the author's opinion, the original $3,000 base

was far too high, and the action of contracting it that was followed in the 1950s and 1960s by having it at a relatively lower, although stable, level was desirable, and the recent ad hoc increases in the opposite direction were undesirable.

While the benefit level seems to have been greatly expanded over the years, this is not the case when consideration in relative terms is made. Under present law, an individual with average earnings during his or her entire working lifetime who retired at age 65 in early 1982 (when the new indexed-earnings approach legislated by the 1977 Amendments first becomes effective for retirees at age 65) will have a benefit of about 40 percent of the earnings rate immediately preceding retirement. Under the Social Security Act as it was amended in 1939, using the assumption that wages would be level in the future, the average-earnings individual, retiring at age 65 in early 1982, would also have had a replacement rate of about 40 percent.[1] For a person with maximum creditable earnings, the 1939 Act would have yielded a replacement rate for the 1982 retiree of 23 percent, whereas under present law such an individual will ultimately have a rate of about 27 percent. Thus, it may be seen that the level of benefits under present law has not been greatly expanded as compared with what the original law would have done.

The very much higher Social Security tax rates now in effect (as well as those scheduled for the future) are, however, a clear indication as

1. It is appropriate to assume static economic conditions for this analysis because the benefit formula was adopted to be appropriate under such conditions as then prevailed. In other words, changes in economic conditions in the future would certainly necessitate changes in the benefit formula.

to the expansion of the program in the past. Although part of the increase is due to the revised financing method—moving from a partially-funded system to a pay-as-you-go one—most of it can be attributed to an expanded scope of benefit protection.[2] The addition of disability benefits by the 1956 Amendments and of hospital benefits by the 1965 Amendments, as well as certain other liberalizations (such as increased benefit rates and lower eligibility ages for widows), resulted in higher costs and thus higher tax rates.[3]

THREE PHILOSOPHIES OF SOCIAL SECURITY

There are three general philosophies of Social Security, regarding its relative role, its extent, and especially its benefit level.

The expansionists believe that Social Security should provide benefits which, for the majority of workers, will provide virtually full replacement of their net take-home pay immediately preceding retirement.[4] In other words, under this belief,

there would be little need for economic security provision to be made by most individuals through the private sector, such as personal savings or pension plans.

At the other extreme are the contractionists who believe that the Social Security program should be reduced in magnitude, and even possibly eliminated eventually. One approach in this direction is to reduce gradually the replacement rates, although maintaining the monetary size of the benefits and their real purchasing power.[5] A more extreme procedure would be to eliminate mandatory Social Security participation and then compel people to purchase private protection.[6]

The moderate philosophy essentially believes that the present benefit level is approximately satisfactory and that it should continue unchanged, on a relative basis, into the future.

Expansionist philosophy

At first glance, the expansionist philosophy has considerable appeal, because "it gets the job done" by providing economic security protection for the vast majority of the populace, leaving only the very highest paid to do something for themselves in addition. The result then seems to be a socially equitable and desirable situation. However, the se-

2. Although it has been widely stated that the original Social Security program was on a fully-funded actuarial basis similar to life insurance companies and private pension plans, this was not the case. At no time was it intended that the fund on hand would equal the accrued liabilities to date. For more details on this matter, see Robert J. Myers, *Social Security* (Homewood, IL: Richard D. Irwin, 1975), p. 143.

3. The addition of survivor and dependent benefits by the 1939 Amendments did not result in higher costs because of the offsetting factors of reducing the retirement benefits payable in the distant future and eliminating the "lump-sum refund of contributions" death benefit.

4. Examples of this view are found in Bert Seidman and Lyndon Drew, "The Injustices of Aging," *American Federationist*, July 1978, p. 16, and in the testimony of the American Association of Retired Persons before the Senate Special Committee on Aging, 8 September 1978.

5. For an example of such a proposal, see *Report of the Consultant Panel on Social Security to the Congressional Research Service* (Washington, DC: USGPO, August 1976), p. 17.

6. For examples of such proposals, see Michael J. Boskin, "Social Security: The Alternatives Before Us" in *The Crisis in Social Security,* Institute for Contemporary Studies, San Francisco, 1977, p. 173; and Charles D. Hobbs and Stephen L. Powlesland, *Retirement Security Reform, Restructuring the Social Security System,* Institute for Liberty and Community, Concord, Vermont, 1975, p. 16.

rious question can be raised as to whether, if the government provides fully for virtually all persons, there will be serious disincentives for individual responsibility and initiative, resulting in insufficient national economic growth.[7] The economic pie might then be divided up in an equitable manner, but the total pie would be much smaller than if personal incentives were not stifled.

Another important disadvantage of the expansionist approach is the effect that its fulfillment would have on the capital market. Without the private savings involved in pension plans and individual savings efforts, there would be far less accumulation of capital. If this were to occur, the productive capacity of the country would stagnate, unless the necessary funds were provided in some other manner, and this would seem to be possible only through government loans. The net result would then be more governmental controls because, naturally, where loans are made, control and regulation must follow. This, too, would undoubtedly have a deleterious effect on the growth of the national economy.

Contractionist philosophy

Many people might well believe that a diminished role for Social Security would be desirable, because this would mean an increased role for the private sector. There would then occur the advantages of greater flexibility and individual initiatives,

7. The evidence seems clear from both national and international experience that over-control by government eventually results in the stifling of productivity. On the other hand, the author does not argue for a return to complete laissez faire in economic and financial matters. It would seem that somewhere between these two extremes lies the optimum situation.

as well as greater accumulation of capital required for economic growth. However, the various proposals that have been made along these lines seem to have inherent, although not readily observable, difficulties.

The extreme proposal of gradually phasing Social Security out by either requiring or permitting younger persons to buy their own economic security in the private sector is, on the surface, very appealing. It is argued that such individuals would thus be able to obtain larger benefits—and this may well be so. However, what is forgotten is the huge residual cost of the Social Security system for the older persons who would remain covered by it. Such cost would have to be met, over the long run, through general taxes on the younger workers who opt out, so that, in the aggregate, they would be no better off—a "catch-22" situation.

The proposals that would not completely eliminate the Social Security program, but rather would bring about contraction of its benefit level are quite seductive. This approach does, however, have great weaknesses. From the standpoint of equity, it seems unfair to require younger workers to pay relatively higher taxes over their working lifetimes than current older workers have paid, and yet receive lower relative benefits. Also, there is the serious question whether Congress would allow the benefit level to slowly wither away, and instead might well make ad hoc increases, possibly in irresponsibly large amounts. The resultant instability would make it very difficult for individuals and their employers to plan for adequate supplementary protection.

Moderate approach

The moderate philosophy has as its basic principle that the Social

Security program should provide a reasonable floor of economic protection upon which people can build. The floor should be high enough so that for the vast majority of persons (say, at least 90 percent) the total retirement income is such that supplementary public assistance is not needed. At the same time, the floor should not be any higher than is necessary to achieve this result, or else individual efforts to achieve economic security will be diminished. The present level of Social Security benefits does approximately achieve this goal, although it may be slightly higher than necessary. This is evidenced by the fact that only about 8 percent of Social Security beneficiaries aged 65 and over also receive payments under the Supplemental Security Income program.

It is desirable, even essential, that if the Social Security program is to serve as a floor of protection, its benefits should have relative stability into the future, regardless of changes in economic elements. If this is the case, then private-sector economic security activities can be reasonably planned and executed.

The moderate philosophy can be criticized on the grounds that it is an effort only to maintain the status quo.[8] It should be remembered, however, that although the status quo is not always best, it may be so at some times, and perhaps this is the situation as to Social Security.

SOLUTION OF CURRENT FINANCIAL PROBLEMS OF SOCIAL SECURITY

For several years prior to the enactment of the 1977 Amendments, there had been considerable public concern about the financial solvency of the Social Security program. Although serious problems were present, much of the criticism greatly over-emphasized them. In any event, the 1977 Amendments did substantially solve the financial problems for the next three decades, unless very unusual circumstances should occur, such as runaway double-digit inflation over a considerable number of years.

Nonetheless, many individuals still proclaim a financial crisis for the Social Security program. They incorrectly assert that huge tax burdens have been imposed by the 1977 Amendments, when actually the scheduled increases in the tax rates are no more than have been effectuated several times in the past.

Some persons have advocated rolling back the scheduled increases in payroll taxes and substituting payments from general revenues. Such procedure is at best very deceptive—and, at worst, dishonest—because it would make people believe that some third party is picking up a substantial part of the costs of Social Security. Hopefully, the nation should be economically mature enough to know that general-revenues payments must either come from other taxes than payroll ones or else from the creation of printing-press money. Under the former circumstances, the same people—namely, the populace of the country—must pay the general taxes as would otherwise provide the payroll taxes. Under the latter circumstances, the resulting inflation will be paid for, once again, by everybody.

Fiscal economists frequently assert that the substitution of other taxes for payroll taxes in financing the Social Security program is desirable, because of the different incidence of these two forms of taxa-

8. Certainly, most people would agree that it is not desirable to change the fundamental principles enunciated by the Ten Commandments. Further, few would argue other than that pi should be 3.14159, inconvenient as that number may be!

tion. Their views are frequently backed up by very scholarly studies based on extensive computer runs and mathematical statistical analyses. However, in the author's opinion, these various studies have no validity—and cannot possibly have any validity.

It is necessarily assumed in the computer models and regression equations that, when a new tax is inaugurated, everything else will remain unchanged. This just does not happen in the real economic world. All elements, such as salaries, self-employment earnings, and prices will react in an unpredictable —and even, in hindsight, an unknown—manner under these circumstances. It may well be said that the attempt to measure the incidence of various types of taxes—although very intellectually interesting and challenging—is really no more useful and productive than the arguments that took place among medieval theologians about how many angels could stand on the head of a pin!

Great debate occurs among economists as to the incidence of the employer payroll tax.[9] The majority view currently seems to be that the employer tax is largely "paid" by the employee, in the form of lower wages than would otherwise have been paid. Some, however, argue that at least some of the employer tax is passed along to consumers (who, after all, are merely the employees and their dependents) in the form of higher prices. It is generally believed that little, if any, of the employer tax is absorbed by the employer in the form of lower profits.

In the author's view, it is absolutely impossible to know what the effects of a new tax or an increase in taxes really are, except possibly in the very short run. The imposition of a tax changes the whole "ball game" in a manner that is impossible to analyze.[10] The economic world is a "one-time" one, and experiments cannot be conducted on alternative approaches as is possible, for example, in a chemistry laboratory.

Accordingly, it seems the straightforward and proper procedure in financing the Social Security program to do so entirely by equal employer and employee taxes, which stand out quite clearly for one and all to see. Essentially, this should be done for psychological reasons, rather than actuarial or economic ones. People should be aware, as they now are, of the substantial costs of the Social Security program. They should then decide whether they would like to pay more through governmental channels by expanding the program, or whether they would prefer the present level and use the remainder of their income for current needs and for the provision of supplementary economic-security protection through the private sector.

This, then, leaves us with the

9. An outstanding example of the difficulty of knowing who really pays for social-insurance taxes arose in the case of the Railroad Retirement system in 1974. Then, the employers agreed in collective bargaining to pay the entire RR contribution rate except for an amount equal to the employee SS rate (which the employees would pay). This meant an increased tax of 4¾ percent to be paid by the employers, which apparently was a great victory for the employees. But at the same time, the bargained wage increase was about 4–5 percent lower than what other workers were obtaining. So, is the RR tax no longer equally shared by the employers and employees, as it was for years? How can one really say?

10. For example, it is extremely doubtful that salaries of executives and fees of professionals would be as high as they now are if we did not have the progressive income tax. Similarly, when an executive's salary is increased, account is taken as to what the net effect will be for him (or her), not the gross rise.

question of how to solve the long-range financing problems of the Social Security program that still remain after the 1977 Amendments. Basically, two procedures seem to be possible if the program is to maintain its same relative standard of benefit adequacy.

One method is to provide additional financing when it will be needed some three decades hence. The higher payroll tax rates that would be required could be eased in gradually, just as has been done frequently in the past. Although the required level of payroll taxes might seem high to us at the moment, it should be realized that there will be significantly lower tax burdens in the future with respect to programs for children, such as education. Specifically, the factor of lower fertility that causes the financial problems with respect to retirement benefits in the distant future will, as the other side of the coin, mean far lower costs for children.

The other method is to reduce total benefit expenditures. This should not be done by lowering the benefit level, but rather by gradually increasing the minimum retirement age, beginning about 20 years hence and slowly moving up from the present age 65 to, say, age 68. The real justification for doing this is that, with the anticipated lower mortality in the future, a retirement age of 68 is, from a cost and longevity standpoint, really lower than the current age 65 when it was first adopted. It seems reasonable to establish the retirement age over the future so that it has the same "real" value—just as, on the other hand, it is desirable to adjust benefits in course of payment so that they maintain their "real" value when prices rise.

CONCLUSION

A great need exists for education of the public both as to the most appropriate role of the Social Security program and as to the basic economics of financing it. Either an expansion or a contraction of the Social Security program would have undesirable social and economic effects. Expansion would mean an overpowering control and influence of people's lives by the government and a resulting hidden deterioration of national character and productivity. Contraction would be deceptive because indirect costs of vast magnitude would arise and because adequate economic security planning in the aggregate would not be possible. People should be educated to realize that a reasonably adequate Social Security program has a significant cost. They should recognize what this cost is and be willing to bear it directly by visible payroll taxes. And, likewise, they should realize that an expansion of the program will have cost effects which should equally be recognized by direct, visible tax rates.

No-Fault Insurance: What, Why and Where?

By JEFFREY O'CONNELL

ABSTRACT: Under the common-law "tort" or fault-finding system, after an accident between Smith and Jones, if Smith is an "innocent" party claiming loss against a "wrongdoer," he is paid not only for his economic loss, but for the monetary value of his pain and suffering. But it is often very difficult to establish not only who was at fault in an accident but the pecuniary value of pain. Under the no-fault solution, after an accident between Smith and Jones, each is paid for economic losses by his own insurance company, regardless of anyone's fault. As a corollary, each is required to surrender his claim based on fault against the other. No-fault insurance then, was designed to make the following improvements in auto accident compensation: (1) to assure that everyone injured in auto accidents is eligible for auto insurance payments, regardless of whether he was able to prove fault-based claims; (2) to spend less on smaller, relatively trivial claims, and more on serious injury; (3) to pay claims promptly; (4) to pay more efficiently by using less of the premium dollar on insurance overhead and legal fees; (5) to reduce, or at least to stabilize, the pertinent costs of auto insurance. In essence, no-fault auto insurance has succeeded in all these goals. Consideration is given to extending no-fault to all kinds of accidents.

Jeffrey O'Connell is a Professor of Law at the University of Illinois. He is the co-author of the principal work which proposed no-fault auto insurance. A graduate of Phillips Exeter Academy, Dartmouth College, and the Harvard Law School, he has taught law at the University of Iowa, Northwestern, the University of Michigan, Southern Methodist University, and the University of Texas at Austin. During 1973, having received a Guggenheim Fellowship, he taught a course in personal injury law at Oxford University, England. Prior to teaching law, he practiced law in Boston, Massachusetts, as a trial lawyer. O'Connell is the author or coauthor of nine books dealing with accident law.

This article is excerpted from a forthcoming book, Jeffrey O'Connell, *The Lawsuit Lottery*, to be published in the Fall of 1979.

UNDER the common-law "tort," or fault-finding, system, after an accident between Smith and Jones, if Smith is an "innocent" party claiming loss against a "wrongdoer," he is paid not only for his economic loss, but for the monetary value of his pain and suffering. Obviously, it is often very difficult to establish not only who was at fault in an accident but the pecuniary value of pain. Under the no-fault solution, after an accident between Smith and Jones, each is paid, regardless of anyone's fault, by his own insurance company, periodically month-by-month as his losses accrue. As a corollary, each is required to surrender his claim based on fault against the other. Only economic losses (essentially, medical expenses and wage loss) which are readily reducible to dollars and cents, and not pain and suffering, which are not so easy to assess, are covered. Payment for additional claims is financed by the savings from simplifying the insured event so as not to pay either for determination of fault and the pecuniary value of pain and suffering, or for pain and suffering itself.

REASONS FOR NO-FAULT INSURANCE

No-fault, then, was designed to make the following improvements in auto accident compensation. First, it was designed to assure that everyone injured in auto accidents is eligible for auto insurance payment, regardless of whether he was able to prove fault-based claims. According to a massive study by the United States Department of Transportation (DOT), about 55 percent of those seriously injured get absolutely nothing from automobile liability insurance.[1]

Second, it was designed to spend less on smaller, relatively trivial claims, and more on serious injury. According to Professor Alfred Conard of the University of Michigan, who conducted an extensive Michigan study, "If there is one thing which [all] the surveys have shown conclusively, it is that the [fault-based] system overpays the small claimants who need it least and underpays the large claimants who need it most."[2]

Third, it was designed to pay claims promptly. According to the DOT study, on the average, a period of 16 months elapses between an accident and any payment based on fault-finding. The larger the loss, the larger the delay. For losses over $2,500, the average delay rose to 19 months.[3]

Fourth, it was designed to pay more efficiently by using less of the premium dollar on insurance overhead and legal fees. No-fault insurance has been called "no-lawyer insurance" by one consumer advocate. Prior to no-fault in Massachusetts, approximately 80 percent of successful claimants under liability insurance there were represented by attorneys. As a corollary, no-fault was designed to reduce the amount of litigation stemming from auto accidents. Without no-fault laws, typically 50 to 80 percent of civil jury dockets are taken up with auto cases.

Fifth, no-fault insurance was designed to reduce, or at least to stabilize, the costs of auto insurance. Prior to no-fault, the number one complaint about auto insurance was its high cost. It was one of the fastest rising items on the consumer price index.

1. U.S. Department of Transportation, "Economic Consequences of Automobile Accident Injuries" (1970), pp. 37–38.

2. A. Conard, *Testimony Before the New York Joint Legislative Committee on Insurance Rates and Regulation*, U. Mich. L. Quadrangle Notes (Fall 1970), p. 14.

3. U.S. Department of Transportation, "Economic Consequences," p. 52.

TYPES OF NO-FAULT LAWS

In response to all these problems, beginning in the mid-1960s, vigorous attempts were begun to initiate no-fault insurance reform. In fact, studies had been urging such reform since the early 1930s, but had been confined largely to academic journals, and were consequently ignored. In 1970, Massachusetts enacted the first no-fault law, followed since by 23 other states. The laws are bewildering in their variety—a fact that adds to the pressure for a uniform federal law—but basically fall into three categories, with some overlap.

In the first category are *modified no-fault laws*, which provide only modest no-fault benefits and eliminate relatively few fault-finding claims. States with modified plans are Colorado, Connecticut, Florida, Georgia, Hawaii, Kansas, Massachusetts, Minnesota, Nevada, New Jersey, North Dakota, Pennsylvania, and Utah.

The second includes *add-on plans* which, arguably, are not no-fault plans at all. Although they usually call for modest benefits to be paid to traffic victims without regard to anyone's fault, they do not eliminate any victim's right to press a fault-finding claim for his pain and suffering against other drivers. Hence, the name add-on: the laws add on benefits but do not take anything away. States with add-on plans are Arkansas, Delaware, Maryland, Oregon, South Carolina, South Dakota, Texas, and Virginia.

In the third category are *plans approaching pure no-fault*. A pure no-fault plan would eliminate all, or almost all, claims based on fault, and substitute relatively unlimited benefits for all medical expenses and wages lost, not matter how extensive. No law goes that far, but Michigan's comes closest. It covers unlimited medical expenses and a maximum of about $58,000 of wage loss, while eliminating fault-based claims unless the victim suffers death, serious disfigurement, or serious impairment of bodily function. Minnesota's law, along with New York's, as amended, also approach pure no-fault. A federal no-fault bill, too, approaches pure no-fault in both benefits and elimination of fault-based claims.

The drive for no-fault reform has been stalled in various states, largely over the question of which type of legislation should be adopted. The trial bar has vigorously asserted, at both the state and federal levels, that no-fault benefits can be paid without eliminating anyone's fault-finding claims for pain and suffering. No-fault backers, on the other hand, oppose add-on laws as a mockery of reform, often labeling them "yes-fault" laws. Trial lawyers in reply argue that under add-on plans auto insurance rates are not increased, but reduced, since people who receive their economic losses promptly from their own insurance companies don't bother to press a fault-finding claim against the other driver. Former President of the Association of Trial Lawyers of America, Leonard Ring, notes that the Delaware add-on experience "has indeed proven that, where the victim has received his medical and wage loss, the incentive to make further claim is extinguished in all but the most serious cases."[4]

Proponents of the purer forms of no-fault that formally ban some fault-based claims argue that statistics for Delaware demonstrate that fault-finding claims are not reduced by add-on plans. Even if fewer people than expected bring fault-finding

4. L. Ring, *The Fault with No-Fault*, 49 Notre Dame Lawyer (1974) pp. 796, 826.

claims when provided with no-fault benefits, despite their right to do so, that situation cannot be expected to remain, given the aggressive personal-injury bar and the money that can be made by pressing fault-based claims.

HOW EFFECTIVE ARE NO-FAULT LAWS?

Several extensive statistical studies appraising the operation of no-fault laws help answer how the various forms of no-fault have fared in practice.

The principal controversy over no-fault has been whether insurance premiums go up or down upon its enactment. A recent study published in the *Rutgers Law Review* evaluates cost-benefit performance of the various types of no-fault laws by measuring the extent to which the laws keep personal injury premiums (as distinguished from property damage premiums) "at or below the level they would have reached had no-fault not been enacted." During the five year period between 1972–77, total personal injury premiums covering fault-based liability and all supplemental coverages increased 22 percent in fault states; in add-on states such premiums (including no-fault coverages) increased 49.5 percent; in modified no-fault states with low no-fault benefits they increased 18 percent; and in modified no-fault states with high benefits they increased 13 percent.[5]

In Michigan, designated pure no-fault, the study found an 11 percent decrease in total personal injury premiums, for both no-fault and fault-finding claims. The Michigan data also showed a 53 percent de-crease in premiums covering fault-finding claims for personal injury, and an 87 percent decrease in the number of fault-finding claims for personal injury. According to the Rutgers Law Review:

> Together, reductions in premiums and [fault-finding] . . . claims are powerful evidence of the efficacy of Michigan's . . . threshold [barring fault-finding claims]. Furthermore, the fact that . . . premium decreases [for fault-finding claims] have more than offset the added cost of [no-fault benefits] suggests that the cost tradeoff envisioned by no-fault proponents is not only a viable concept, but can be implemented effectively for even the most generous [no-fault benefit] packages.[6]

However, simple premium aggregates are only one rather crude way of measuring costs. An arguably better measure is the *value* of the insurance purchased. The improved value per insurance dollar under no-fault is most graphically illustrated by the Michigan experience. Coverage under Michigan's no-fault law pays unlimited medical expenses plus over $58,000 in wage losses, in addition to coverage of $20,000 for those fault-based claims against a motorist which are preserved under the law. All this insurance is provided at a cost no greater, and apparently less, than the costs prior to no-fault, of only $20,000 of traditional liability insurance based on fault, under which few seriously injured victims were paid much, if at all. The Michigan Bureau of Insurance estimates that the proportion of premium dollars paid out as benefits has increased by 58 percent under no-fault.

These comments raise another goal of no-fault insurance: namely, spending less on small, rather trivial claims,

5. *Rutgers Law Review* (1977), pp. 909, 953–54, 960, 964, 966, 970.

6. Ibid., p. 978.

and conversely, more on serious injuries. Professor Joseph Little of the University of Florida Law School found in a study of Florida's no-fault experience that a "shift to greater payments for more serious injuries is clearly seen" under no-fault compared to fault-based payment. The percentage of total personal injury payments to more seriously injured victims almost doubled after two years' experience under no-fault.[7]

A 1978 Michigan Insurance Bureau study similarly found more compensation for genuine losses and for serious victims under no-fault.[8] Under the fault system, it will be recalled, payments for pain and suffering are most often made to the less seriously injured—often really as "bribes" to get rid of the "nuisance" value of smaller claims. But under Michigan's no-fault laws, much more of the insurance dollar is being paid for genuine dollar losses and, given the fact that no-fault law eliminates smaller fault-based claims, what is paid for pain and suffering goes to more seriously injured victims (who do after all suffer the most pain from accidents).

As to the aim of prompt payment under no-fault, a Massachusetts survey by Professor Alan Widiss of the University of Iowa Law School, discloses some striking figures regarding timeliness of payment under no-fault as opposed to fault. The figures indicate that the time lapse between receipt by the insurance company of documentation "sufficient for payment of medical expenses" and the first no-fault medical payment re-

ceived by the victim was between 4 and 7 days in over 50 percent of the cases. Eighty percent received the first payment within a month, and 97.9 percent within 180 days. The time lapse between the date of accident and date of receipt of first no-fault payment was necessarily longer, dependent as it is upon the filing of claims and supporting documents by claimants. Even here, 63.3 percent of the claimants received the first no-fault payment within 90 days and 84.8 percent within 180 days. Under the fault system, according to the U.S. Department of Transportation, only 40.5 percent of claims were settled and paid within 90 days of the accident, and only 57.6 percent within 180 days.[9] Reports to the Department of Transportation from the insurance departments of Colorado, Connecticut, Michigan, and New Jersey show comparable statistics, with Michigan's Insurance Bureau reporting that "almost all auto accident claims are settled within 30 days."

As to no-fault's aim of more efficiency by using less of the premium dollar on legal fees and insurance overhead, the Massachusetts study by Professor Widiss suggests a radical reduction in the need for lawyers under no-fault claims. In contrast to the use of attorneys in about 80 percent of the cases prior to the institution of no-fault, attorneys were used for no-fault claims in substantially less than 15 percent of the cases. According to Widiss, "No-fault insurance claims are usually paid without disputes over either the existence of coverage or the amount due the claimant." He states: "A majority of

7. J. Little, *No-Fault Auto Reparation in Florida*, 9 Michigan Journal of Law Reform (1975), pp. 1, 36.

8. Insurance Bureau, Michigan Department of Commerce, *No-Fault Insurance in Michigan: Consumer Attitudes and Performance* (1978), p. 34.

9. A. Widiss, *A Survey of the No-Fault Personal Injury Experience in Massachusetts* in Council on Law-Related Studies: *No-Fault Automobile Insurance in Action* (1977), pp. 209, 211, Tables 28, 30.

the claimants and defense attorneys surveyed felt that the average [no-fault] . . . claimant did not require legal assistance because the forms were not complicated. Typical of this group was the response of one attorney who observed: 'It's just like Blue Cross or any health or accident claim.' " In Florida, too, overall lawyer involvement per claim diminished.

Considering reduced litigation under no-fault, another Massachusetts study found that the filing of personal injury cases in Massachusetts courts was "precipitously lowered in the wake of no-fault," including a remarkable reduction of over 50 percent in courts of unlimited jurisdiction, and an astonishing decline of about 90 percent in courts limited to claims under $2,000.[10] The reduction of litigation in Michigan was also significant.

On the other hand, under Delaware's add-on plan, according to a study there, "[t]ort litigation is continuing substantially unabated by the no-fault legislation." Professor Roger Clark, of Rutgers-Camden Law School, who conducted the Delaware study, concludes "It is now clear that, whatever beneficial effects it has had, the Delaware legislation has not discouraged any significant number of potential tort plaintiffs from suing."[11]

PUBLIC RESPONSE TO NO-FAULT

The 1978 Michigan Insurance Bureau Report contains the results of Michigan public opinion surveys re-

garding public attitudes to various individual aspects of no-fault, and regarding no-fault in general. The results show that the public favors by a 62 percent to 23 percent margin the idea of providing full medical and rehabilitation benefits to all accident victims. The public also favors by a vote of 79 percent to 10 percent, the concept of curtailing rights to pain and suffering in order to provide more adequate medical and wage loss benefits. Furthermore, by a vote of 53 percent to 18 percent the public said they would relinquish their own rights to damages for pain and suffering in exchange for prompt and complete payment of medical bills and lost wages. Finally, a vote of 65 percent to 26 percent favored coordination of no-fault benefits with other insurance benefits in order to prevent double payments for the same economic loss. The Report concludes that, "[t]he responses . . . show that people do not support the tort system as an effective means of providing accident reparations and that no-fault is clearly preferred."

It is thus somewhat surprising to discover that, in response to questions regarding attitudes to no-fault in general, only 17 percent of those polled said that Michigan no-fault is a "good system." Those who said it was a "poor system" included 55 percent of those polled. The Report states, however, that when these responses were analyzed, it became clear that almost two-thirds of those giving a "poor" rating identified the reasons for that rating as being due to problems which plague the entire automobile insurance system, and not directly related to fault versus no-fault systems. Another 38 percent indicated that the basis of their dissatisfaction lay in problems related to car damage, not to the aspects of the law pertaining to injury to per-

10. R. Bovbjerg, *The Impact of No-Fault Auto Insurance on Massachusetts Courts,* New England Law Review 11 (1976), pp. 325, 329; A. Widiss, *A Survey of No-Fault,* p. 141.

11. R. Clark, *Delaware No-Fault: 1974 and 1975 Court Filings Arising From Personal Injury Incurred in Motor Vehicle Accidents,* an update of R. Clark and G. Waterson, "No-Fault" in Delaware, 6 *Rutgers-Camden Law Journal* (1974), pp. 225, 232, 260.

sons. When the Insurance Bureau evaluated consumer needs in conjunction with the actual performance of Michigan's no-fault law, the stated result was that Michigan no-fault is successful in "meeting the real needs of the people."

In summary, the U.S. Department of Transportation has concluded that:

State experience with no-fault automobile insurance would appear to confirm the basic soundness of the theory and feasibility of the theory's implementation. No-fault plans of sharply varying objectives and character are widely seen as successes. No problem has arisen in the implementation of no-fault for which there does not appear to be a readily available and feasible solution, given the political will to make the necessary change. No-fault insurance works.[12]

ELECTIVE COMPENSATION AS A PROPOSED SOLUTION

If state or federal no-fault auto laws were to become effective in all states in the foreseeable future, they would still apply only to some auto accident victims. Present laws do little for victims of non-auto accidents, including those presently covered (or, better said, not covered) by fault-finding liability rules for medical malpractice, defective products, and accidents. For those who suffer losses in non-automobile accidents, the prospect of securing adequate compensation is poor, whether the losses are large or small. The areas of products liability and medical malpractice probably account for the largest losses and the largest number of seriously injured victims outside of automobile accidents. In both areas one finds: (1) liability turning

12. U.S. Department of Transportation, "State No-Fault Automobile Insurance Experience, 1971–1977" (1977), p. 80.

on very complicated fact situations, almost always calling for expensive expert witnesses; (2) litigation so expensive that only the largest claims are brought; (3) relatively little of the total loss being paid from liability insurance; (4) defendants winning approximately three-quarters of the cases that reach a verdict; (5) rapidly rising claims and premiums; and (6) most of the money going to lawyers and insurance companies rather than accident victims.

Some have proposed that "market" mechanisms might remedy this situation. Certainly the exigencies of present conditions require remedy. What might the product in such a market look like?

The scheme proposed here is elective first-party no-fault insurance which could work as follows: An insurance company would offer no-fault coverage to its insureds in increments of, say, $10,000 up to any amount, including a million dollars or more. The coverage would be for economic loss, consisting mainly of medical expenses (including rehabilitation rarely covered under health insurance today) and wage loss, resulting from personal injury in any kind of accident. Nothing would be paid for noneconomic loss, such as pain and suffering, nor would payment be made if the loss had already been paid from another source such as sick leave or health insurance. In return for such a guarantee of no-fault benefits payable regardless of how the accident happened, the insured would transfer to his no-fault insurance company his entire fault-based claim against any third-party who caused the accident.

In accordance with the concept of no-fault insurance, *any* person buying the coverage would be paid in the event of suffering loss from an accident, not just those with valid fault-finding claims. The no-fault benefits would be paid periodically as loss accrued. Furthermore, the insurance company would also agree to pay the insured the equivalent of any amount in excess of his no-fault benefits for his economic losses which the insured could gain in a fault-finding claim against any third-party, without subtracting any legal expenses incurred in gaining such payment. The no-fault insurance company is in a position to offer such free legal services to its insured because it must pay its lawyer to pursue its own claim anyway, just as today it defends an insured against a fault-finding claim under liability insurance at no additional cost to the insured beyond his initial premium.

By this device the insured would be guaranteed whatever level of no-fault benefits he wishes to purchase, plus whatever amounts of economic loss in excess of that limit he is eligible for under a fault-finding claim. But, to repeat, he would have transferred to his no-fault insurance company any fault-based claim, including amounts due for pain and suffering, that had accrued to him as a result of the injury. The transfer of the fault-finding claim would have to be made prior to any injury, at the time the agreement for potential payment of no-fault benefits is instituted. Otherwise, if after an accident a victim could choose whether to press a fault-finding or a no-fault claim, those with valid fault-finding claims would press such claims and others would collect no-fault benefits, which would mean an insurance company would not have any fault-finding claims to provide income to pay no-fault benefits.

The complex questions of fault and the value of pain and suffering would still have to be settled between the no-fault insurance company and the insurance company of the third-party who injured the no-fault insured. But those issues would now arise between two insurance companies and they would be more likely to settle the matter expeditiously by informal means and without expensive litigation, as now happens with many intercompany claims. If the matter couldn't be settled quickly, at least the protracted, expensive litigation would take place between large, impersonal corporations, without forcing its agonies of expense, delay, trickery, and uncertainty on lonely, frightened, wounded accident victims.

This plan for no-fault benefits would not be mandatory. Rather it would be elective—allowing but not compelling any insurance company to offer it, and similarly allowing any potential accident victim to refuse it. Given the apparent public preference for certainty of insurance payment versus the gamble of a law suit, evidenced by many polls, widespread adoption of no-fault can be expected. Recall that in Michigan, after experience with the most sweeping no-fault auto insurance law in the nation, the public favors by a 79 percent to 10 percent margin curtailing rights to payment for pain and suffering in exchange for larger medical and wage loss benefits; furthermore by a 53 percent to 18 percent margin, members of the public said they would relinquish their own rights to sue for payment for pain and suffering "in return for prompt and complete payment of medical bills and . . . lost wages." These Michigan results confirm many earlier studies showing a strong public preference for certainty of payment for out-of-pocket loss caused by an accident versus a gamble for payment of out-of-pocket loss plus pain and suffering.

The advantages to the insured under elective no-fault insurance are that he is assured of automatic payment of economic loss at whatever level he chooses in the event of any kind of accidental personal injury; and he is, in addition, assured of payment of whatever additional economic losses he would have received under a fault-finding claim, without the necessity of incurring attorneys' fees or other litigation expenses for either no-fault or fault-based payment. This will mean that his net payment will often be almost as great as—and sometimes greater than—whatever payment he would have received from a fault-finding claim, while suffering much less uncertainty and anxiety.

Thus, for an example: if after an accident between Smith and Jones, Smith had a valid fault-based claim against Jones and recovered all his loss of $55,000 ($30,000 economic loss plus $25,000 in noneconomic loss), he would normally pay at least a third of that to a lawyer (or $18,333), leaving him with a net of $36,667. Under elective no-fault insurance, if Smith had bought $30,000 or more of no-fault insurance, he would be paid for all his economic losses automatically without the uncertainty or anguish of a fault-finding claim and without paying anything to a lawyer. If Smith had instead elected $10,000 of no-fault insurance, he would still receive a net of $30,000, with $10,000 (the amount he chose) payable automatically without the uncertainty of fault-finding litigation. Assuming litigation expenses of 50 percent (not that unusual), Smith would have received net payment of $27,500 from liability insurance versus $30,000 under elective no-fault insurance.

It is true that there are legal rules which at first blush might seem to inhibit the implementation of elective no-fault insurance: legal rules prohibiting the sale of personal injury claims and rules against "maintenance" and "champerty" which supposedly prohibit others from sharing in the proceeds of a suit. But these rules were instituted long ago to prevent desperately injured accident victims from being taken advantage of—forced to sell their claims for a pittance to speculators in order to get something to live on—and to prevent "officious intermeddling" in others' affairs by such speculators. Neither of these will result when an insurance company promises to pay promptly for economic losses of accident victims in return for the right to press their claims against third parties causing injury. After all, the law already allows the accident victim to, in effect, sell a third or more of his claim to his lawyer in the form of a contingent fee in order to pay his lawyer, thereby creating an exception to rules against maintenance and champerty.

Why shouldn't insurance companies, once again à la Adam Smith, step in to fill the desperate need of injury victims and allow potential personal injury victims to pool their risks with the best risk bearers of all—those same insurance companies. After all, an insurance company is a much better risk bearer than a lawyer. In addition to its actuarial safety, an insurance company has all the stability and fairness that the law demands of such an enterprise through extensive governmental regulation of insurance. (Admittedly that regulation is often weak, but it's still much more rigorous than for most enterprises—and much greater than for law firms.) In other words, why *not* go a step further than the contingent fee and allow anyone who wants to sell his *entire* fault-finding claim to a highly regulated, financial entity like an insurance company, whereby the risk of an accident victim's uncompensated loss is removed? In still other words, why should plaintiffs' lawyers be the only ones allowed to buy fault-finding claims—and then only in return for legal services?

Elective no-fault insurance could be offered in a variety of ways. An auto insurance company could offer no-fault insurance benefits for auto accidents to its insureds in states without, or with inadequate, no-fault auto laws. Workers' compensation insurance companies could offer employees—pursuant to collective bargaining—benefits supplementing inadequate no-fault workers' compensation benefits for injuries in the course of employment; workers' compensation insurance companies could also offer no-fault benefits to employees and their families for off-the-job accidents. Health and disability insurance companies, either writing individual policies or through group coverage, or casualty companies writing homeowner's coverage, could offer to their policyholders no-fault coverage for all kinds of accidents. Credit unions, professional or trade associations, and others could also offer such coverage to their members.

CONCLUDING REMARKS

Daniel Patrick Moynihan, in urging favorable consideration of elec-

tive no-fault insurance, calls no-fault auto insurance "the one incontestably successful reform (proposed in) . . . the 1960s."[13] Since elective no-fault insurance is self-executing, without the need for a new cumbersome bureaucracy such as those ordained by OSHA and other such regulatory bodies, it is, for Moynihan, a prototype of the kind of innovative, pragmatic, cooperative, and mutually beneficial reform that is essential to our society.

Moynihan has also stated that the proponents of no-fault insurance "are right in the all-important perception as to what it is Americans are good at. We are good at maintaining business relationships once a basis of mutual self-interest is established."[14] Elective no-fault insurance allows insurance companies and their insureds to bypass lawyers with all their self-serving cumbersomeness in dealing with all kinds of accidental injuries. It is therefore an excellent example of a relationship based on mutual self interest. As such, Moynihan wrote, it is not "merely . . . concerned with aspects of tort liability (it is concerned with) . . . those particulars whereby a free society remains free."[15]

13. D. P. Moynihan, *Foreword* to J. O'Connell, *Ending Insult to Injury* (1975), p. xi.

14. *A New Auto Insurance Policy*, 27 Aug 1967, section 6, *New York Times Magazine*, pp. 26, 82.

15. D. P. Moynihan, Foreword to O'Connell, *Ending Insult to Injury*, p. xx.

Medical Malpractice Problem

By CHARLES P. HALL, JR.

ABSTRACT: The medical malpractice problem is extremely complex and is perceived very differently by health care providers, patients, and other segments of society. As a widely recognized problem, it is of relatively recent origin. Its potential societal consequences include disruption of health services, waste and maldistribution of economic and human resources, and a severe strain on a variety of our traditional social institutions. The "crisis" of malpractice is a product of many forces, including a disturbing level of negligent and improper medical care, frequently unrealistic patient expectations, and the growing "philosophy of entitlement" which is rampant among Americans. Responses to the problem have sometimes been ill-advised and emotional. Most often, the problem is seen as one of inadequate or overpriced malpractice insurance, though careful analysis suggests that insurance issues are merely symptoms of the real problem. Nevertheless, insurance-based solutions have proven to be politically expedient and have produced at least temporary alleviation of the problem. Ultimately, though, other approaches will be necessary, and careful, objective research is required to identify and test long-term options.

Charles P. Hall, Jr., received his BBA from the University of Wisconsin and his Ph.D. from the University of Pennsylvania. He currently holds a joint appointment as Professor of Insurance and Risk and Health Administration at Temple University, where he is also Adjunct Professor of Community Medicine. He has previously taught at the University of Washington and was with the American Medical Association's Department of Economics. He is President-elect of the American Risk and Insurance Association.

MALPRACTICE, like so many other problems relating to risks and their treatment in our society, is multifaceted and disturbingly complex. From a macro point of view, the malpractice problem has potentially far-reaching societal consequences in four major areas. These, in turn, can be broken down into a multitude of interrelated issues. The first major concern has to do with the potential paralysis of the delivery of medical services. This can be manifested dramatically, as it was during the "work slowdown" (strike) carried out by members of the New York State Medical Society in several New York counties from June 1–10, 1975. In less dramatic fashion, hospitals and physicians may, either individually or collectively, choose to withhold certain types of service or treatment if they are perceived to involve excessive potential for malpractice claims.

It has been argued by some that the spectre of malpractice suits has already, or surely will eventually, also have an impact on the supply of health manpower. As will be noted later, this "service paralysis" is often associated with either the unavailability of professional liability insurance or "excessive" premiums for the desired coverage. This often blurs the issues and results in what many believe to be the erroneous diagnosis of an "insurance problem," rather than an insurance symptom of a malpractice problem.

A second major societal concern has to do with the potential waste of resources that arises from the practice of "defensive medicine," which is an alleged outgrowth of the malpractice problem. To the extent that this leads to unneeded tests or procedures, it can only exacerbate the already serious problem of rapidly escalating health care costs. The socioeconomic impact of health care costs has been one of the most persistent and troublesome political issues of the last decade, having given rise to a plethora of proposals for various forms of national health insurance as well as a variety of medical welfare programs.

Closely related is the concern over the distribution of costs associated with malpractice. There is overwhelming evidence that the costs are high and rising. Should they be borne exclusively by physicians and other providers? Or are they more properly the responsibility of individual patients? Perhaps society in general should shoulder the burden.

Finally, society has a stake in the impact of the malpractice problem on its related institutions, including both the legal and insurance systems. In the face of the "malpractice crisis," there has been a flurry of proposed solutions. These encompass such diverse tactics, for example, as scrapping the tort system altogether or, alternatively, retaining the traditional concept of tort liability but altering rules of evidence, statutorily limiting amounts of recovery, and mandating the creation of special insurance and other risk handling mechanisms. Some of the proposals involve fundamental constitutional issues. Others may create problems more serious than the one they purport to solve. Most are politically controversial.

DEFINITION OF PROBLEM

One of the difficulties in discussing "the malpractice problem" is getting agreement on its definition. Even the most extensive and prestigious of all malpractice studies, that called for by President Nixon in February 1971, suffered from this basic confusion. Under the heading of "Historical Perspective," it stated that, "During the 19th Century and the first two or three decades of the 20th, there was essentially no such thing as a malpractice 'problem' in the United States . . . sickness was accepted as a usual and expected thing . . . medicine itself was comparatively limited and adverse results of treatment more often than not were either regarded as the natural outcome of disease or attributed to the 'will of God.' The first significant change began in the 1930's. California . . . suddenly surpassed all other states in the number of malpractice suits."[1] Though the central part of this statement cannot be challenged, the first and last parts cannot be accepted unless one takes the narrow, parochial view that the malpractice problem is solely the problem of health care providers, and one which is defined exclusively in terms of the number of malpractice suits brought against them. Yet such a definition is clearly inadequate.

A more appropriate characterization of the problem was enunciated by a special Advisory Panel on Medical Malpractice for the state of New York. "The common law definition of medical malpractice in use in New York since 1898 provides that a physician or surgeon can be held liable for damages resulting from his failure to exercise the degree of reasonable and ordinary care, diligence, and skill in the diagnosis and treatment of his patient that is ordinarily possessed and exercised by physicians engaged in the same line of practice during the same period of time. Medical malpractice may consist of negligence in doing some act

which such a reasonable physician would not have done under the same circumstances or of a failure to do something which such a physician would have done."[2]

Malpractice, then, is simply another word for negligent or improper medical treatment in the eyes of the law. Logic suggests that such negligence, when present, is certainly a problem for the patient, whether or not he/she decides to sue, which would then create a problem for the physician or other provider. The facts are that the potential pool of malpractice claims is substantially greater than the number actually submitted.[3]

However, it would be a gross oversimplification to suggest that this fairly straightforward legal definition of malpractice adequately describes the problem.[4] Unfortunately, there is another growing dimension as well. There has been a tremendous increase in the volume of "illegitimate" claims in recent years, claims which allege malpractice under circumstances which, by any reasonable definition, involve neither negligence nor wrongdoing on the part of the provider. These illegitimate claims are particularly frustrating to providers. This is especially true in the face of changes in the social climate which have made it increasingly difficult and costly to defend such suits and to obtain insurance protection against them. In this more hostile environment, the results of suits often give the impression that the concept of malpractice has been

1. U.S. Department of Health, Education and Welfare, Report of the Secretary's Commission on Medical Malpractice (Washington, DC: DHEW, 1963) pp. 2, 3.

2. Report of the Special Advisory Panel on Medical Malpractice, State of New York (New York, NY, 1976) pp. 32–33.

3. Ibid., p. 141.

4. For a more extensive but clear discussion of basic malpractice law, see Sylvia Law and Steve Polan, Pain and Profit: The Politics of Malpractice (New York: Harper & Row, 1978), Chapt. 1.

greatly expanded beyond the common law definition quoted above.

A predictable response to these changes has been that medical malpractice insurance premiums soared at the same time the available market dwindled. Little wonder, then, that many providers perceived the malpractice problem to be primarily an insurance problem. Similarly, because of the organized response of physicians in many states to what they viewed as unacceptable changes in the medical malpractice insurance market, politicians and the public in general were also sometimes misled into believing that insurers were the real culprits, along with the "greedy lawyers" who, many doctors are convinced, encourage groundless suits by any patient who experiences less than prompt, complete recovery from any and all medical injury or disease.

In any case, when the number and severity of negligent acts by physicians and/or the number and magnitude of suits by patients (whether legitimate or not) become large enough to either disrupt the delivery of medical services, create economic hardship for patients or providers, produce significant levels of physical and emotional stress for either group, or threaten the viability of existing social institutions, then society as a whole has a problem.

History

No one has produced evidence that medical professionals are any more or less negligent today than they were in the first three decades of this century. Surely, negligent and incompetent medical practice existed in this country at the turn of the century too. The famous Flexner Report documented many of the deficiencies of medical education

and practice at that time.[5] Early efforts to control the quality of medical performance centered on setting standards for medical schools and the licensure of practitioners, but this did not eliminate negligence, even though it probably upgraded the general level of care available.

Most observers note that significant increases in the number and magnitude of malpractice claims have occurred primarily since the end of World War II, and in large part they merely reflect a general pattern which has developed in relation to most tort actions. Americans have become widely identified as the most litigious people in the world. The increase in malpractice suits has more or less paralleled the experience in such other areas as automobile liability, product liability, and worker's compensation, though with marginally different timing and with a number of specific operative factors which have tended to magnify the changes.

Generically, one observer has aptly referred to the general increase in claims and litigation as the result of the emergence of a "philosophy of entitlement" among many Americans.[6] Whether as the real or imagined victims of negligence, or as members of a jury determining the presence or absence of same, Americans have become increasingly willing to claim (or dispense) dollar damages. Sometimes, it seems, the claimants simply feel that somebody ought to "owe" them whenever

5. Abraham Flexner, *Medical Education in the United States and Canada: A Report to the Carnegie Foundation for the Advancement of Teaching* (New York: Carnegie Foundation, 1910).
6. Archie R. Boe, "A Call to Reason," speech delivered to the New York Chapter, Chartered Property & Casualty Underwriters, New York, 26 April 1976.

things are not quite right, and jurors occasionally leave the impression that the question of fact they consider is not whether or not culpable negligence was present but, rather, who is better able to bear the burden of loss?

As noted above, some factors unique to the medical milieu have played an important role in the emerging malpractice crisis. Advances in medical science and technology have increased exponentially for the past several decades. This has created an atmosphere of great expectations which is not always justified by the facts. People tend to forget that medicine is a mixture of art and science, and imperfect science at that. Nevertheless, when expectations are high, failure to fulfill them prompts dissatisfaction. A tentative indication that frustrated expectations rather than negligence may be at the root of some claims can be found in "testimony to the panel in December, 1975, which stated that over $60,000,000 of malpractice claims were at that time outstanding against medical school department heads in the state of New York alone. More than likely, some of these claims reflected disappointment with less-than-perfect results in extremely complicated cases which could only have been undertaken by these particularly skilled individuals. Inadequate results were probably more a reflection of the state of the art of medicine than of incompetence or negligence."[7]

Advances in medicine have also been reflected in the composition of medical manpower. A sharp drop in the role of the "family doctor" (usually a general practitioner) has accompanied the vast array of medical advances, with the majority of physicians now practicing in one of the many available specialties or subspecialties. When combined with the great mobility of the American public, this means that few individuals or families develop the close and lasting personal relationships with their physicians which were characteristic of earlier, simpler times. "An operation takes only a few hours, while a foundation of trust takes much longer to establish."[8]

In recent literature on malpractice, much has been made of this deterioration of the doctor-patient relationship as a causal factor though it is hardly a new notion.[9] Yet, little organized effort has been made to remedy the situation. Modern doctors, perhaps partially victimized by the very technology which has made them more effective, are frequently charged with treating the disease rather than the patient. This is probably never a good strategy, but it is particularly inappropriate during a decade dominated by consumerist causes. Furthermore, it has been accompanied in recent years by a decline in the overall prestige of the medical profession.

As a group, doctors no longer command the respect they once enjoyed. This loss of prestige is fostered, at least in part, by general dissatisfaction with the rapidly escalating costs of health care, widely reported

7. Charles P. Hall, Jr., "Medical Malpractice—Some Reflections on the New York Experience," paper delivered to the annual meeting of the American Risk and Insurance Association, Boston, 16 August 1976, pp. 13-14.

8. Ronald E. Gots, The Truth About Medical Malpractice (New York: Stein and Day, 1976) p. 16.

9. See, for example, Michael E. Zahn, The Unmerited Medical Malpractice Case (Diss., University of Pennsylvania, 1961); see, also, Ronald E. Gots, The Truth About Medical Malpractice (New York: Stein and Day, 1976), Chapt. 1.

incidents of claim fraud by providers under medicare and medicaid, and equally well publicized studies which suggest that large numbers of unneeded medical procedures, especially surgery, are performed each year in this country.[10]

The kindly, house-calling, Dr. Welby-like physician of a generation ago may well have been insulated from lawsuits by the love and respect of his patients, but the same can seldom be said of the $100,000 per year surgeon who barely has the time of day for his block-scheduled referral patients, many of whom he barely knows, as he moves quickly and efficiently from cubicle to cubicle in his modern medical office. Some physicians, in an attempt to protect themselves from possible claims, seem to have relied largely on the execution of "consent forms" signed by patients for protection. However, these forms must be carefully designed; the test of "informed consent" is not easily met, and there is danger in the false sense of security that can be generated by their improper use.[11]

At the institutional provider level, the tradition of charitable immunity from malpractice claims which existed under common law has been largely eliminated by statute since the end of World War II, thus creating virtually overnight a huge liability exposure which did not previously exist.

More recently, providers have faced better informed, more innovative and, some have suggested, more "hungry" plaintiffs' attorneys. With respect to the latter, there are those who see more than coincidence in the fact that the biggest surge in malpractice claims has taken place during the 1970s. It has been speculated that trial lawyers who had their case loads adversely affected by the growing adoption of no-fault insurance laws in the automobile insurance field simply shifted their attention to malpractice. This same cynical view is sometimes used to explain the more recent surge in product liability claims, as states during the mid-1970s were busily enacting malpractice reform legislation. No documentation exists to support this view.

With respect to innovation, negligence-based claims have sometimes been discarded in favor of breach-of-contract suits against unwary physicians who tried to reassure worried patients with a promise that "everything will be all right," only to find out later that everything was not all right.

Other changes in the legal environment also took place which aggravated the malpractice problem, including some changes in rules of evidence and the adoption, in many jurisdictions, of the doctrine of *res ipsa loquitur*, or "the facts speak for themselves," in certain malpractice cases. Where invoked, this doctrine shifts the burden of proof from the plaintiff having to show negligence to the defendant physician or hospital having to prove its absence. This obviously makes successful defense more difficult.

As the number and size of claims grew, professional liability insurance premiums rose sharply. Annual increases of fifty to one hundred percent and more were not uncommon in some jurisdictions and specialties during the mid-1970s. As annual premiums for individual physicians climbed—in some cases to over

10. "Unnecessary Surgery Still a 'Monumental' Problem, Report Says," *The Wall Street Journal*, 27 December 1978, p. 6.

11. "Attorney Discusses Advantages and Pitfalls of Using Consent Forms," *Malpractice Digest*. Nov/Dec., 1978, pp. 2–5.

$20,000—and the premiums for hospitals in some cases equalled the face amount of the protection provided, providers began to balk.[12] Furthermore, many insurers also "bailed out" by refusing to offer malpractice coverage at any price. By 1975, only twelve insurers were actively selling malpractice insurance in the country, and the American Insurance Association reported that in some areas physicians might not be able to secure insurance at any price.[13]

Providers, especially physicians, became increasingly agitated over developments in the malpractice field. They were frustrated, confused, and angered by what they viewed as unjustified suits and confiscatory premiums. They lashed out at "ungrateful" patients, "greedy and unethical" lawyers, and "gouging" insurers. They began to exercise their considerable political clout to demand redress of the situation. This not only spawned the massive study of medical malpractice by the Secretary's Commission, but it also triggered a variety of special investigations at the state level. Private foundations and individual researchers also launched studies.

A plethora of findings and recommendations ensued.[14] Frequently, the public response, was favorable and the proposals—in New York for example—were endorsed by such diverse groups as the state medical society and the medical malpractice committee of the Association of the Bar of the City of New York.[15] Never-

theless, political expediency frequently dictated the application of a band-aid rather than a cure, and many of the most far-reaching and fundamental recommendations for reform were virtually ignored.

Again using New York as an example, Governor Carey made clear that his primary concern "was to continue the uninterrupted delivery of medical care," because failure to do so would have been political suicide. To achieve that, at least in the short run, it was not necessary to become embroiled in the highly controversial process of implementing all suggested reforms, such as, for example, the replacement of the tort system by an as yet undefined compensation system, no matter what the longer term merits of such a switch might be.

From a practical point of view, the more expedient answer was to forestall any further job actions by physicians or other health providers. This was possible by assuring the availability of a malpractice insurance market which had one or both of two characteristics; it must have reasonably stable premium rates and/or reasonable opportunities for passing costs beyond the providers.[16]

Much of the reform legislation adopted around the country in the mid-1970s focused on the assurance of a viable insurance market for providers, with the legislative creation of joint underwriting associations and authorization of various self-insurance arrangements for physicians and hospitals. Some controls were also introduced via limitations on lawyers' contingency fees, the introduction of maximum dollar limits for noneconomic (that is, pain and suffering) losses, and introduction of modified statutes of limita-

12. Hall, "Medical Malpractice," p. 4.
13. *Report of the Special Advisory Panel*, p. 17.
14. See, for example, *Report of the Secretary's Commission*, "Summary of Recommendations," pp. xix–xxviii, and *Report of the Special Advisory Panel*, "Summary and Recommendations," pp. 1–8.
15. Hall, "Medical Malpractice," p. 16.

16. Ibid., pp. 17–19.

tions for malpractice. There were both legislated and voluntary efforts to assist in the prevention of unnecessary malpractice claims as well as the more efficient resolution of disputes. Included here were such devices as patient grievance mechanisms, state offices of consumer health affairs, screening panels, and various forms of arbitration arrangements.[17]

Unfortunately, less attention has been devoted to the prevention of medical injuries, the real root of the malpractice problem, than to making the financial consequences less onerous. After all, "patient injuries, real or imagined, are prime factors in the malpractice problem."[18] Pennsylvania, however, did include in its malpractice reform legislation, effective since January 1976, a requirement that "all health care providers maintain a plan of risk management." It also adopted a fairly rigorous set of "Guidance Standards for Review and Approval of an Institutional Plan of Risk Management." The scope of these standards assures implementation of far more than a traditional safety program. "Those persons familiar with the nature of medical professional liability are in agreement that, if any significant change is going to occur in frequency and severity of losses, it will require considerable effort on the part of providers to control the sizeable exposure."[19] Many feel that Pennsylvania's focus on risk management is one of the most promising approaches yet tried.

17. See *Report of the Secretary's Commission*, Chapts. 7, 8, for a description of several of these.
18. Ibid., p. 14.
19. Robert L. Archer, "Professional Liability Risk Management in Pennsylvania," *Risk Management*, vol. 25, no. 11 (November 1978): 52–54.

Because of the very recent implementation of most of the reform movements, few firm conclusions can be drawn regarding their long run effectiveness. For the short run, prices of malpractice coverage have stabilized somewhat, and most providers have been able to obtain desired coverage. Few experts believe that the problem has really been solved, though, and many fear that it will reappear soon in even greater intensity unless more basic reforms are undertaken.

INCREASES IN LITIGATION AND MALPRACTICE INSURANCE PREMIUMS

As noted in the historical outline above, sharp increases in the amount of malpractice litigation have occurred in recent years. This phenomenon cannot be attributed to any one cause; rather it results from the interaction of many forces, several of which have been enumerated. The inevitable result has been the sharp increase in malpractice insurance premiums.

There is no mystery involved in identifying the causes for premium increases. Malpractice insurance, a form of liability insurance, is essentially an outgrowth of our system of tort law. The basic purpose of tort law is "to find fault for wrongdoing and to deter the wrongdoer by assessing damages to be paid to the victim of his wrongdoing." In this setting, the purpose of malpractice insurance is to protect the assets of the provider.

This protection is achieved in two ways. First, the insurer agrees to pay for all costs of defending claims, whether or not those claims are fair or fraudulent; second, it indemnifies the insured for the actual amount of any judgments rendered against

him. However, "in medical malpractice, as in so many other fields
of our technological society, there
has developed the third expectation that proper and just compensation to injured persons will be
achieved under the tort law/liability
insurance system. The common law
definition of insurance and associated legal procedures and doctrines
were [sic] apparently adequate in
simpler times to limit the concept
of compensation to the concept
of damages associated with negligence. Although the definition has
not changed, the way the system
works has, so that the system is now
often expected to be a generalized
compensation system . . . The rise
in frequency of claims, the liberalized rules of procedure, the use of
mediation panels, the dramatic
awards—all tend to create a new
theory, namely that victims of adverse medical outcomes or injuries
resulting from medical treatment
ought to be compensated."[20]

There is an element of contradiction in these three objectives
of deterrence, protection of assets,
and injury compensation. But there
is no contradiction in their impact
on premiums. Greater expectations
of compensation, whether or not
negligence is present, lead to more
suits, which result in greater costs
of defense. And, since asset values
have also increased, claims and
awards have multiplied in size as
well as number.

While the reasons for increasing
premiums are easily explained, the
amounts of the increases are far
more difficult to justify. In the sim-
plest possible terms, one must recognize that malpractice insurance is
sold at a particular point in time;

typically, it offers to the insured a
promise to defend and pay for claims
based on injuries incurred during an
immediate future time period (one
year, for example). Insurers, however, must contend with the in-
famous "long tail" problem of malpractice claims. That is, a physician's
error may not manifest itself as a
recognizable injury for several years,
and the victim may then defer the
filing of a claim for an additional
period of time, perhaps in an effort
to be certain that the full costs can
be known. Finally, liability claims
are notoriously slow in proceeding
through the courts.

The bottom line is that an insurance carrier may pay claims out of
a single year's premium income over
the subsequent ten years or more,
and "it is not atypical for 50 percent
of loss payments to occur more than
five years after the collection of the
premium."[21] Admittedly, this means
that the insurer will hold a portion
of the premiums for some time, possibly earning considerable interest.
Historically, however, this has been
more than offset by the sharply increased size of awards in recent
years, based partially on simple inflation and partially on changing
attitudes and legal procedures.
Nevertheless, it is virtually impossible for insurance actuaries to explain satisfactorily to a physician
or hospital with a good claims history
why premiums continue to rise
exponentially.

The problem is complicated by
the fact that, in comparison to most
forms of insurance such as life, fire
and auto, there are relatively few

20. *Report of the Special Advisory Panel*,
pp. 13–14.

21. Patricia Munch, "Causes of the Medical Malpractice Insurance Crisis: Risks and
Regulation," in Simon Rottenberg, ed. *The
Economics of Medical Malpractice* (Washington, DC: The American Enterprise Institute for Public Policy Research, 1978), p. 135.

exposure units in the malpractice liability field, so a few large claims can have a more significant impact on premiums than would be true in a more mass market. Since insurers are traditionally conservative, many have chosen to simply withdraw from the malpractice market altogether rather than face the many imponderables of premium computation in a changing environment, especially since their best judgment has only served to antagonize both their customers and regulators, while at the same time generating losses (real or potential) for the insurer.

RESTRICTED INSURANCE MARKET AND PROPOSED SOLUTIONS

It has already been noted that only a few companies still make medical malpractice insurance available on a voluntary basis. Most of the direct efforts to address the problem of availability of insurance have involved group activity and political action. Initially medical societies and hospital associations intervened and attempted to negotiate group insurance programs for their constituencies. This produced some premium savings. Some of these efforts have been around for many years. Such plans, however, were not much help when insurers began to withdraw from the market. More recently, these groups have sought and obtained special legislation or administrative rulings permitting the establishment of either self insurance options or captive insurance companies to serve their needs. Examples include the Medical Mutual Liability Insurance Company in New York and the Pennsylvania Hospital Insurance Company in Pennsylvania. Companion legislation has been passed in many states to create joint underwriting asso-

ciations (JUA's). In New York, the facility is called the Medical Malpractice Insurance Association. Some states created special state insurance funds as back-up systems.[22]

The layman will recognize JUAs as variations of the assigned risk plans which have operated in the automobile insurance field for many years. They differ, however, in at least one very important respect. In auto assigned risk plans, only insurers which were actually in the automobile insurance market were required to participate. JUAs typically required participation of all insurers writing any form of personal injury liability insurance in the state. Because of the specialized nature of malpractice insurance and the relatively few insurers with any experience in the field, these laws are particularly distasteful to the companies and, along with other elements of the growing body of reform legislation, may even be of questionable constitutionality.[23] The reform legislation often also extended special rate making or other authority to insurance commissioners; it also generally established mandatory limits of coverage, reserves and, sometimes premiums.

Many reform measures do not deal directly with insurance, but they will have an impact on it. For example, changes in collateral source rules, limits on lawyers' contingent fees, and limits on awards for noneconomic losses all serve to reduce

22. See, for example, Report of the Special Advisory Panel, pp. 119–20.
23. For two very useful discussions of these issues, see Martin H. Redish, Legislative Response to the Medical Malpractice Crisis: Constitutional Implications (Chicago: American Hospital Association, 1977), and Martin H. Redish, The Constitutionality of Medical Malpractice Reform Legislation: A Supplemental Report (Chicago: American Hospital Association, 1978).

malpractice insurance payouts. Modified statutes of limitation may help to reduce the "long tail" under policies written on an occurrence basis, thus taking some of the speculation and "sorcery" out of the actuarial process. Claim screening panels and arbitration arrangements could serve to lower insurance costs by reducing legal costs.

Naturally, some of the more radical proposals could have far-reaching implications for the legal and insurance systems. Suggestions to scrap the tort system in favor of some form of compensation or no-fault system have surfaced in recent years.[24] This could easily lead to governmental handling of the risk, though there is no theoretical reason why private insurers could not function along the lines of workers' compensation insurance. Such an approach could produce higher rather than lower costs and might significantly alter their distribution as between patient, provider and public; both might be justified on grounds of equity or social desirability.

EFFECTS ON SOCIETY AND THE MEDICAL PROFESSION

The malpractice problem has had and will continue to have manifold effects on society and the medical profession. Individual patients and society in general suffer grave damage from negligent and improper treatment. There are many evidences of this, but a recent House of Representatives Subcommittee report gives one indication: ". . . about two million unnecessary surgical

procedures were performed (in the U.S.) in 1977, costing more than $4 billion and resulting in the deaths of more than 10,000 people."[25] While not every unnecessary surgical procedure represents culpable malpractice, many do. The damage, then, is both physical and economic.

Firm cost figures are not readily available on a nationwide basis, but it was estimated that the actual cost of medical malpractice insurance in New York alone amounted to about $244 million in 1975. Those costs were projected to rise to $500 million by 1979. The initial impact of these premium costs falls on providers, but it is estimated that 70 to 90 percent of the total cost is ultimately passed on to the consumer.[26] This is more readily accomplished by institutional providers than by individual physicians, because of the cost basis of reimbursement for hospitals under many forms of public and private health insurance. What is initially perceived as an economic problem for providers, however, is in reality a problem for society in general. Nearly 26 percent of hospitalization in New York in 1975 consisted of Medicaid patients; under its 50-50 cost sharing formula with the federal government, that meant that the state (that is, the taxpayers) was paying the full costs for 13 percent of the patients. In some hospitals, malpractice costs translated into daily room charges of $15.00 per day and more, based on number of beds and average occupancy.[27]

Hidden costs abound, frequently attributed to the wide-spread practice of "defensive medicine." With high and rising health care costs, unnecessary tests designed to build

24. *Report of the Special Advisory Panel*, pp. 4–5, 57–63; see also, Clark C. Havighurst and Laurence R. Tancredi, "'Medical Adversity Insurance'—A No Fault Approach to Medical Malpractice and Quality Insurance," *The Milbank Memorial Fund Quarterly* 51 (Spring, 1973): 125–168.

25. "Unnecessary Surgery Still a 'Monumental' Problem."
26. *Report of the Special Advisory Panel*, pp. 22–24.
27. Hall, "Medical Malpractice," pp. 4–7.

a defense against future malpractice claims may be extremely expensive. Yet this is a two-edged sword, and "one suspects that most patients, given a choice, would prefer to be cared for by a defensive physician, if the implication of the label can be translated as 'conservative' or 'careful'"; this is especially true to the extent that defensive medicine could impact on the unneeded surgery cited previously.[28]

Clearly, the impact on providers of care has had economic, emotional, and professional overtones. Individual physicians feel this most acutely. Claims that insurance costs are impacting on choice of specialty and geographic distribution of physicians, however, have not been well documented. Furthermore, this, too, can be viewed as a two-edged sword, with at least as much potential for good as for mischief.[29] If, for example, "service paralysis" results in a decline of unnecessary surgery, and a decision by would-be surgeons to practice primary care, and if high malpractice premiums in metropolitan areas led more physicians to locate in rural areas, society might well benefit from the changes.

Increasing constraints on professional freedom, too, may not be all bad. Proposals for reform of educational and licensure standards, as well as various criteria for review of performance, hold significant potential for solving the root issues of the malpractice problem; so, too, do some of the risk management provisions of reform legislation. Recent research also suggests that a more rational approach by insurers to the process of risk classification and premium setting could also be helpful.[30]

Finally, the societal impact of changes in the entire structure of the reparations system for dealing with malpractice or other medical misadventure could be most significant of all. It would be well to proceed carefully when implementing either major reform of the tort system (that is, limits on recovery) or introducing a substitute system. These kinds of changes, as noted previously, often raise serious constitutional and philosophical issues, and they may have spillover effects on other institutions and structures of society. They should not, therefore, be entered into lightly.[31]

CONCLUSION

As stated at the outset, the malpractice problem in this country is multifaceted and complex. Like the proverbial blindman who tried to describe an elephant after being permitted to touch but one part of the animal, various parties have differing perceptions of the problem. Despite the necessary brevity and, therefore, incompleteness of this treatise, it should be clear that there are unlikely to be any panaceas at hand. The seemingly intractable nature of the problem demands that carefully designed and controlled research be undertaken to explore the many possible strategies for dealing with the problem. Emotionally and politically inspired flurries of activity are unlikely to produce satisfactory results.

28. Ibid., p. 11.

29. Ibid., pp. 7–10. See, also, Galen Burghardt, Jr., "Medical Malpractice and the Supply of Physicians," in Simon Rottenberg, ed. *The Economics of Malpractice*, pp. 103–123.

30. Deborah J. Chollet, *The Effect of Physician Liability Insurance on the Severity of Medical Injuries* (Diss., Syracuse University, December 1978, Chapt. 5).

31. See, for example, *Report of the Special Advisory Panel*, "Minority Report," pp. 283–92.

Products Liability Problem

By BARRY B. SCHWEIG

ABSTRACT: This paper presents an analysis of the changing impact of products liability risk on various individuals, firms, and institutions in today's society. After defining products liability and products liability risk, the pendulum-like evolution of products liability law is documented. Then an analysis of some of the most important factors responsible for the recent increases in the frequency and severity of products liability litigation is presented. Several of these elements have apparently combined to produce a synergistic increase in products-related lawsuits. These elements include recent development in the law of products liability, together with a newly emerging products claim consciousness, public concerns about product safety, and the plethora of old and new products in use today. Finally, the paper concludes with an analysis of the potential impact of enacting one or more of the many proposed solutions to the problem of products liability risk.

Barry B. Schweig is Visiting Assistant Professor of Finance at the University of Nebraska-Lincoln. He received his M.A. and Ph.D. degrees in Business and Applied Economics from the Wharton School of the University of Pennsylvania, where he studied under a Huebner Foundation Fellowship. Professor Schweig has published articles concerning products liability in the Journal of Products Liability and the Journal of Insurance Issues and Practices.

PRODUCTS liability may be defined as the legal obligation(s) of a manufacturer, distributor, or seller of products, to indemnify persons who have suffered bodily injury or property damage attributable to a defective product or a product defect.[1]

Products liability risk, moreover, may be conceptualized as the subjective probability that a person who suffers a products-related injury or loss will later seek legal redress or indemnification from the product's manufacturer, distributor, or seller. For example, a person who suffers a products-related loss may initiate a lawsuit on the basis of breach of expressed or implied warranty, or on the basis of strict liability in tort, or on the basis of any of several distinct negligence doctrines.[2]

The most troublesome aspect of today's product liability risk appears to be the seemingly endless spiral of escalating products-related lawsuits. For example, a California jury recently awarded the largest judgment on record, $128,466,280—after one person was killed and another badly burned in a Ford Pinto automobile that was hit from behind.[3] In another automobile products-related suit, in Alaska, a suit for $9,341,683 was brought, based upon alleged defects in an automobile's seat-belt design.[4] Besides automobiles, sporting goods also seem to spawn spectacular products-related cases. The paralysis of a Florida high school football player in 1975, for example, resulted in a $5,200,000 judgment against a football helmet maker, when the jury decided that the youth's helmet was improperly designed.[5]

According to a prominent consumer plaintiff's attorney, Philip H. Corboy, "A product liability case is nothing more nor less than litigation arising because a manmade product has some part, some characteristic indigenous to the product, that fails or produces a result it was not intended to produce."[6]

In an attempt to cope with the uncertainty generated by the increasing frequency and severity of products-related lawsuits, and other troublesome aspects of the products liability risk problem as well, the property and liability insurance industry has resorted to restrictive underwriting practices.[7] Moreover, for at least some businesspersons, regardless of their products liability loss experience, insurance coverage may not be available at any (acceptable) price.[8]

The developments in the law of products liability that have facilitated plaintiffs' actions are the result of a lengthy and convoluted process. Therefore, in order to better understand the complex legal milieu surrounding products liability today, it is first necessary to review some of the rich legal heritage of products liability.

1. A. S. Weinstein, "Products Liability: An Interaction of Law and Technology," *Duquesne Law Review*, vol. 12, no. 3, (Spring 1974):425–64.

2. Rajan Chandran and Robert Timmerman, "Planning to Minimize Product Liability," *Sloan Management Review*, vol. 20, no. 1 (Fall 1978):33–45.

3. David F. Pike, "Why Everybody Is Sueing Everybody," *U.S. News & World Report*, 4 December 1978:50–54.

4. Ibid., p. 53.

5. Ibid., p. 53.

6. Grace W. Holmes, *The Product Liability Case: Preparation and Trial* (Michigan: The Institute of Continuing Legal Education, 1975):3.

7. Office of the Secretary, U.S. Department of Commerce, "Options Paper on Product Liability and Accident Compensation Issues," *Federal Register*, vol. 43, no. 67 (6 April 1978): 14612–14632.

8. Ibid., p. 14623.

HISTORICAL EVOLUTION OF THE PRODUCTS LIABILITY RISK

Products liability risk is far from being a new problem. For example, one of the first references to products liability risk is found in a series of English criminal statutes which were enacted in 1266 A.D.[9] These statutes imposed pillory confinement or cash fines on victualers, butchers, cooks, and any other persons caught dispensing "corrupt" food or drink.[10]

The influence of the Medieval guilds further expanded the products liability risk to include all kinds of defective products. For example,[11]

The rigid regulation of the guild craftsmen made scamped workmanship . . . as dangerous in industry as was adulteration in food. The severity of the punishments inflicted for fraud or even carelessness is astonishing. . . . The artisan was subject to constant control of municipal overseers, who had the right to enter his shop by day or night and also to that of the public, under whose eyes he was ordered to work at his window.[12]

Privity of contract

Products liability lawsuits were a rarity until quite recently, primarily because of a potent defense known as privity of contract. Privity of contract was interpreted in the United States as follows:

the original seller of goods was not liable for damages caused by their defects to anyone except his immediate buyer, or one in privity with him.[13]

In 1916, the question of whether or not to continue a strict interpretation of the doctrine of privity of contract in the United States, was presented to Judge Benjamin Nathan Cardozo, in the case of *MacPherson* v. *Buick Motor Company*.[14]

This case involved the liability of a manufacturer of an automobile with a defective wheel, to the ultimate purchaser of the automobile, who was injured when the defective wheel collapsed. Judge Cardozo ruled that,

If the nature of a thing is such that it is reasonably certain to place life and limb in peril when negligently made, it is then a thing of danger. Its nature gives warning of the consequences to be expected. If to the element of danger there is added knowledge that the thing will be used by persons other than the purchaser and used without new tests, then irrespective of contract, the manufacturer of this thing of danger is under a duty to make it carefully.

Thus, Cardozo found the manufacturer negligent, despite the absence of privity of contract between the manufacturer and MacPherson, the ultimate consumer.

Although the Cardozo decision helped to breach the "citadel" of privity of contract, it was still very difficult for an injured consumer to pursue a products liability case successfully on the basis of negligence.

9. Reed Dickerson, *Products Liability and the Food Consumer* (Westport, CT: Greenwood Press, 1951), p. 20.

10. Mary Coate Houtz, "The Insurance Response to a Shifting Caveat," *Proceedings*, American Bar Association Section of Insurance Law, 1944, p. 296.

11. Henri Pirenne, "Urban Economy and the Regulation of Industry," Part Six, *Economic and Social History of Medieval Europe* (New York: Harcourt, Brace, and Company, 1933), p. 179.

12. Ibid., p. 173. The minute regulations of the tailors' guild are demonstrated by the fact that details as small as the number of stitches to be made on a man's collar were stipulated, and any deviation in the number of stitches was a punishable offense.

13. William L. Prosser, *Law of Torts*, 4th Ed. (Minnesota: West Publishing Co., 1971), p. 461. Prosser often referred to "privity of contract" as a "citadel" against products liability lawsuits.

14. 217 N.Y. 382, 111 N.E. 1050. (1916).

For example, the plaintiff first had to prove a duty owed by the manufacturer or seller. Then the breach of that duty had to be demonstrated. Finally, the breach of duty had to be shown to be the actual or proximate cause of the plaintiff's injury. The defendant had defenses in such negligence cases as well. For example, it could be argued that the plaintiff was contributorially negligent; or that the risk of injury had been assumed by the plaintiff.

Breach of warranty

It also became possible to win a products liability action based upon breach of warranty liability, instead of negligence. Breach of warranty is an action in contract law, rather than a tort. If a plaintiff could show reliance upon one or more express representations concerning the product, then the manufacturer or seller could be held liable. The idea originated in *Baxter* v. *Ford Motor Co.*[15] The court held that a statement concerning an automobile's "shatterproof" windshield, which was contained in a widely circulated piece of advertising material, made the defendant liable.

In addition to express warranties, some courts have also allowed recovery on the basis of implied warranty. The leading breach of implied warranty case is *Henningsen* v. *Bloomfield Motors*, Inc.[16] In this case the plaintiff alleged that the steering mechanism of her husband's new automobile had malfunctioned, just ten days after purchase, causing her to be injured. The plaintiff sued, relying upon theories of negligence, express warranty, and implied war-

ranty. The plaintiff won her case on the implied warranty count.

Strict liability in tort

The real breakthrough in products liability law occurred after the Henningsen case. The development concerned extending the concept of strict liability in tort. Prosser describes the development as follows:[17]

. . . it gradually became apparent that 'warranty', as a device for the justification of strict liability to the consumer . . . is more trouble than it is worth. The American Law Institute drafting group of the Second restatement of Torts therefore discarded the term [warranty], and offered a Section as follows:[18]

(1) One who sells any product in a defective condition unreasonably dangerous to the user or consumer or to his property is subject to liability for physical harm thereby caused to the ultimate user or consumer, or to his property, if,
   (a) the seller is engaged in the business of selling such a product, and
   (b) it is expected to and does reach the user or consumer without substantial change in the condition in which it is sold.
(2) The rule stated in Subsection (1) applies although
   (a) the seller has exercised all possible care in the preparation and sale of his product, and
   (b) the user or consumer has not bought the product from or entered into any contractual relation with the seller.

Note that (2a) largely eliminates the requirement of proving negligence, while (2b) eliminates any privity of contract requirements.

---

15. 166 Wash. 456, 12 P. 2d 409, affirmed on rehearing 15 P. 2d 1118 (1932).
16. 32 N.J. 358, 161 A. 2d 69 (1960).

17. William L. Prosser, *Law of Torts*, pp. 656–657.
18. Restatement of Torts, Section 402A. Special Liability of Seller of Product for Physical Harm to User or Consumer. (1965).

Products liability law —summary

Today, a product liability lawsuit can be brought under the doctrines of breach of expressed or implied warranty, strict liability in tort, or under any of the following theories of negligence: a) improper product design; b) improper manufacture or assembly of the product; c) failure to inspect and test for product defects in premarketing stages; d) failure to warn of dangerous characteristics inherent in or built into the product; e) deceptive advertising or excessive "puffery" concerning product attributes; f) inadequate instructions for product use; or g) manufacturer's failure to forsee possible dangerous uses or misuses of the product.[19]

Given the legal evolution of products liability risk just described, it would certainly appear that *caveat venditor* (let the seller beware), is probably a better description of the nature of products liability risk today, than is the traditional *caveat emptor* (let the buyer beware).

THE CHANGING IMPACT OF THE PRODUCTS LIABILITY RISK

Pre-industrial society

Products liability risk was not an important or serious problem during the age of pre-industrial society. The rights and responsibilities of handicraft workers and individual or family-unit consumers were approximately equal. Therefore, disputes could often be settled quickly and with a minimum of intervention on the part of government or the courts.

Industrial society

During the Industrial Revolution (circa 1760 in Great Britain and later

19. Chadran and Timmerman, "Planning to Minimize Product Liability," p. 34.

in the U.S.), however, society mandated a substantial shift in products liability risk. Consumers were made to suffer the burden of products-related losses, so that industrialization in the United States and Great Britain could proceed at an enlivened pace. During this era, society obviously preferred the protection of "infant industries," and industrialists, to the protection of consumers and workers.

Post-industrial society

In the modern era of post-industrial society, the rights and duties of consumers became favorably balanced against the rights and duties of products' manufacturers, distributors, and retailers. For consumers, the advantageous shift in products liability risk begins with Judge Cardozo's (1916) decision against privity of contract whenever "inherently dangerous" products are concerned. The shift in products liability risk continued with the development of consumer "offenses" such as breach of expressed or implied warranties in products-related lawsuits. The culmination of the shift in favor of consumers, and against products' producers, however, can be conveniently reckoned with the inception and spread of the doctrine of strict liability in tort (1965).

In addition to the evolution of products liability law which is favorable to consumer plaintiffs, additional impetus for the expansion of products liability tort litigation may be found in the newly emerging claim consciousness of the American people, along with their concern about product safety, and the sheer volume of products in use today.

Claims consciousness

As previously mentioned, products liability lawsuits were largely a rarity prior to the 1960's.[20] By 1963, however, nearly fifty thousand products liability lawsuits were filed in a single year.[21] The number of products liability lawsuits had swollen to one hundred thousand per year by the end of 1966.[22] During the period of time between 1967 and the present, not only had the frequency of products liability lawsuits been increasing at an alarming rate, but the settlement costs associated with these lawsuits had also been subject to rapid increase.[23]

Product safety

The publicity generated by several recent pieces of Federal consumer protection legislation may also have contributed to the propensity of consumers with products-related injuries to sue. For example, the 1970 Occupational Safety and Health Act, and the Consumer Product Safety Act of 1972, have both been credited with stimulating products liability claims and lawsuits.[24]

The saccharin controversy, the debates about potential dangers to the Earth's ozone layer from aerosol sprays, and the "tris" childrens sleepware dilemma, probably further stimulated a new consumer awareness concerning unsafe products.

20. D. J. Hirsch, ed. *Products Liability: Guide for Management*, vol. 1972, no. 2 (Wisconsin: Defense Research Institute, Inc. 1972), p. 7.

21. R. M. Bieber, "Products Liability Loss and Its Control," *Products Liability An Area of Growing Concern* (Pennsylvania: The Society of Chartered Property and Casualty Underwriters, Inc., 1976), p. 43.

22. Ibid., p. 43.

23. *Federal Register*, vol. 43, no. 67 (6 April 1978), p. 14612.

24. S. J. Paris, "Analysis of the Consumer Product Safety Act of 1972 and Its Effect on Products Liability Litigation," *Products Liability An Area of Growing Concern* (Pennsylvania: The Society of Chartered Property and Casualty Underwriters, Inc., 1976), pp. 111–12.

A *plethora of products*

A third aspect of the products liability risk problem concerns the huge volume of new and used products in use today in the United States. The bountifulness of science and modern technology, when combined with the American public's penchant for gadgets, results in the production and distribution of a staggering number of products each year.

For example, the U.S. Consumer Product Safety Commission recently announced that it is focusing its efforts this year on those consumer products involved in more than 650,000 annual deaths and injuries to Americans. A sample of those "high priority" products include: a) power mowers; b) unvented gas heaters; c) miniature Christmas tree lights; d) skateboards; and public playground equipment.

Note that the recent developments in the law of products liability that have been favorable to consumer plaintiffs, plus the new products liability "claims consciousness," the new awareness concerning product safety, and the public's penchant for new products, are all individually capable of promoting an increase in the frequency and severity of products liability litigation.

Realizing that each of these three components of the problem of products liability risk are complimentary in nature, it is notable that their separate development in recent years tends toward a synergistic result. This result is an unprecedented increase in the frequency and severity of products liability claims and lawsuits.

Beginning in June of 1976, the U.S. Department of Commerce initiated an in-depth probe concerning all aspects of the products liability problem or "crisis." The results of the Commerce Department's Interagency Task Force study offers the most comprehensive and thorough analysis of products liability risk to date.[25]

A summary of the task force findings include: (a) recent products liability insurance premiums had been increased substantially for many types of industrial manufacturers, in a few cases, annual premium increases in excess of one thousand percent had been alleged; (b) products liability problems had contributed to the failure of some small manufacturers of high-risk products; (c) it appeared as if the increased cost of products liability insurance had not been successfully passed on to consumers, except by large manufacturers; (d) the impact of increased products liability insurance premiums appeared greater on small versus larger businesses; (e) some firms are "going bare," that is, at least some firms have dropped their products liability insurance protection and are continuing in business despite the possibility of substantial adverse products liability judgments; (f) at least some new product development had been retarded by the prospect of further products liability premium increases; (g) some manufacturers consider products liability to be their most pressing business problem; and (h) some products liability insurers appear to have engaged in restrictive underwriting practices—including "panic-pricing" of products liability insurance coverage.[26] Taken together, these developments have been referred to as the products liability insurance availability/affordability problem.

PROPOSED SOLUTIONS TO THE PRODUCTS LIABILITY RISK PROBLEM

A long list of potential solutions to the products liability risk problem has been suggested.[27] The analysis presented here, however, includes only a sample of the major solutions aimed at reducing the frequency and severity of products liability claims and lawsuits.

Tort liability reform

The following proposed solutions to the products liability problem intend primarily to reduce the frequency and/or severity of today's products liability lawsuits—while retaining the present tort-litigation system.

I. Methods to reduce the frequency of today's products liability claims and lawsuits.
1) Enact a statute of limitations defense.
2) Enact a state of the art defense.
3) Enact a product alteration, modification, or misuse defense.
4) Enact a compliance with governmental standards defense.
5) Enact a limitation of attorneys' fees uder the contingency fee system.
6) Enact a measure requiring the settlement of products liability claims via installments, rather than in lump sum amounts.
7) Enact a measure requiring the assessment of all court costs

25. Interagency Task Force on Product Liability, *Final Report*, (Washington D.C.: U.S. Department of Commerce, 1977).

26. Ibid., pp. I-1-21 and VI-11-35.

27. A discussion of many of the proposed solutions not analyzed in this paper may be found in the *Federal Register,* vol. 43, no. 67, (6 April 1978) pp. 14612–24, and Federal Register, vol. 43, no. 176 (11 September 1978) pp. 40438–40448.

in the event of a nugatory or fraudulent lawsuit.

II. Methods to reduce the severity of today's products liability claims and lawsuits.
   1) Elimination of the collateral source rule.
   2) Elimination of punitive damages in products liability lawsuits.
   3) Elimination of the plea for specific monetary damages (*ad damnum*).
   4) Enforce separate trials on the issues of liability and damages.
   5) Enforce comparative responsibility in strict liability lawsuits.
   6) Enforce contribution among joint tortfeasors.

SOME CONSEQUENCES OF ADOPTING THE PROPOSED SOLUTIONS

Each of the seven proposals aimed at reducing the frequency of today's products liability claims and lawsuits, while retaining the present tort-litigation system, are intended to "prohibit" a class of currently viable products liability claims or lawsuits.

For example, the enactment of a statute of limitations defense, would call for passage of a state law that stipulated that a manufacturer's or seller's liability for alleged product defects would be subject to a nine-year statute of limitations after the product was first purchased for use or consumption. In other words, nine years after the product was first purchased for use or consumption, a consumer who suffered a product-related loss associated with that nine year old product would not be able to pursue a products liability lawsuit.

Similarly, passage of a state of the art defense would imply that if the design or method of manufacture of a product conformed with the prevailing industry state of the art at the time the product was designed or manufactured, the product should not be considered defective today.

Passage of a product alteration, modification, or misuse defense would provide a complete defense to a product liability claim or lawsuit if there is evidence that the alleged injury was caused by the alteration, modification, or misuse of the product by the plaintiff.

Enactment of a compliance with governmental standards defense is intended to eliminate products liability claims and lawsuits where there is evidence that a product complies with applicable federal or state regulations with respect to the design, manufacturing or testing of that product.

The limitation of attorney fees under the contingency fee system is designed to discourage attorney "financing" of products liability cases, especially in cases where an unsophisticated plaintiff is induced by an attorney to bring suit, based upon the assurance that the attorney charges nothing—unless the lawsuit is successful.

Settlement of products liability claims via installments, rather than in lump sum amounts, is designed to discourage attorneys from taking modest injury cases on a contingency fee basis, because the attorney will not be interested in cases that take many years to pay off only small amounts of money.

Assessment of all court costs in the event of a nugatory or fraudulent law suit is intended to discourage attorneys from accepting marginal products liability cases. At present, the attorney invests only time, if the lawsuit or claim is unsuccessful. With the passage of this type of rule, however, a substantial amount of the attorney's funds could be at stake.

The remaining six proposals in this category are intended to reduce the severity of today's products liability claims and lawsuits. Elimination of the collateral source rule would mean that a plaintiff with products-related injuries, that had already received at least partial indemnification from other sources, such as his or her own group health and disability insurance at work, would not be able to collect again for these same losses from a products' manufacturer, distributor, or retailer. Hence the dollar cost of settlement in such a case should be substantially reduced.

If punitive damages are eliminated from products liability cases, then spectacular cases such as the previously discussed recent California Ford Pinto Case, where the jury award was in excess of one hundred million dollars in punitive damages against Ford Motor Company, would not be possible. It can be argued that punitive damages were designed for criminal rather than civil lawsuits, and that their continued presence only adds greater uncertainty as to the future severity of products liability settlements.[28]

Elimination of the *ad damnum*, or the plea for specific monetary damages, ought to help prevent the American public from receiving a distorted view of the "value" of products liability personal injury claims. The *ad damnum* is an anachronism that ought to be removed from the products liability scene. Enforcing separate trials on the is-

sues of liability and damages in products liability lawsuits is thought to promote less emotional and more realistic court awards.

Enforcing comparative responsibility in strict liability lawsuits is designed to reduce the severity or dollar settlement amount in strict liability in tort products liability cases. By including the plaintiff's share of the responsibility in regard to the product-related loss, for example, his or her percentage of contributory negligence or assumption of the risk involved, the dollar value of any final settlement would be diminished in proportion to the amount of responsibility attributable to the plaintiff's actions.

The final proposal within the category of tort liability reform would enforce contribution among joint tortfeasors in the settlement of all products liability lawsuits. The doctrine of contribution is an equitable rule based upon notions of fairness. It was first recognized in suretyship cases and other areas of the law before it was applied to tort actions. Contribution is defined as the right of one, who has discharged a common liability, to recover from another, his or her proportionate share of that liability. In a products liability action, there may be several joint tortfeasors, and the fact that one defendant is found liable on the basis of negligence and another is found liable on the basis of breach of warranty, should not preclude either defendant from seeking contribution from the other. Note that this proposal is designed to reduce the severity of products liability lawsuits by spreading the risk among several defendants; this proposal will not, however, reduce the amount of any settlement received by the plaintiff.

28. For an excellent and comprehensive analysis of the role of punitive damages in insurance situations, see John D. Long, "Should Punitive Damages be Insured?," *The Journal of Risk and Insurance*, volume 44, no. 1 (March 1977), pp. 1–20.

SUMMARY AND CONCLUSIONS

This paper presents an analysis of the changing impact of products liability risk on various individuals, firms, and institutions in today's society. After defining products liability and products liability risk, the pendulum-like evolution of products liability law is documented. Then an analysis of some of the most important factors responsible for the recent increases in the frequency and severity of products liability litigation is presented. Several of these elements have apparently combined to produce a synergistic increase in products-related lawsuits. These elements include recent developments in the law of products liability, together with a newly emerging products claim consciousness, public concerns about product safety, and the plethora of old and new products in use today. Finally, the paper concludes with an analysis of the potential impact of enacting one or more of the many proposed solutions to the problem of products liability risk.

ANNALS, AAPSS, **443**, May 1979

The Changing Societal Consequences of Risks from Natural Hazards

By HOWARD KUNREUTHER

ABSTRACT: In recent years, the federal government has provided substantial relief to victims of natural disasters. A primary reason for this assistance is that many of the individuals suffering damage have not protected themselves with insurance. Standard coverage, normally required as a condition for a mortgage, offers protection against fire, wind, and hail damage; flood and earthquake policies can be purchased separately, and most residents of hazard-prone areas have not voluntarily bought this coverage. Recent empirical evidence on individuals' decision processes with respect to protection against events which have a relatively small chance of occurring but can result in severe losses is summarized. Unless individuals have been made graphically aware of the consequences of disasters, typically through past experience, they are unlikely to even consider purchasing insurance protection. Once their interest is stimulated they use informal networks such as friends and neighbors to guide them in their actions. Tradeoffs between using voluntary means of promoting insurance or some other form of required coverage are discussed. Policy decisions have to reflect both the decision processes of individuals as well as value judgments on the appropriate role of the private and public sectors in natural disasters.

Howard Kunreuther is Professor and Chairman of the Decision Sciences Department at the Wharton School, University of Pennsylvania. His recent research has been on individual decisionmaking with respect to low probability events. Recent publications explore the relationship between decision processes and policy in the areas of natural hazards, health, and safety.

This article draws on the findings of an interdisciplinary study supported by funds from the National Science Foundation reported in more detail in Howard Kunreuther, Ralph Ginsberg, Louis Miller, Philip Sagi, Paul Slovic, Bradley Borkan and Norman Katz, *Disaster Insurance Protection: Public Policy Lessons* (New York: John Wiley & Sons, 1978). Preparation of this article was supported by funds from NSF Grant PFR 77-26363.

TROPICAL Storm Agnes, which wreaked havoc on many areas of the northeast in June 1972, brings into sharp focus the question of appropriate roles for the public and private sectors in dealing with risks from natural disasters. Total damage caused by flooding was estimated at over $2 billion, making Agnes the costliest natural disaster in the nation's history. The Red Cross estimated that over 5,200 dwellings and mobile homes were completely destroyed by Agnes and that an additional 45,000 suffered major damage. Total damage to private housing was estimated at over $750 million.

Even though a number of the communities in the affected regions qualified for the federal government's subsidized National Flood Insurance, very few people had acquired coverage prior to the flood. In fact, only 1,580 claims, totally $5 million, were paid under the National Flood Insurance Program. As a result of the financial burden imposed on many of the victims by Agnes, Congress provided generous relief through its Small Business Administration Disaster loan program. Residents and businesses suffering damage were able to obtain forgiveness grants up to the first $5,000 of the loss and loans at an attractive 1 percent annual rate for the remaining portion.

The statistical story of Agnes illustrates two general points: (1) few individuals voluntarily protect themselves against the financial consequences of disasters, and (2) Congress is likely to respond to the plight of victims with liberal relief if large numbers of them are uninsured.

Since 1972, there has been a concern by Congress with shifting some of the financial burden of disasters away from the federal government to hazard-prone communities and their residents. This philosophical change has been reflected by emphasizing the importance of pre-disaster protection rather than large-scale relief following severe catastrophes. There is still no consensus by policy makers on how best to achieve this objective. We shall argue below that there is a need for better understanding the decision processes of different actors in the natural hazard drama if effective programs are to be designed. After briefly summarizing the changing federal and private sector role in disasters, current knowledge about the decision processes of residents of hazard-prone areas is reviewed. The concluding portions of the paper discuss the policy implications of these descriptive findings.

CHANGING FEDERAL AND PRIVATE ROLE IN DISASTERS

During the period from 1953 to the present, the federal government has played an increasing role in providing disaster relief. While the dollar amount of damage from natural disasters has climbed rapidly since the early 1950's, federal financial assistance has grown even more rapidly. This pattern appears to reflect an attitude by victims of natural disasters that the federal government has a responsibility to relieve them financially from Acts of God beyond their control. This feeling is in marked contrast to the attitude of victims even one generation ago. For example, following a tornado in San Angelo, Texas in 1953, federal representatives advised certain local school officials to apply for federal funds to repair a school damaged by the twister. They were reluctant to do so because most of the repair cost was covered by insurance. Eventually they did make a request. It was promptly granted. A year later, they returned the money in an act of conscience. Today one rarely hears of such independent conduct.

Evidence on increased federal disaster relief is provided by comparative data on the Small Business Administration disaster loan program. The growth of the program is easily seen in Figure 1; the increase is particularly significant in the case of home loans where both the total number and total dollar values in the 1966–76 period were more than 25 times what they were in the first 12 years of the program. It is striking that the $1.2 billion approved by the SBA for victims of Tropical Storm Agnes represented almost four times the entire amount allocated by the SBA for all disasters between fiscal years 1954 and 1965. Over $540 million of the amount approved by

FIGURE 1

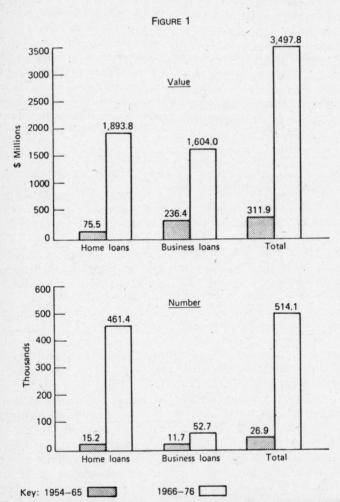

Comparison of value and number of SBA Disaster Loans, by category, for fiscal years 1954–1965 and 1966–1976. *Source:* Small Business Administration, Office of Reports.

the SBA for victims of this disaster were in the form of forgiveness grants which did not have to be repaid.

The financial repercussions of Tropical Storm Agnes led to the formation of a Presidential Task Force whose principal charge was to compare the cost and benefits of federal disaster relief with those of an insurance program.[1] Since the Task Force Report, Congress conducted an extensive set of hearings and appraisals on federal disaster assistance. In April 1973 legislation was passed (PL 93-24) rescinding the $5,000 forgiveness grants authorized after Tropical Storm Agnes and increasing the annual interest rate from 1 percent to 5 percent. The interest rates were further raised to 6⅝ percent in August 1975 (PL 94-68). Spring flooding in Appalachia during 1977 led Congress to liberalize the disaster relief provisions once more. Legislation passed in August 1977 (PL 95-89) permits individuals to obtain 1 percent interest loans on the first $10,000 loss, 3 percent on the next $30,000, and 6⅝ percent loans for that portion of a loan covering uninsured losses exceeding $40,000. The current SBA program provides loans to homeowners and businesses at cost of money which at this time is 7⅜ percent. There is, however, a proposal before Congress which would provide loans to businesses at 5 percent for the first $250,000, cost of money thereafter and to homeowners at 3 percent for the first $55,000, cost of money thereafter.

This program would be retroactive to 1 October 1978.

The primary reason for the special Congressional legislation in 1977 regarding SBA loans was that most of the victims from these disasters had not voluntarily purchased insurance. The standard policy normally required as a condition for a mortgage covers damage to property from fire, wind, or hail. Insurance against damage from flooding or earthquakes is available as separate policies to residents in hazard-prone areas.

Flood insurance

The National Flood Insurance Program, which was initiated in 1968, is the first positive step taken by the federal government to induce individuals to protect themselves against flood disasters.[2] The program, which is administered by the Federal Insurance Administration, encouraged homeowners and businesses, through federal rate subsidies, to purchase coverage while, at the same time, inducing communities to control unwise development of flood plains. Specifically the sale of this insurance was restricted to communities who agreed to adopt permanent land-use and control measures in special flood-hazard areas. Property owners residing in the community at the time it entered the flood program were able to buy coverage at highly subsidized rates. After flood insurance rate maps had been determined for a given area, premiums reflecting the actual risk were charged on new construction.

There is substantial evidence that most individuals in flood-prone areas

---

1. A detailed analysis of the data collected for this task force for three severe disasters (the San Fernando earthquake of 1971, the Rapid City flood of 1972, and Tropical Storm Agnes) can be found in Howard Kunreuther, *Recovery from Natural Disasters: Insurance or Federal Aid* (Washington, DC: American Enterprise Institute, 1973).

2. Private firms had discontinued offering the insurance since the mid-1920s because of catastrophic losses.

do not voluntarily purchase insurance despite highly subsidized rates. For example, less than 3,000 out of 21,000 flood-prone communities in the United States entered the program during its 4 years of operation, and less than 275,000 homeowners voluntarily bought a policy. This lack of interest in the program by communities and homeowners induced Congress to pass the Flood Disaster Protection Act of 1973. Its principal provision is that no federal financial assistance for the construction or acquisition of buildings in special flood hazard areas would be available to any flood-prone community that did not join the National Flood Insurance Program. All homeowners on the flood plain are now required to purchase this coverage as a condition for new FHA and VA financed mortgages if their community is enrolled in the program. Thus, by invoking sanctions on communities and residents in flood-prone areas, the program has grown markedly since 1973.[3]

Earthquake insurance

Earthquake coverage is privately marketed by American insurance companies and is available throughout the country. Approximately three-fourths of all policies are purchased in California where policies have been available to residents since 1916. Premiums for wood-frame homes in California, which comprise almost all residential structures in the state, average 20¢ per $100 coverage (with a 5 percent deductible). Coverage can easily be written as an endorsement to a standard policy. Nevertheless, today less than 5 percent of all homeowners

in California are protected against earthquake damage.

There is some evidence that the low subscription rate is due to the unwillingness of consumers to purchase coverage rather than to the unwillingness of the industry to market it aggressively. As an experiment following the San Fernando earthquake of February 1971, the Insurance Company of North America mounted a serious campaign to promote earthquake insurance in California by placing newspaper ads in the major dailies, advertising on TV, and enabling all their California agents to mail special brochures and announcements to their customers. The following month only 61 policies were sold, and then sales dropped off during the next 7 months to an average of seven per month.[4] The Hartford Insurance group and Kemper Companies ran similar campaigns to market earthquake insurance. Their efforts also bore little fruit.

The history sketched above suggests that few individuals purchase insurance against natural disasters unless they are required to do so. In the absence of compulsion what factors influence their knowledge of and behavior toward risk? Can an understanding of these factors provide insight into how more of the cost burden of disasters can be shifted from the public to the private sector through some form of insurance?

UNDERSTANDING DECISION PROCESSES TOWARD LOW PROBABILITY EVENTS

Alternative models of choice

Economists have relied on the expected utility model as a basis for

---

3. A more detailed description of the flood insurance program can be found in paper 12 in this issue.

4. Robert Syfert, "The Unwilling Market for Earthquake Insurance," Best's Review 73 (1972): 14–18.

recommending alternative courses of action under uncertainty.[5] According to this theory, a person determines whether insurance is an attractive option by considering the insurance premium, the estimated damage to his property from future disasters of different magnitudes, and the probabilities that each of these events will occur. In other words, he is assumed to behave as if he engaged in a detailed analysis of the costs and benefits associated with the purchase of insurance. When the expected benefits of protection exceed the costs of a policy, coverage is desirable; otherwise it is not.

As an alternative way of viewing the decisionmaking process, Herbert Simon introduced the concept of "bounded rationality" to signify that the decisionmaker's cognitive limitations force him to construct a simplified model of the world. Simon argues that in actual choice situations people have a difficult time making the computations required to maximize some objective. Furthermore, it may be difficult for them to gather the information to make these decisions.[6] Hence, a person will be reluctant to collect data on insurance or other protective mechanisms unless motivated to do so by some external event such as a recent disaster. Then the search process is likely to be very similar to the one followed by individuals who are considering the adoption of a new innovation.[7] An individual generally will first be made aware of the existence of insurance through the mass media or an insurance agent. Before buying he is likely to discuss the subject with friends or neighbors to obtain more information about the terms of a policy and the need for such protection. If he learns that his friend or neighbor has purchased coverage, his need to process information is further reduced, and he then may decide to buy a policy. This approach implies that an individual will neglect to purchase insurance because his knowledge of the subject is limited —not because he has studied the matter carefully and concluded that the cost-benefit ratio is unattractive.

One reason for contrasting these two models of choice is that they imply radically different policies regarding insurance purchases. According to the expected utility model, homeowners currently residing in hazard-prone areas will purchase insurance voluntarily if they perceive the premiums to be sufficiently low and are convinced that liberal disaster relief will not be forthcoming after the next catastrophe. By contrast, a model based on the concepts of bounded rationality implies that homeowners must be made graphically aware of the potential losses from the hazard before considering insurance. Because of the individual's reluctance to seek new information, friends and neighbors, as well as insurance agents, can play

5. For illustrations of the application of this theory to insurance purchases, see Isaac Ehrlich and Gary Becker, "Market Insurance, Self Insurance and Self-Protection," *Journal of Political Economy* 80 (1972): 623–48; Kenneth Arrow, "Optimal Insurance and Generalized Deductibles" Rand Report R-1108-OEO, Santa Monica, CA; and John Marshall, "Insurance as a Market in Contingent Claims: Structure and Performance," *Bell Journal of Economics and Management Science* 5 (1974):670–82.

6. A more detailed description of bounded rationality and its relationship to individuals' decision processes can be found in Herbert Simon, "Rational Decision Making in Business Organizations," *American Economic Review* (forthcoming).

7. For a comprehensive summary of the literature on the diffusion of innovations, See Everett Rogers with F. Floyd Shoemaker, *Communication of Innovations: A Cross Cultural Approach* (New York: The Free Press, 1971).

an important role in providing data on the availability of coverage and the terms of insurance. However, if the individual views the event as having an extremely low probability, he still may not be interested in data on potential losses and insurance even if the information is spoon-fed to him. These people will have little desire to purchase a policy voluntarily even when the rates are subsidized.

Empirical evidence

The empirical data from studies in the natural hazards area lend support to the bounded rationality approach as a descriptive model of choice under uncertainty. Results from a series of cross-cultural field surveys suggests the limited ability of individuals to deal with information and their reliance on past experience as a guide to action.[8] These observations are consistent with an earlier hypothesis of Kates that individuals in hazard-prone areas have an extremely difficult time dealing with complex information on probability distributions and potential losses from future disaster. Hence, they "simplify the world in order to deal with it" by relying on their own experience as a guide to the future.[9]

One explanation as to why individuals rely on past experience for making decisions has been offered by Tversky and Kahneman on the basis of a series of controlled laboratory experiments. The two psy-chologists hypothesize that individuals utilize a heuristic which they call availability, whereby the probability of an event is judged by the ease with which such instances are retrieved from memory.[10] Past experience may thus be necessary to raise the probability to a level where a person feels that it is a problem worthy of attention.

Further light has been shed on the accuracy of the expected utility model in explaining insurance purchase behavior and the relative importance of factors central to the bounded rationality model through a field survey in hazard-prone areas and controlled laboratory experiments.[11] The field survey involved face-to-face interviews with 2,055 homeowners residing in 43 areas throughout the United States subject to coastal and riverine flooding, and 1,006 homeowners living in 18 earthquake-prone areas of California. Half the respondents had purchased flood or earthquake insurance, the other half had not. The controlled laboratory experiments undertaken by Paul Slovic, Baruch Fischhoff, and Sarah Lichtenstein, at Decision Research, shed light on the causal relationships between variables entering into the insurance decision. A few of the key findings from this study which relate to individual decision processes are now summarized.

Although most uninsured homeowners interviewed were aware that flood and earthquake coverage existed, the majority were unaware

8. See Gilbert White, ed. *Natural Hazards: Local, National and Global* (New York: Oxford University Press, 1974), and Ian Burton, Robert Kates, and Gilbert White, *The Environment as Hazard* (New York: Oxford University Press, 1978).

9. Robert Kates, *Hazard and Choice Perception in Flood Plain Management* (Chicago: University of Chicago, Department of Geography Research Paper No. 78, 1962).

10. Amos Tversky and Daniel Kahneman, "Availability: A Heuristic for Judging Frequency and Probability," *Cognitive Psychology* 5 (1973):207–32.

11. A more detailed discussion of the research design and the findings can be found in Howard Kunreuther, et al., *Disaster Insurance Protection*.

that they were eligible to purchase a policy. And those who were aware had no reliable knowledge of the terms of a policy. When homeowners were asked to estimate the chances of a severe flood or earthquake damaging their property in the next year, 15 percent of the respondents in flood areas, and 8 percent of those in earthquake areas, were unable to provide any sort of estimate. Among those who did respond, some of the estimates defied logic. Some people thought the probability of a disaster hitting them was quite high—1 chance in 10—yet they said they had purchased no disaster insurance. Others believed the chance of a disaster affecting them was almost nil—1 in 100,000—yet they had purchased disaster insurance. It seems evident that a number of individuals participating in the field survey do not understand the concept of probability.[12]

It is tempting to attribute this casual attitude about the risks of natural hazards and protective activities to homeowners' beliefs that the federal government will bail them out in a crisis. But the field survey data revealed that the majority of *uninsured* residents anticipate *no* aid at all from the government in the event of a disaster. Most of these people were aware that the SBA provides aid to the victims, but they had little knowledge of the loan terms

or whether they could receive forgiveness grants. On the basis of these results, one can conclude that most homeowners in hazard-prone areas have not even considered how they would recover should they suffer flood or earthquake damage. Instead they treat such events as being so unlikely that they ignore the consequences altogether.

What variables influence a person's decision to purchase insurance? A key factor is a belief that the hazard is a serious problem. This concern is found primarily among people who have had past experience with the hazard. "You ask me why I didn't have insurance before the June 1972 flood" said one homeowner in Norristown, Pennsylvania. "We had the flood in September of '71 and I had two feet of water in my basement. And I felt this I can tolerate and this is probably as high as it will ever get." To his chagrin, this man suffered severe property damage in 1972. Only then did he decide that he needed insurance. Another uninsured flood victim, said that his rationale was that "the $60 in premiums they could use for something else. But now they don't care if the figure was $600. They're going to take insurance because they've been through it twice and they've learned a lesson from it."

Another important factor in influencing the purchase of a policy appears to be knowing someone who has purchased coverage or discussing insurance with a friend, neighbor or relative. The following example graphically illustrates this point. In a pretest of the questionnaire in San Francisco, a homeowner responded to one of the questions by saying that he did not have earthquake insurance. A friend of his who was listening to the interview commented that he had himself purchased

12. These findings are consistent with the heuristics and biases implied by controlled laboratory experiments over the past decade. See Amos Tversky and Daniel Kahneman, "Judgment Under Uncertainty: Heuristics and Biases," Science 185 (1974):1124–1131. For a discussion of the implications of these findings in the context of natural hazards, see Paul Slovic, Howard Kunreuther, and Gilbert White, "Decision Processes, Rationality, and Adjustments to Natural Hazards," in G. White, ed. *Natural Hazards: Local, National and Global.*

such insurance a few years before. The respondent was dumbfounded and asked his friend about the availability of earthquake coverage and how much it cost. "I'm going to have to look into earthquake insurance myself," he added.

The expected utility model appears to be an inadequate description of the choice process regarding insurance purchases even for those who elicited sufficient information to compare the costs with the benefits. Data from the field study revealed that people frequently behave in a manner that is inconsistent with what would be predicted by the theory. For example, over 40 percent of the uninsured homeowners had benefit/cost ratios which made purchasing a policy an attractive option for them; almost 30 percent of the *insured* homeowners estimated the cost of insurance to be so high in relation to its benefits that coverage should have been unattractive to them.

The controlled laboratory experiments on insurance undertaken at Decision Research provide insight into these unexpected findings.[13] Subjects were exposed to a variety of risks that had different losses and probabilities associated with them. By keeping the premium constant for all risks and varying the losses and probabilities in such a way that the expected loss (loss multiplied by probability) was the same, it was possible to test the adequacy of utility theory in explaining insurance behavior.

13. For more details on the study, see Paul Slovic, et al., "Preference for Insuring Against Probable Small Loss: Implications for Theory and Practice of Insurance," *Journal of Risk and Insurance* 44 (1977):237–58. A description of the experiments also appears in Howard Kunreuther, et al., *Disaster Insurance Protection*, Chapt. 7.

According to utility theory, individuals should prefer to insure themselves against events having a low probability of occurrence but a high loss rather than against those having a high probability and low loss. The reverse was found to be true for a variety of experimental formats. These results suggest that if the chances of an event are sufficiently low, people do not even reflect on its consequences. In other words, people are primarily interested in buying insurance if they feel the probability of a disaster is high enough for them to stand a good chance of getting a return. They thus view insurance as an *investment* rather than as protection.

IMPLICATIONS FOR POLICY

The viewpoints of the individual and the policy maker toward low probability events often conflict. For example, a homeowner residing near a river may picture a damaging flood as having a small probability of occurrence or may not perceive his potential property losses to be very large. The policymaker must look at risks aggregated over many residents in numerous locations, or in one place over a period of time; for example, the risk of a major flood or earthquake occurring in California within the next 25 years. From this perspective, the probability of a disaster and the expected aggregate costs are high enough to warrant concern.

Private and public risks

The public policy issues associated with this conflict revolve around private and social risks. Private risks refer to actions taken by an individual which affect himself but not society. An example is a decision by a person to construct a house near a fault line even though he knows full well that he would have to bear the entire financial burden should the structure suffer damage from an earthquake. Social risks arise when the general public bears the costs of negative outcomes associated with a particular action. The above location decision would be classified as a social risk if the federal government were to pay for all earthquake losses to private property.

Most actions involve both types of risks.[14] The relative magnitude of the private and social costs depends on the nature of the public policies in force and the reaction of individuals to them. The findings described above suggest that policies must recognize the lack of concern by most residents of hazard-prone areas with the private risks of a future disaster. Hence the tendency of so many not to purchase insurance coverage. After the event, these victims will be faced with severe private costs and are thus likely to clamor for government assistance. The extent of the social costs will depend on the type of relief provided to the private sector for recovery. Disaster related programs must thus study the interaction between mitigation and recovery measures given our understanding of individuals' decision processes.

Criteria for evaluation

The relative merits of alternative policies are reflected in two types of costs. First, there are resource

allocation costs. These are likely to be incurred if homeowners and businesses choose to locate in a hazard-prone region with misperceptions about the potential consequences from future disasters. If location decisions are made with limited or imperfect knowledge, then individuals may focus on the advantages of a particular area without fully appreciating the costs.

The recent empirical evidence discussed in the previous section suggests that the traditional market forces of supply and demand are unlikely to achieve the most desirable allocation of resources because of information imperfections.[15] Suppose people could be made more aware of the true risks of locating in hazard-prone areas through differential insurance premiums. If their actions reflected these risk considerations, this should lead to more efficient allocation of land, labor, and capital than currently exists.

Second, there are distributional costs. These costs represent the relative financial burden of a disaster to the victims and the rest of society. Governmental policy implies some value judgment as to what subsidies will be paid by the general taxpayer and how much by the residents of hazard-prone areas.

To evaluate the distributional impact of alternative programs, it is useful to understand the decision processes of individuals after a disaster. For example, there is considerable evidence that many victims do not utilize the federal loan program

14. For an interesting discussion of private and social aspects of risk in the context of safety, see Lester Lave, "Risk, Safety and the Role of Government," in Perspectives on Benefit-Risk Decision Making (Washington, DC: National Academy of Engineering, 1972).

15. See Kenneth Arrow, "Uncertainty and the Welfare Economics of Medical Care," American Economic Review 53 (1963):941–73, and Oliver Williamson, Markets and Hierarchies: Implications for Antitrust Policy (New York: The Free Press, 1975) for a fuller discussion of information imperfections and market failure.

to the extent possible.[16] Some families may have had negative feelings toward incurring large debts, while others may have had their loan size limited by the SBA because the agency felt that they could not afford to repay the loan. Whatever the reason, this self-reliance has resulted in many victims not recovering completely from the disaster because they were uninsured. Furthermore, those victims who availed themselves of generous SBA loans are then saddled with large debts for long periods of time. Vinso has shown that many elderly victims from Tropical Storm Agnes were financially crippled despite the generous SBA loan policy provided them after the disaster.[17] A typical lament in Wilkes Barre was "I wish that I had known about flood insurance and purchased a policy before Agnes."

Specifying policy options

Both resource allocation and distributional considerations suggest that insurance is likely to have both private and social benefits. Two broad alternatives deserve consideration for overcoming the lack of awareness and interest in coverage.

Voluntary coverage

One course of action is to make flood and earthquake coverage more attractive by presenting information through normal channels. The insurance agent may serve an important and useful function in this regard.

To the extent that he has the trust of his clients, he can stimulate their awareness of the hazard by telling them the chances of a disaster occurring and the potential losses that could result. One way for the agent to increase the client's concern with the hazard may be to present information on the probability of a disaster on a different time interval than the traditional one year period. For example, in describing the chances of a 100 year flood, the agent could note that for someone living in a house for 25 years, the chances of suffering damage at least once will be .22. He can also provide details as to what coverage is available and how much it costs.

Since most individuals seem to treat insurance as an investment, the agent should educate his clients that the biggest return on their policy is to have no return at all. At the moment, insurance agents have little incentive to promote disaster coverage among their clients. Commissions are based on a percentage of the total premium, which is usually a small amount in the case of earthquake and flood insurance. A 1975 study of the federal flood insurance program in New York state found that many agents had little interest in the program because they felt that the volume of flood policy business would be low and that they would be unlikely to pick up new business as a result of the contacts made.[18]

Required coverage

If voluntary methods of promoting insurance are viewed as too costly and time-consuming, financial insti-

16. For a more detailed discussion of this point, see Harold Cochrane, *Natural Hazards and Their Distributive Effects* (Boulder: University of Colorado, Institute of Behavioral Science, 1975).

17. Joseph Vinso, "Financial Implications of Natural Disasters: Some Preliminary Indications," *Mass Emergencies* 2 (1977) 205–17.

18. J. C. Preston, D. E. Moore, and T. Cornick, "Community Response to The Flood Disaster Protection Act of 1973" (Ithaca: Community and Resource Development Series, Bulletin 10, 1975).

tutions may play a key role by requiring some type of natural hazard insurance as a condition for a mortgage on residential property. Several types of policies deserve consideration.

One option would be a broader form of homeowners insurance which combines flood and earthquake coverage as part of a package. On the surface this has the element of simplicity, but it also presents problems. Such coverage would undoubtedly require a subsidy by the federal government on the flood portion of the policy, and some form of reinsurance against losses from a catastrophic disaster. This would mean that the government would be injecting itself into areas of property insurance which have traditionally been in the private domain. In the past, the industry has resisted such encroachment unless they feel it is absolutely essential. Institutionally, we are further away from this cooperative arrangement than we were two years ago; until the end of 1977 the National Flood Insurance program was a joint private-federal partnership with the private companies providing risk capital, whereas today the underwriting of flood risks is assumed completely by the federal government, although private insurance agents still market policies. There are several other problems associated with such a proposal: if the rates are uniform throughout the country, as has been proposed, then states having less than average exposure to hazards may be reluctant to approve these rates through their regulatory commissions. Furthermore, it is likely that tax laws would have to be modified to handle the huge reserves accumulating for a catastrophe.[19]

19. For a more detailed analysis of this

A less extreme proposal would be to add only earthquake coverage to a standard homeowners policy and maintain the current flood insurance program. The principal stumbling block to implementing such a proposal revolves around the reinsurance problem should there be a severe quake in a populated portion of California. The insurance industry would then have to address the following question: "If such coverage was only required on new residential structures, how much of a financial burden would be placed on the reinsurance capacity of the industry?" Practically all homes in California are wood-frame structures where the damage from even the most severe quakes will be relatively small. Hence, it is conceivable that if required insurance was restricted to just the residential sector, the industry may be able to absorb the loss in a catastrophic disaster without having to turn to the federal government for reinsurance assistance.

A third option would be to maintain the current insurance coverage and provide disaster relief to special groups or for special situations. Distributional cost considerations suggest that special treatment be given to low-income or elderly residents who may be uninsured. Similarly, after a catastrophic disaster, there may be a need to offer special relief to victims to cover the uninsured portion of their loss. If Congress deems such measures to be important, then it would be wise for them to pass legislation prior to a catastrophe rather than having to react to each situation with a new disaster bill.

proposal, see C. Robert Hall, "Major Disaster Proposals Invite 'Feds' Into Areas Now Well Handled," *The National Underwriter*, 21 March 1975.

CONCLUSIONS

Policy makers responsible for protecting society from the consequences of natural hazards need to understand how individuals and organizations think and behave with respect to risk and uncertainty. Most recent research on behavior toward low probability events has focused on the way residents in hazard-prone areas obtain information and process it in making decisions. The findings suggest that the consumer is not as "rational" as may have commonly been believed. This general conclusion suggests that future studies should focus on the creative types of partnerships which are possible between the private and public sector in both the pre- and post-disaster periods. By analyzing the behavior not only of individuals but of organizations, laws and social institutions (markets, regulatory agencies), it should be possible to propose efficient and equitable policies for coping with the risks of natural hazards.

ANNALS, AAPSS, 443, May 1979

Guarantees Against Loss to Transnational Corporations

By HAROLD C. KROGH

ABSTRACT: Guarantees and funding to cope with possible losses to transnational corporations, alternatively referred to as multinational corporations, encompass risk management principles, theory, and applications. The paper analyzes the risks faced by multinational corporations in their overseas operations, including credit and political risks; the latter treating of such risks as currency devaluation, expropriation of plants, kidnapping of key executives, and ransom demands. Risks to property valuation receives emphasis, but often risks to persons reflect an intertwine in risk management by transnational enterprises. Various private and public insurance mechanisms are available to meet these problems, and the effects of these approaches on society are examined.

Harold C. Krogh is a Professor of Business Administration, School of Business, The University of Kansas, with teaching and research responsibilities in the areas of finance, risk management, and insurance. He received his Ph.D. in business administration at The University of Iowa and has had post-doctoral study and research activities at graduate schools of business: Harvard, Stanford, Northwestern, and Wisconsin Universities. He has presented papers in research workshop sessions: export-import political risk guaranty funds, at the 1977 International Insurance Seminar, Oslo, Norway; and managing by multinational firms of employee insurable benefits, I.I.S. Program, Manila, Philippines, 1978.

THIS PAPER examines a number of the risks faced by multi-national, increasingly referred to as transnational, corporations in their overseas operations, and includes political risks such as currency de-duction, expropriation of plants, and credit inflation.[1]

Although kidnapping of key exec-utives, ransom, and terrorist activ-ities against persons are suggestive of "personal risks," as is risk man-agement of employee insurable benefits programs, these personal risks are intertwined with "property and liability risks" for the trans-national corporation.

Various private and public insur-ance mechanisms are available to meet these problems, and attention is focused on the effects on society of a representative number of these effects.

Findings from the study are pre-sented in three major sections: In-surance Funded and Export Credits Investment Guaranty Systems; The Employee Insurable Benefit Pro-grams of Transnational Corpora-tions; and Private Sector Responses to the Threat of Terrorism Impact-ing on the Transnational Business Community.

INSURANCE AND GUARANTEE SYSTEMS FOR EXPORT CREDIT SYSTEMS

Objective of export credit insurance/guarantee

The purpose of export credit in-surance/guarantee systems is to place a nation's exporters on an equal basis with foreign competitors and to pro-mote exporting with the effective assistance of private financial insti-tutions. Export credit insurance is used by the United States and is also used in most leading countries in Europe and elsewhere. The terms "guaranty" and "guarantee" are used synonymously for this discussion.[2] The evolution of export-import in-surance and guaranty programs con-tinues to be a vital influence in sus-taining the development and growth of international trade and payment reconciliations.

Protecting against political risks

Some protection against political risks ranging from excessive taxes to total confiscation without com-pensation is available in the form of government guarantees. Never-theless, it is difficult to develop guidelines for a firm to cope with the conditions under which it should purchase investment guarantees. To a considerable extent, the guarantees are provided by a government agency, and there is little knowledge as to whether such guarantees reflect the average loss for such investments plus a small charge for administrative expenses, as they would if charged by private companies. The govern-ment may not be charging enough, thereby subsidizing foreign invest-ment, or it may be charging too much, thus gaining something at the ex-pense of those who purchase invest-ment guaranties. The experience for guarantees, at least with reference to United States multinationals, has

---

1. In this paper "transnational," "multi-national," "international" firms will be used interchangeably as synonyms. Another form that is used at times is "conational." Milton Hochmuth, "Multinationals, Transnationals and now Conationals," *European Research in International Business*, Michael Ghert-man and James Leontiades (Amsterdam,

The Netherlands: North-Holland Publishing Company, 1978), pp. 169–87.

2. In books and articles treating of finan-cial institution insolvency funds, the terms "guaranty" funds and "guarantee" funds find acceptance.

been quite short and there are little data with which to extrapolate experiences; and the incidence of investment losses because of various forms of expropriation is very uncertain.

The foreign credit risk

Many factors contribute to the foreign credit risk. Mark Greene has divided these into hazards and perils:

Hazards of credit losses abroad include:

- Language barriers and differences in accounting make it difficult to interpret financial information to the buyer.
- Credit reports on foreign buyers often involve delays.
- Reduced tariffs (for example, among European Economic Community countries) have opened huge markets to relatively efficient producers, causing insolvencies among less efficient producers operating in previously protected territory. Insolvency figures attest to the dangers involved.
- Increased world trade has put financial pressures on firms whose capital has not been able to expand sufficiently fast to accommodate the rising volume of trade.
- In many countries the supply of trained and experienced managers has not been adequate for the rising volume of business.
- In certain developing countries, unsound fiscal controls have existed, resulting in shortages of international currencies with which to pay debts. Developing countries often run trade deficits for long periods. This problem tends to become more

severe as rising debt repayments put a strain on a nation's ability to retire new debt commitments on schedule. Demand for longer credit terms greatly increases the credit hazards and the chances for occurrence of unknown perils.[3]

The Export-Import Bank of the United States credit and insurance functions relate particularly to U.S. transnational enterprises, and are representative of similar programs by other leading industrial-commercial nations, and of the United States Overseas Private Investment Corporation, a principal structure for stimulating U.S. private investment by private enterprise in the developing nations.[4]

UNITED STATES—EXPORT IMPORT BANK

The Export-Import Bank of the United States (Eximbank) supports a broad range of U.S. exports in keeping with its legislative mandate to facilitate the export of U.S. goods and services. Major export support programs include:

Fixed-rate direct credit to foreign buyers for the long-term maturities —generally those over five years —usually in participation with private market financing.

Medium-term loans to foreign financial institutions to help finance U.S. exports through the Cooperative Financing Facility (CFF).

3. Mark R. Greene, *Risk and Insurance*, 4th ed. (Cincinnati, OH: South-Western Publishing Company, 1977), p. 654.
4. At a research-in-progress panel discussion, 13th International Insurance Seminars, Inc., Oslo, Norway, August 9, 1977, in which the author participated, some of the observations were similar to those presented in the first section of the paper.

Discounting of medium-term export obligations that carry fixed interest rates.

Credit insurance and guarantees for commercial and political risks.

Short-term and pre-shipment export financing is available from commercial banks at market interest rates.

About 11 to 13 percent of U.S. exports were officially supported during the recent four-calendar year period.

Overcoming deficiencies in private financial markets is one of the major objectives of Eximbank. Market deficiencies include the lack of adequate long-term export financing, limited knowledge of foreign markets and buyers by small- and medium-size banks and exporters, and a generally exaggerated assessment of the risk of financing foreign transactions.

In accordance with its statutory directive, Eximbank also seeks to maintain the competitiveness of its credit and insurance programs within limits that reflect the Bank's need to remain self-sufficient—a need which is unique among the major export credit agencies of Europe and Japan. The Bank has not resorted to extraordinary credit programs such as the mixing of development aid with export financing, or to extraordinary insurance schemes such as inflation indemnity. The United States opposes these schemes which distort free-market competition for export sales and give dangerous impetus to an export credit race.

Export credit insurance is provided to U.S. exporters and, by assignment, to commercial banks by the Foreign Credit Insurance Association (FCIA)—a private company including 54 of the leading U.S. casualty insurance companies— in cooperation with Eximbank. FCIA, which was formed in February 1962,

insures commercial risks for its own account, reinsured in part by Eximbank. Under contract, FCIA serves as Eximbank's agent for political risk coverage. In certain cases Eximbank may provide both commercial and political risk coverage on its own account. Commercial credit risks are normally covered up to 90 percent while political risks receive 95 percent cover.

Several different policies are offered, depending on the product and coverage desired: a short-term policy provides an exporter with blanket coverage for all his foreign buyers who purchase consumer items, parts and accessories, or other products normally sold on terms of 180 days or less. Exceptionally, certain U.S. agricultural commodities may be insured under this type of policy on payment terms up to one year, with 98 percent coverage for both commercial and political risks.

A medium-term policy is offered on an individual buyer basis to cover capital equipment exports. The buyer is required to make an initial cash payment, and coverage applies only to the portion of the transaction being financed. A medium-term political risk only policy is available with coverage up to 90 percent of the contract value. A combined short-term/medium-term policy is offered to protect U.S. manufacturers who export capital equipment, including related parts and accessories, to overseas distributors. A master policy is also offered which provides blanket coverage up to 90 percent for both political and commercial credit risks for all of an exporter's eligible short and medium term credit sales, or a reasonable spread of risks on terms of up to five years. This type of policy includes a deductible provision for first loss on commercial risks.

Premiums for FCIA insurance are payable as a one-time, front-end fee based on the amount of credit or, for short-term cover, on the invoice value. Premium rates are generally determined by three factors — the term of repayment, the extent of supplier retention, and the country of destination. Premiums for short-term coverage range from $0.54 to $1.42 per $100; for medium-term cover they range from $1.61 to $4.24 per $100.

Independently of FCIA, Eximbank provides guarantees to commercial banks to cover the commercial and political risks associated with supplier credits. These guarantees are available to any U.S. commercial bank which purchases a foreign buyer's promissory note without recourse to the exporter; and are normally restricted to transactions with repayment terms ranging from 181 days to five years. The fee for this guarantee varies according to the length of the credit, the country of destination, and the extent of supplier retention. Medium-term Eximbank guarantees are assessed the same way as insurance premiums. They range in cost from $1.35 to $3.55 per $100.

Eximbank also provides financial guarantees for buyer credits—usually to commercial banks in participation with Eximbank direct loans. On occasion, guarantees of up to 85 percent of contract value may be provided, eliminating the need for an Eximbank direct credit. Eximbank charges a fee for these guarantees of 0.75 to 1.5 percent per annum on loan amounts outstanding.

Insurance is not offered for exchange rate fluctuations or for inflation risk. It is emphasized that there is at present no United States inflation insurance program for export-import credit guarantee activities as has been established quite recently in France and the United Kingdom.

THE UNITED STATES OVERSEAS PRIVATE INVESTMENT CORPORATION

The Overseas Private Investment Corporation (OPIC) is the U.S. Government's principal structure for stimulating U.S. private investment in the developing nations. Formally organized in January 1971, its programs and those of its predecessor organization in the Agency for International Development (AID) have covered $5.3 billion of some $6.5 billion of investments in these countries during the last 6 years (through the end of the fiscal year 30 June 1976).

In keeping with the objectives set forth by Congress, the Corporation is encouraging economic progress and development in some 87 lesser developed countries in Latin America, Asia, Africa, and Eastern Europe. It does this by providing qualified U.S. investors—large and small—with political risk insurance and financial assistance to support their investments in these countries.

OPIC programs are extended to new projects or for the expansion of existing projects which are financially sound. All projects OPIC supports must assist in the social and economic development of the host country, and must be consistent with the economic interest of the United States. Collectively, the countries identified with OPIC activities contain more than 70 percent of the world's population, and may very well represent the great markets of the future. The Corporation's insurance program provides coverages in friendly developing nations against: inconvertibility of local currency earnings, expropriation, war, revolution, and insurrection.

Insurance funded and exported credits guaranty systems in a world of relatively free trade markets might continue to grow with trade and balance of payment expansion. Nevertheless, a sustained counter trend, over at least the past four years, to a pronounced rising protectionism in the United States and Western Europe may have significant effects on such programs.

THE EMPLOYEE INSURABLE BENEFIT PROGRAMS OF TRANSNATIONAL CORPORATIONS

Employee insurable benefit programs are administered for nationals in foreign countries, and for employees who are citizens (indigenous persons) to those countries. Admittedly, the subject of employee insurable benefit programs is closely identified with management of "personal risks," but the implications of successful establishment and evolvement of such programs are apparent in both the costs and the losses to property values experienced by transnational firms entering and withdrawing business operations in foreign nations. There is a cause and effect relationship of such programs. Successful coping with political risk and with expenditures by firms confronting international terrorism in risk management in these subject areas involves an intertwine of personal and property risk situations.

Scope of study

The author, in continuing research over several years on the management by international firms of employee insurable benefits, has concentrated on the activities by U.S. multinational firms which treat of employee benefit planning for em-

ployees of affiliates abroad.[5] The conceptual pattern of employee benefit planning includes private pension plans in their possible integrative relationship with life, disability, income, health, and medical, unemployment insurances, as well as programs by firms for disabled persons in job-related injuries or diseases (workers' compensation and occupational disease programs). Plans for future study of multinational firms originating in other nations, operating in the United States would conceivably lead to more comprehensive understanding of evolving programs.

Although in recent years there has been increasing management attention given to employee benefit planning by firms operating abroad, the literature available in the subject area has remained generally fragmentary and sparse until very recent years when this situation reversed in spectacular fashion. Multinational firms do have executive talent that is responsive to inquiries by researchers, and this responsiveness has led to the growth of knowledge supplanting the relative scarce information available ten to fifteen years ago. The expanding knowledge has made persons studying managerial aspects of transnational firms aware of some problems in the specific management of international insurance benefits plans for employees.[6]

5. The author presented at a research panel discussion (workshop session) 20 June 1978, some of these ideas and findings from surveys and interviews, conducted in the United States during 1977 through the Spring, 1978 at the 14th International Insurance Seminars, Manila, The Philippines.
6. Norman A. Baglini in his book, *Risk Management in International Corporations*, (New York: Risk Studies Foundation, Inc., 1976), incorporates some interesting findings pertaining to employee benefit plans

Extent of parent company involvement

The growth and expansion of United States companies overseas has had a rapid acceleration in the past two decades. In general, since large firms principally identified with this expansion are more likely to provide employee retirement benefits as well as other insurable benefits than are small firms, a greater use of retirement plans abroad by such large firms might reasonably have been anticipated. However, the incidence of these plans has been less than for smaller domestic firms operating solely in the United States. The approaches being used by international companies in managing employee insurable benefits vary in managerial style from authoritarian, centralized control to a consultative approach involving a greater mixture of input from the parent company.

The extent to which the parent company involves itself in local (host country) benefit decisions is reflected in transnational firm typical activities, including:

1. Making decisions based on a broader perspective and longer-term considerations.

2. Maximizing the advantages of multinational financing.

3. Obtaining objectivity.

4. Achieving greater worldwide consistency in the treatment of employees.

5. Making parent company benefit expertise available.

6. Coordinating benefit programs of the international employee whose career includes employment in several countries.

7. Achieving consistency in approaches to benefit financing.

"Possible disadvantages of parent company involvement (as opposed to subsidiary autonomy) include:

1. Discovering that local conditions are best coped with by local management.

2. Weakening of local manager's profit responsibility if his authority is decreased in the employee insurable benefit area."[7]

The most easily established reason that a multinational would exercise parent control in the area of financing of benefits is in order to employ operational leverage derived from volume, such as the purchasing of group insurance under employee benefit programs. The more employees covered under a group insurance contract, the better the terms that can be negotiated with the insurer.

The development of a cohesive program of employee insurance benefits to achieve better terms from operational leverage can result in lower unit costs, speedier delivery, and better after-sales service. The development of a program or network is a natural outcome of the U.S. transnational companies seeking more efficient and economical means of providing benefits for their foreign employees. Such a network has these objectives: to provide local insurance contracts, and to pool these contracts in such a way that the firm derives maximum advantage

---

gathered from the responses to his questionnaire (Appendix A of the book), "Problems and Practices of Risk Management in Foreign Subsidiaries of American Multi-National Corporations." See also: David Callund, *Employee Benefits in Europe 1976*; A review of employee benefit practice in 16 countries, Employee Conditions Abroad Ltd., (London, England: Callund & Company Ltd., 1976), pages xv to xvii and 1-10.

7. William D. Welsford, "International Employee Benefits: A Current Overview," *Viewpoint: The Marsh and McLennan Quarterly*, vol. 1, no. 3, (Winter 1973) pp. 26-31.

from the total number of employees covered.

The contracts are established by a multinational firm either through utilization of an insurance company's foreign subsidiary or affiliate in a country or, alternatively, by entering into an agreement with a local company. In the former arrangement the pooling of interests is under the control of the parent insurer; but under the latter arrangement the pooling must be handled by some form of reinsurance arrangement.

Socio-economic implications

As Donald E. Boden observes: "There is not any bright future in the pooling of self-administered pension funds across country borders. Despite the best efforts of many people to utilize the world-wide size of a multinational firm by applications of techniques to save money, there has been no successful solution of the tax and currency problems inhibiting the creation of such pooling."[8]

While there are certain combinations of countries where the possibility of pooling appears technically possible, questions persist:

1. How long will pooling continue to be possible and what is the expectancy that laws and regulations may remain unchanged?

2. How can investment be designed to overcome the problem of currency fluctuations?

3. How are employee relations best dealt with when employees see the funds for their pensions going out of their country and currency of their nation being subject to conditions over which neither they nor their government have any control?

Acknowledging that the goal of the composite fund is attractive from an investment and control standpoint, the potential gain is substantially offset by these problems and complications. There are other problem areas that require attention; specifically, employee benefit plans and unionization; requirements that a private plan be integrated with the public social security system of the foreign country; and awareness of the cost of the employee benefits as they affect a firm's foreign operations.

With the objective of providing some further insights into employee insurable benefits of transnational firms, the author sought interviews during 1977 and 1978 with professionals in several firms specializing in employee insurable benefits and with executives of several U.S. based international firms.[9] Some of the responses obtained were informative.

For U.S. citizens in other countries, an attempt is made by these firms generally to maintain a U.S. benefits

8. Donald E. Boden, "Managing International Employee Benefits," *Viewpoint: The Marsh and McLennan Quarterly*, vol. 3, no. 1, (Fall 1974), pp. 3–4.

9. The author is indebted to executives of several insurance management and pension consulting firms for remarkable input of information from timely articles and publications. Consultants of the American Management Association furnished library listings and references of current articles. The AMA research studies of a decade ago, available in university libraries, *Source Book of International Insurance, and Employee Benefit Management of Selected Countries of the World*, provide invaluable material. Similarly, officers with Marsh and McLennan, Inc., and its affiliate, William M. Mercer, Inc. have furnished a wealth of worthwhile articles. Invaluable support in the assemblage of considerable information, recent publications, references and data resumés were given in the responses by executives with Charles D. Spencer Associates, Hewitt Associates, and the International Foundation of Employee Benefit Plans.

profile which will be augmented if the public policies of other countries generate additional benefits for the individuals. The respondent of one firm did assert that employee benefits policies and practices were entirely up to its prominent, sizeable subsidiary (affiliate) in another nation.

Should an international firm attempt to extend for foreign employees the pattern of benefits applicable to domestic employees, or should a different plan be developed for each country?

Should the potential cost of employee benefits be given consideration in the foreign investment decision?

What is the importance of union organization abroad in setting the patterns and levels of employee benefits?

How should the employee benefit structure be integrated with the social security system of the foreign country?

Whether the transnational firm programs are privately or publicly generated, the benefits profiles from country to country are often quite similar in their impact on employees. It is likely that this is because people in various parts of the world have similar basic needs for security and income augmentation which group-based mechanisms can provide. Yet, differences in unionization and bargaining practices do cause variances in plans among many areas and nations of the world.

Severe frictions arise when a transnational firm withdraws from a foreign nation. Direct costs of meeting (continuing) employee insurable benefit commitments to foreign nationals and indirect costs such as retributions and terrorism activities or reprisals against the firm upon severance of employees, and withdrawal from within-country business operations fall particularly within the area of property value risks.

Executives of transnational firms are usually in agreement with the principle of having a foreign national paid in accordance with the policies in the country where he or she is employed. This is also true for foreign nationals employed by a company in a third country. Basically, then, an attempt is made by firms to adopt employee benefit plans in accordance with the conditions existing in the country of their employment. Executives of companies affirm that such a policy is followed usually for foreign nationals employed in the United States as well. Companies do observe some distinctions for the latter classification, and formal naturalization results in the former "foreign" national being integrated into plans identified with standards existing in the U.S.

The growing prominence of international educational programs, seminars, conferences, and meetings among executives and employee benefit plan consultants, bespeak constructive programs. Consortiums of U.S. transnational and transnational companies of other nations have entered into a more extensive interchange of ideas in recent years.

PRIVATE SECTOR RESPONSES TO THE THREAT OF TERRORISM IMPACTING ON THE TRANSNATIONAL BUSINESS COMMUNITY

The acts of terrorists may have an international effect even though they are committed wholly within a state's territory. Terrorism is aimed primarily at obtaining political ends to embarrass the government or to drive out foreign business interests.

Fear of terrorism spurs U.S. companies to bolster security measures. Terrorism refers to acts or activities that usually are not performed by or under the control of a recognized government or governmental agency. This section will treat as practically as possible with the nature of terrorist activities faced by transnational business operations in order to arrive at several suggestions for combatting this problem.

Within this subject area there has traditionally been a dearth of information. This situation, in the main, continues today. Scarcity of published texts and journal articles on private sector security, risk management, and insurance measures and effective response to terrorism reflects the complexity of the problem. There is a clear necessity for limiting hazard exposures to property values as well as lives by avoiding publicity of specific countermeasures and specific details about insurance coverages applied to clientel firms.

Some risk management alternatives available to multinational firms

As countermeasures in dealing with the problem of international terrorism there are several alternative possibilities.

Preventive measures may utilize a set of rules to cope with kidnapping, hijacking, and ransom. One approach is based upon strength in numbers and thus numerous armed security guards are utilized. An alternative approach is based on the assumption that armed guards only invite attack and thus it is better to rely on the stance of the "loner," who can move quickly, quietly, and unplanned from location to location. In both approaches movements of executives as well as the policy of the company in the event of kidnapping are kept highly confidential. Executives will not discuss their position on ransom, contact of police, or withdrawal of their company expatriots. This is, for the most part, a passive stance.

Underwriting the benefits by refusing to pay ransom to kidnappers is the position of many governments, including the United States; maintaining a low profile and avoiding releases to news media except for instances of terrorist failures; furthering the development of prosecution of terrorists by redefining acts of terrorism as acts of international crime.

The refusal to pay ransom in several spectacular instances proved nonfeasible because of blackmail and terrorist threats to kill additional employees if the ransom is not paid. Maintaining a low profile may boomerang under charges of company-governmental censorship. Furthermore, terrorists often furnish publicity to the media with the intent of gaining public sympathy. Treatment of kidnappings as international crimes, comparable to the historical definition of piracy and slavery, may be a more effective countermeasure. Still, there must be a comity among nations for extradition and trial. This also is difficult to realize and accomplish in the typical "politically motivated" act of terrorism, and the reluctance of the state having custody over the alleged offender.

If perhaps 300 major transnational enterprises are United States based companies, accounting for 75 to 80 percent of all foreign investment, with several thousand companies conducting transnational business operations through thousands of affiliated companies around the world (two hundred world-wide major transnational companies account for approximately 25 percent of total world trade), some approximation of the importance of managerial concerns to cope with international terrorism is gained.

Existing private sector responses against threat of terrorism include: the internal security of the enterprise, cooperation within the private sector and between government agencies and other enterprises, ways of self-restraint, and risk combination through insurance.

Hostage insurance as a form of risk management furnishes an ability to spread losses or damages out of specified risks among a number of persons or organizational units exposed to the same risks. It enables the management of a firm to gain "peace of mind" and permits better planning. Potential losses from terrorist risks can be estimated on the basis of experience and budgeted for a period of time among such units. The resulting costs are pooled through periodic payments to a commercial underwriter or to a captive insurance subsidiary. Alternatively, the plan may be to establish a reserve on the company accounting statements as a form of insurance. Similar principles may be applied to losses and damages arising from bombings, incendiary attacks, kidnappings. Criminal loss insurance coverage has been applied for several years as an endorsement to bankers blanket bond coverages, but the implications of such perils as blackmail, extortion, international air hijackings, and a widened range of political characteristics of terrorism in a world-wide setting impels the development of more specialized, detailed insurance coverage. Hostage insurance is identified more particularly with the specific risk of kidnappings and ransom payments.

The financial loss that is incurred through the surrender of property as a result of a threat to do bodily harm to an employee, or one of his relatives, has impelled executives and employees, especially of transnational companies, to purchase policies for themselves and for their families. There is a wide variance in premium rates, depending on the "underwriters" evaluation of the individual's exposure.

Often the policy will be carried by the company because of the increasing trend to make corporations the targets of kidnappings, rather than executives. Where the policy is owned by the firm, premiums, as well as *ransom payments not covered by insurance* are deductible as ordinary and customary business expense. *Individuals* can deduct ransom payments as losses arising from theft, but there is some difficulty in aligning kidnap insurance within the cost-of-business concept. *Self-insurance* allows a company to retain insurance reserves for its own use, but it restricts tax deduction to amounts paid at the time of the loss.

Hostage insurance for large, transnational enterprises is usually structured on a group basis. The less expensive type of insurance limits the group to designated employees or to positions that the company determines have a high risk of kidnapping. The more expensive type covers an unspecified number of employees based on defined job classifications or categories.

The *cost* of hostage insurance to corporations also varies widely, depending on such factors as the size of the enterprise, the states or regions for which coverage is to apply, the amount of coverage, the group insured (for example, executives or all employees), the company's public silhouette. "In the

United States the resolution of kidnapping cases exceeds 90 percent and, therefore, the country factor for the premium rate is relatively low compared to that for most other nations. The *annual premium cost* for a $500,000 policy could be about $1,000 per executive insured, annual sales of the company under $1 million."

"A company with annual sales of over $500 million might pay $5,000 per executive for the same coverage. A recent estimate of a "typical" or "representative" group policy indicates an annual premium of $10,000 on a $1 million policy with a $100,000 deductible. For coverage outside the United States, the premium rate multiplies to a prohibitive amount, such as *an annual premium of $100,000 per executive insured*, on a maximum $1 million coverage in some of the developing countries."[10]

Absolute secrecy is normally required by the policy, both as to the existence of insurance and its coverage. Fear that kidnapping might be encouraged if hostage insurance is believed to be widespread, leaves underwriters reluctant to talk about it in any specific sense. The policies may be cancelled if the existence of insurance is disclosed during the kidnap negotiations. Most underwriters refrain from involvement in such negotiations themselves.

10. Clarence J. Mann, "Personnel and Property of Transnational Business Operations," Alona E. Evans and John F. Murphy, eds., *Legal Aspects of International Terrorism* (Lexington, MA: D. C. Heath, 1978), p. 401.

Several *implications* are apparent. No reliable estimate can be given of the prevalence of hostage insurance among transnational corporations. It is reported that some countries, such as Italy and France, do not legally permit hostage insurance because of the conviction that it would encourage kidnapping. In other countries, as a matter of government policy, the payment of ransom may be discouraged or prohibited.

Proposals for governments to subsidize hostage payments directly or through special tax treatment could engender serious "backlash" effects. Terrorists might reason that such plans provided an "open sesame" to public treasuries and would tend to strengthen the symbolic link that terrorists already see between transnational enterprise and the target government.

One example of a governmental measure to counteract terrorism is in proposal form at present: to change U.S. tax law to provide that individuals may deduct premiums paid for hostage insurance and that companies may fully deduct ransom payments as ordinary and necessary business expenses even when the payments are made on behalf of a foreign subsidiary.

Exciting challenges for management of transnational corporations are manifestly increasing in coping with terrorism; and similar awareness of increasingly complex risk situations continues to expand challenges in export-import credit, political risk operations, and in risk management of employee insurable benefit programs.

ANNALS, AAPSS, 443, May 1979

A Review and Evaluation of Selected Government Programs to Handle Risk

By MARK R. GREENE

ABSTRACT: Six government insurance programs are described and evaluated against three criteria: (1) size and significance of the economic burden imposed by the risks covered, (2) public acceptance of the program, and (3) necessity of government initiative to accept the risk if private insurers could not do so. It is concluded that government handling of flood and swine flu liability risks are justified, but the government programs in riot reinsurance, crime insurance, and nuclear energy liability should be terminated. Federal crop insurance is of questionable necessity in view of the basic insurability of this risk by private insurers.

Mark R. Greene is Distinguished Professor of Insurance, Department of Risk Management and Insurance, at the College of Business Administration, The University of Georgia. He received his Ph.D. degree from The Ohio State University, and the A.B. and M.B.A. from Stanford University. He is past president of the American Risk and Insurance Association, a member of the Board of Governors of the International Insurance Seminars, Inc., and has been a member of the Board of Directors, Southern Risk and Insurance Association. He is author of many scholarly articles and several books, including Risk and Insurance and Risk Aversion, Insurance, and the Future. Greene's latest book, of which he is coauthor, is Risk Management: Text and Cases.

RISK is generally considered to be a burden on society and upon individuals alike. Individuals tend to be risk averse in many circumstances and seek ways which reduce or eliminate risk. The question is often raised as to whether private business or government should bear risk. Many say they prefer to use private means, but transfer of risks to government is apparently seen by others as a way to handle them at least cost or with greatest total efficiency.

In this paper the question is approached by examining (a) measures of risk and reasons for governmental insurance programs, (b) how successful and vital government insurance programs in selected areas have worked out to be, and (c) an evaluation of government's performance and rationale for assuming the risk. In the following sections, we consider objective and subjective measures of selected risk burdens, and general reasons for government assumption of selected risks, vis á vis private sector assumption. Selected government insurance programs, including riot reinsurance program, crime insurance, nuclear energy liability risks, crop failure risks, flood risks, and influenza and disease control risks are then examined in detail.

In evaluating why or the extent to which a risk may be viewed as "burdensome," it seems important to distinguish between two major dimensions of risk: objective and subjective. Objective risk may be defined as the statistical uncertainty that predicted financial losses of a given type will be realized in practice. It is common to employ some measure such as variance or standard deviation as the measure of this risk. Subjective risk, on the other hand, refers to the uncertainty perceived by individuals or groups about a given set of possible losses. Specifically, if citizens are frightened of some peril they may seek political means to transfer it even if objective facts would hardly justify their fear or need for government insurance. Thus, the concepts of objective and subjective risk are important in measuring the significance of risk and in determining why some risks are handled by governments rather than by the private sector.

REASONS FOR GOVERNMENTAL RISK ASSUMPTION

Although in principle the U.S. economy is based on private enterprise, the role of government—national, state, and local—has steadily increased in most areas of citizens' lives. In the area of risk management and insurance, the government has expanded its role to the point that approximately half of all the insurance premiums now written in the United States (including OASDHI) are collected by a federal, state, or local government.[1]

The question arises as to why governments are assuming a larger share of those activities described under a "risk management" heading. Several types of rationale have been advanced to explain it, but underlying all of these is a general tendency for society to become more risk averse.[2] This tendency not only increases the number and variety of risks people wish to transfer to others but, to some extent, it reduces the willingness of private organizations

1. Mark R. Greene, "The Government as an Insurer," *Journal of Risk and Insurance,* vol. 43, no. 3 (September 1976), pp. 393–406.
2. Mark R. Greene, *Risk Aversion, Insurance and the Future* (Bloomington, IN: Indiana University Press, 1971), Chapt. 4.

to assume risk. To apply the terminology in the last section, subjective risk perceptions tend to be greater, and in the absence of willing takers in the private sector (who also perceive greater subjective risk), the burden of risk assumption increasingly falls upon governments.

The dominant rationale employed for many government programs, particularly those discussed in this paper, is the residual market philosophy. Under this philosophy, governments move into an area of risk assumption because private insurers are unable or unwilling to handle all the risk. What private insurers reject is "residual," left-over, representing an unfilled market.

Other types of rationale are also used by governments as justifications for inaugurating insurance programs. These are: convenience, achieving some collateral social purpose, need for compulsion, efficiency, and handling risks produced by adverse conditions of society itself. Obviously, one or more of the above types of rationale may occur simultaneously.[3]

Flood risks, for example, may be assumed by the federal government for several of the above reasons. First, private insurers view the flood risk essentially uninsurable because of adverse selection—the tendency for only those subject to loss to take coverage, thus inviting catastrophic losses which are difficult to spread out over a larger number of clients. The flood risk becomes residual and if it is to be transferred at all, the government must accept it. Second, a collateral social purpose may be achieved by the government in setting up flood insurance programs—

3. Mark R. Greene, "The Government as an Insurer." A discussion of these types, with examples, is developed in this article.

that of achieving reforms in land use and discouraging building in flood plains without proper safeguards. Third, there is a need for compulsion, in that without it most individuals do not voluntarily purchase flood insurance, even if they are exposed to high loss probability, because their subjective perception of the risk tends to be minimal. Fourth, the rationale of convenience, and perhaps efficiency, influenced the way the flood insurance program has developed.

Although at first the government worked with private enterprise in distributing flood insurance, it later ran into difficulties with its partnership with the National Flood Insurers Association and set up a government-controlled corporation to operate the program. Presumably the Federal Insurance Administration believed the government could administer the program more efficiently and conveniently than by working through private insurers.

A final rationale for government risk bearing, closely related to achieving a collateral social purpose, is to handle those risks produced by society itself. The argument is that if for various reasons societal conditions (such as riots in cities) are responsible for the inability of private industry to handle certain burdensome risks, then society, through its government, should accept the task of handling them. Conversely, if a risk could be handled well privately, then government should not perform this task. As George Bernstein stated, ". . . Government should not perform functions that can better be accomplished through private means; and the private sector should not be compelled to assume the responsibilities that are primarily social and governmental in nature, and which are therefore the proper function of local, state, or federal government entities. . . ."[4]

Studies demonstrate that private insurers are still preferred by the public whenever possible.[5] Thus, the justification for government operated insurance programs needs to be demonstrated.

NATURE OF SELECTED GOVERNMENT INSURANCE PROGRAMS

The federal government has set up programs for handling specific areas of public risk, most of which supplement or compete with those of private insurance institutions. Data reveal that for 1977 expenses exceeded revenues for the programs as follows (in millions): crime insurance, $8.7; flood insurance, $81.1; crop insurance, $65.9; nuclear energy insurance, $254; swine flu vaccination, $134. Only one program, riot reinsurance, produced revenues greater than expenses of $5.9 million.[6] The subsidy totalled well over a half billion dollars in 1977.

4. George K. Bernstein, "P & L Insurance Field Identified as That Most in Need of Reform," Special Report by the *Journal of Commerce, The Federal Insurance Agency Administrator's Recommendations on High Risk Insurance* (undated), p. 20.
5. Insurance Information Institute, *The Tornadoes of April, a Public Evaluation of the Insurance Industry's Performance* (New York, 1947), pp. 47–48. *National Opinion Study: A Profile of Consumer Attitudes Toward Auto and Homeowner's Insurance* (Stevens Point, WI: Sentry Insurance Co., 1974), p. 84. This study was carried out by Louis Harris and Associates and by the Department of Insurance, The Wharton School, University of Pennsylvania. *Businessmen's Attitudes Toward Commercial Insurance* (Stevens Point, WI: Sentry Insurance Co., 1974), p. 28.
6. *Budget of the U.S. Government*, 1979, pp. 142, 506, 507, 912. Swine flu losses were reported in *Swine Flu Immunization Program*, Supplemental Hearings Before the

The obvious questions arise, "Are these programs justified? Is the cost to general taxpayers worth more than the relief obtained by specific groups in being able to transfer risks to the government?"

Riot reinsurance

In 1968 the U.S. Congress authorized the establishment of special state plans, known as FAIR plans, which would qualify for federally sponsored reinsurance if certain requirements were met.[7] The purpose of the program was to facilitate the establishment of private insurance capacity at "affordable rates" against loss to property located in areas not eligible for coverage from private insurers on a regular basis. Private insurers had withdrawn or greatly restricted coverage in certain areas, principally in the centers of larger urban areas of the United States, due to riots and other factors creating unfavorable underwriting conditions in those areas. The residual risk philosophy was the central rationale of the program. There appeared to be a sufficient need for governmental help to cause Congress to act. The reinsurance mechanism was the device through which Congress hoped to achieve the goal of restoring private coverage.

Subsequent market acceptance of FAIR plans supported the belief

Sub-Committee on Health and the Environment of the Committee on Interstate and Foreign Commerce House of Representatives, 94th Congress, 2nd Session, June 28, July 20, 23, and Sept. 13, 1976 (USGPO, Washington, D.C. 1976), p. 441. Data represent total costs of the program, not just that portion representing risk transfer costs of the government, for which no estimates exist.
7. Fair Access to Insurance Requirements as outlined in Section 1102 (a) and (b) of Title XI-Urban Property Protection and Reinsurance Act of 1968.

of Congress that there was indeed a public demand for a program to enable transfer of specified physical damage risks. Following the 1968 legislation, 26 states, Washington, D.C., and Puerto Rico adopted FAIR plans. Volume of premiums written grew steadily until by 1976 a total of over 750,000 FAIR policies were in force in all states, representing an increase of 16 percent over the level of 1974. FAIR plan premiums in 1976 totalled $193.5 million, representing a 75 percent increase over the 1974 level. New applications in 1976 were up 141 percent over the 1974 level. New applications increased in all but eight jurisdictions where modest declines were registered in new applications.[8] In the largest three FAIR plan states— Michigan, California, and Illinois— new applications in 1976 were up 165, 141, and 258 percent, respectively, over their 1974 levels. Among the large states only New York had a decline in new applications, totalling 16 percent in 1976 below the 1974 figure.[9] It is estimated that FAIR plan premium volume nationally is about five or six percent of total premium volume of fire and allied lines insurance.[10]

While the above facts do not suggest that FAIR plans are being depopulated or that the demand no longer exists for the FAIR plan mechanism, the demand for federal government reinsurance has slacked greatly, in spite of considerable reductions in the premium charged for reinsurance. Data show that reinsurance premiums have declined from an initial level of over $35 million to only slightly more than $1 million in 1976–1977. The government's losses and expenses totalled only about $15 million, compared to premiums of $82 million, for an average profit of $.82 for each dollar of premium.[11]

In spite of the continued growth of FAIR plan activity, these plans have been relatively unprofitable for commercial insurers. Over the nine-year period 1968–1976, commercial insurers lost a total of $260,000,000, about $.28 for each dollar of premium collected from insureds. Losses occurred in almost all states and areas where FAIR plans were operated. Exceptions occurred in California, Washington, D.C., Georgia, Indiana, Louisiana, New Mexico, and Puerto Rico, where underwriting and investment returns were positive instead of negative. Gains in these states totalled $4.9 million. This represented about two percent of the total loss of $260 million suffered by all plans. These losses are, in effect, borne by other (non-FAIR plan) purchasers of fire and allied lines insurance whose premiums must be ultimately enlarged sufficiently to pay them.[12]

8. New York, Iowa, Maryland, Delaware, Louisiana, Virginia, Puerto Rico, and Washington, D.C.

9. J. Robert Hunter, Administrator, Federal Insurance Administration, in *Extension of Urban Riot Reinsurance and Crime Insurance Programs*, Hearings before the Subcommittee on Housing and Community Development of the Committee on Banking, Finance, and Urban Affairs, House of Representatives, 95th Congress, First Session, 16 February 1977, pp. 33–37.

10. Based on the ratio of FAIR plan volume of $193.5 million to $3,500 million of total fire and allied lines premiums written in 1975–76, as reported in *Insurance Facts*, 1976 Edition (Insurance Information Institute, New York, N.Y., 1976).

11. Federal Insurance Administration in *Hearings* before the Subcommittee on Housing and Community Development of the Committee on Banking, Finance and Urban Affairs, House of Representatives, 95th Congress, First Session, February 16, 1977 (Washington: USGPO, 1977), p. 40.

12. HUD 1603 Reports, December 1976.

In analyzing the social and economic effect of FAIR plans, it seems obvious from the above that the government (really taxpayers as a group) is not subsidizing the above average risk represented by FAIR plan customers; rather, the cost of the subsidy (as is the case in many "assigned risk" plans in auto insurance) is incurred by those other insureds who must pay higher premiums than otherwise would be the case without FAIR plans. To some extent the burden may be shared by stockholders of commercial insurers who have a somewhat lower return on their investments than would otherwise be the case.

It may be concluded that FAIR plan legislation has not transferred the environmental risk to society as a whole. It operates similarly to other types of assigned risk plans. Presumably FAIR plan underwriting losses could be eliminated through higher rates and better loss control. In this case, government reinsurance would become largely unnecessary.

Crime insurance

In the same act which created FAIR plans, Congress also authorized the establishment of a means to make crime insurance[13] more readily available. In contrast to FAIR plans, Congress authorized the federal government to sell crime insurance directly to the customer, rather than indirectly through reinsurance. Thus, for the first time, the federal govern-

ment was authorized to underwrite a form of property insurance which previously had been exclusively handled by the private insurance market. The Federal Insurance Administration was directed to conduct studies to determine in which states crime insurance, as defined, was not being offered at "affordable rates." Affordability was defined as a rate which "would permit the purchase of a specific type of insurance coverage by a reasonably prudent person in similar circumstances with due regard to the costs and benefits involved."[14] As a result of these investigations, federally sponsored crime insurance was offered in 1971 in about ten states. The program was gradually expanded until by 1978 there were 24 states and jurisdictions where this coverage was offered. The policies are distributed through normal channels, established insurance agents and brokers.

Crime insurance has been sold mainly in only three or four of mainly industrial states—New York, Massachusetts, Pennsylvania, and Florida. In January 1977, New York alone accounted for about a third of all crime policies in force. The top four states accounted for about 80 percent of the total of 31,675 policies in force. More than two thirds of the policies are to residential, rather than business clients.[15]

Testimony by Robert J. Hunter, an administrator in the Federal Insurance Administration (F.I.A.), is revealing as to the difficulties the government has had in selling crime insurance to the public. Hunter testified that when crime coverage was first offered it was believed there

13. Crime insurance was defined to include robbery, burglary, and larceny insurance. Broad form personal theft, mercantile open stock, mercantile robbery and safe burglary, storekeeper's burglary and robbery, office burglary and robbery, and business interruption insurance from the crime peril, were also included if the HUD secretary so designated. Crime insurance in the act was so defined, however, that it did not include automobile or embezzlement crimes.

14. Urban Property Protection and Reinsurance Act of 1968, as amended, Sec. 1203(a)(1).

15. Federal Insurance Administration, Jan. 21, 1977, *Hearings*, cited in note 11, supra, pp. 38–39.

was a seller's market, but when applications did not flow in, the F.I.A. tried to encourage sales through a number of activities. These included the easing of requirements for protective devices, commissioning studies to learn more about the crime insurance market, advertising campaigns, installation of toll-free lines in inner city areas to help potential customers reach the F.I.A. office directly, and offering agents a finders fee for new customers rather than relying upon commissions alone.[16] Hunter testified that property-liability insurance agents and brokers are often reluctant to attempt to sell coverage in crime areas since they realize that placement of other coverage, including homeowners' policies which cover the crime peril, are difficult to place in the commercial insurance markets. Thus, agents are not working the areas the Federal Insurance Administration most needs to reach.

In addition to the cited reasons, other factors may account for the failure of federal crime insurance to capture a larger segment of the crime insurance market. The crime program requires rather strict safety and loss prevention measures in order to qualify for coverage. In many areas, if these standards are met, the customer becomes eligible for standard types of commercial crime coverage. The time, trouble, and cost of loss prevention measures would seem to constitute a significant barrier to the expansion of crime insurance. Limits on coverage, the requirement of five percent deductible, and the relatively high rates may constitute other barriers to rapid acceptance of crime insurance.[17]

A more basic explanation of the failure of the federal crime insurance program to develop much of a following is the nature of crime insurance itself. The crime peril is difficult to insure because of high moral hazard. Rates are high and coverage restricted. Crime is probably one of the most underinsured perils of any major insurable peril. For example, according to statistics of the Federal Bureau of Investigation covering 1975, property valued at $3.2 billion was stolen in the United States, of which only $961 million, or 30 percent, was recovered.[18] Yet total premiums collected by commercial insurers under burglary and theft policies are estimated at only $120,000,000 (1975) and $215,000,000 for fidelity bonds. If insured losses are, say, 60 percent of premiums, it is clear that only a small portion of total loss exposure, perhaps five or six percent, is insured.

One cannot conclude that the social and economic effects of the federal crime program, or commercial crime insurance for that matter, are especially great. Furthermore, basic conditions of the crime peril are such that it is not likely that this condition will change materially in the foreseeable future. The attempt by Congress to solve a "problem" of lack of availability of affordable crime insurance by putting the federal government in the crime insurance business suffered from misconceptions. Lack of understanding of the difficulties surrounding crime insurance itself, lack of

---

16. Robert J. Hunter, Hearings, cited in note 11 supra, pp. 16 passim.

17. The author analyzes the barriers to

growth of crime insurance more fully in *The Government and Private Insurance* (Chicago, IL: National Association of Independent Insurers, 1974), pp. 52–58.

18. *Uniform Crime Reports 1975* (Washington, D.C.: U.S. Department of Justice, 1976), p. 178.

knowledge about the unfilled demand for crime insurance (which turned out to be embarrassingly low), and unrealistic expectations about how easy it would be to market crime insurance, all existed.

NUCLEAR ENERGY RISKS

A significant demand for transfer of the nuclear energy liability risk emerged when private firms first developed plans for building thermal reactors to produce electrical energy after World War II. To respond to this demand, two private nuclear energy liability insurance pools were developed by the commercial insurance industry. These were the Nuclear Energy Liability Property Insurance Association (NEL-PIA) and the Mutual Atomic Energy Liability Underwriters (MAELU). In 1957 the federal Price Anderson Act was passed authorizing government liability insurance on atomic energy installations in the amount of $560 million, a level established as the maximum liability for which private corporations would be held liable for all those injured in a single nuclear incident. The Price Anderson Act (which later was extended through 1987) was challenged in a federal court in 1977, and the $560 million limitations section was declared unconstitutional. However, the lower court ruling was reversed by the U.S. Supreme Court in 1978.[19]

Under the Price-Anderson Act, liability for nuclear incidents would be funded through a combination of private insurance—an assessment liability, if needed, of up to $5 million for each nuclear power plant—and government funds. As the number of new power plants is increased (there were reported to be 63 in operation in 1978), the assessment liability and private insurance capacity will equal or exceed the $560 million limit, and government liability for loss will be eliminated eventually.

It is unknown how potential investors really view the nuclear liability risk or the effect that this risk has upon society or business investment. Will the absence of total insurance protection above the $560,000,000 deter nuclear investments? What are the potential losses from nuclear accidents? Answers to these questions can only be guessed at since to date nuclear accidents have been minimal, and no accidents have arisen which have caused liability to the government for that portion of the exposure covered by it. For example, it was reported that between 1957 and 1973 only 24 nuclear incidents were reported to private insurance groups underwriting nuclear risk, none of them arising out of the operation of a nuclear reactor. Over the period, aggregate losses related to nuclear exposure paid by private insurers amounted to less than $1,000,000, although nuclear energy liability premiums average about $4,000,000 annually.[20]

In a report by the NEL-PIA an analysis was made of the operating experience at nuclear power plants and related facilities covering the period 1962–1976.[21] Some 30 inci-

19. *Carolina Environmental Study Group, Inc.* v. *U.S. Atomic Energy Comm.* 431 F. Supp. 203.

20. L. R. Rockett, "Issues of Financial Protection in Nuclear Activities," *Selected Materials on Atomic Energy Indemnity and Insurance Legislation*, 94th Congress, 2nd Session (Washington, DC: USGPO, March, 1974), pp. 89–90.

21. *NEL-PIA Reports* (Farmington, CT: Nuclear Energy Liability-Property Insurance Association, October, 1976).

dents were analyzed. No radiation accidents have occurred at a commercial nuclear power plant that resulted in bodily injury. Only one claim alleged harm from the normal operation of a power reactor. Many of the 30 incidents involved leakage of radioactive materials and modest claims resulted for clean-up expense. The largest single claim of $300,000 (1963) involved radioactive contamination from a loading platform exposing seven employees to radioactivity, one of whom lost an arm due to cancer and died five years later. In another case a workman died following exposure to radioactivity when he poured some highly enriched uranyl nitrate from one container into an unsafe tank. A settlement of $70,000 was made.

The cost of government's risk management of nuclear energy in the economy, while as yet not involving the payment of liability losses, may in some sense be measured by the cost of inspection and safety activity. The Nuclear Regulatory Commission spent $253 million in 1977 on such items as nuclear reactor regulation, standards development, inspection and enforcement, nuclear safeguards, research, and administration.[22]

It seems probable that without at least the level of protection now available, private investors would have been unwilling to risk capital in nuclear energy facilities. During the period of 1977–1978, when considerable uncertainty existed because of the court decision about the constitutionality of the $560 million liability limit of the Price Anderson Act, much publicity was given to the dangers of nuclear reactors and much effort was undertaken

22. *Budget of the U.S. Government*, Fiscal 1979, p. 912.

by environmental groups to slow or halt nuclear construction. It seems that subjective risk levels in society may have been substantial, but that objective risk is low. (The absence of reported injuries from the serious nuclear reactor accident in 1979 in Pennsylvania underscores this conclusion.) The problem was sufficiently serious that the legal action to overcome the $560,000,000 Price Anderson limitation on nuclear liability was attempted.

In contrast to the other areas of risk discussed in this paper, the government's role is being confined to loss control, research, and safety regulation, and the risk-bearing function is being shifted to private enterprise.

CROP INSURANCE

A significant example of risk transfer to the federal government is in the field of all-risk crop insurance. In increasing numbers farmers have elected to purchase federal crop insurance against loss due to perils such as insect and wildlife damage, plant diseases, fire, drought, flood, wind, and other weather conditions. Federal crop insurance does not cover loss due to poor farming, negligence of the farmer, or other avoidable loss, nor is profit from farming covered.

In 1978 crop insurance in force was estimated at about $2 billion, and crop insurance premiums, $95,000,000. Federal crop insurance in 1978 was sold in about 1500 U.S. counties, about half of the total number in the nation. In 1976 farmers insured crops of 23 different commodities on nearly 24 million acres, averaging 13 percent of the total number of acres on which insurance potentially could have been written.

Federal crop insurance has grown

steadily over the years. For example, in 1948 crop insurance was sold in only 324 counties, compared to an estimated 1467 counties in 39 different states in 1978, nearly a fivefold increase. Total premiums increased about eightfold over this period. Roughly similar premium growth occurred in a more restricted type of crop insurance sold by commercial insurers known as crop-hail insurance, covering only the perils of fire and hail. In crop-hail insurance, however, premiums are roughly three times the level of all-risk crop insurance. In one study covering the year 1967, it was found that 41 percent of all farms in the United States had some form of crop insurance, and 13 percent had all-risk crop insurance.[23] Crop insurance acceptance appears to reflect a significant desire on the part of farmers to transfer to others some of the risks of farming.

Statistics of the Federal Crop Insurance Corporation (FCIC) suggest that the insurance mechanism works reasonably well as a way to handle unavoidable losses in farming. In examining underwriting experience in crop insurance over the period 1948–1975 for 23 different crops, it may be demonstrated that loss ratios in excess of 100 percent were incurred in about half of the years, and underwriting gains were experienced in the remaining years. Eleven crops, about half of the total number of crops, produced aggregate loss ratios in excess of 100 percent over the period 1948–1975. Thus, farmers in some crops are subsidizing farmers of other crops. Yet, no single crop produced losses continuously over

the period, but rather were subject to good years and bad years. For example, apples produced an aggregate loss ratio of 1.36 over the 12-year period for which they were insured, with losses in seven years and gains in five.[24]

The federal crop insurance program is subsidized by the government. Over the years, premiums exceeded indemnities by about 8.0 percent, although in 1977 the government's loss was 57 percent due to drought in that year. By law, premium rates do not reflect direct costs of loss adjustment, administrative or operating expenses, which include actuarial and program development, marketing and collections, and contract servicing and claims.

The price paid by taxpayers for subsidizing the crop insurance program seems modest enough. Yet the question arises as to the need for having a government corporation perform the task of handling the program. Private insurers are already operating in the field through their crop-hail programs. Since, as noted above, crop risks lend themselves well to the insurance mechanism, there appears to be no compelling reason for having the taxpayers subsidize farmers in an area which could be serviced by private enterprise. Higher premiums would be required if private insurers took over all-risk crop insurance because such agencies would not have a subsidy. If insurance rates were raised by the FCIC, private insurers could compete in the field. It might be difficult for any but nationally operating insurers to handle crop insurance, for regional insurers could not di-

23. Warren R. Bailey and Lawrence A. Jones, *Economic Considerations in Crop Insurance* (U.S.D.A. Research Service, August 1970), p. 36.

24. James Deal, Federal Crop Insurance Corporation, Hearings Before a Subcommittee of the House of Representatives on Appropriations, 95th Congress, 1st session, 14 March 1977, p. 395.

versify risks over different crops which are grown in different regions. Absence of private insurers in this field, however, suggests that all-risk crop insurance rates are now too low for a free market to operate.

FLOOD INSURANCE

Federally sponsored flood insurance was first established under the Housing and Urban Development Act of 1968 after a long history of rising flood losses which appeared to be unabated in spite of large sums spent annually by the U.S. Corps of Engineers on flood control activities.[25]

Provisions of the 1968 act proved to be inadequate, so Congress passed the Flood Disaster Protection Act of 1973 in which coverage limits were doubled, and it was required that all construction in designated flood-prone areas receiving federal financial assistance be covered by flood insurance. Emergency (subsidized) rates were authorized. All communities having identified flood-prone areas were required to participate in the flood insurance program or be denied federally related financing for projects that would be located in such areas. It was the intent of the 1973 act to have flood insurance eventually replace federal disaster relief for flood occurrences, thus relieving flood victims of the necessity to repay disaster loans and to be more fully indemnified than would be the case if individuals relied solely on disaster relief. In order for a community to qualify for flood insurance, certain land use measures, including building code requirements to safe-guard property against flood, are required.

In general, unsubsidized flood insurance from private insurers is not available, with only a few exceptions. (For example, certain DIC [Difference in Conditions] policies cover flood, as does automobile insurance under comprehensive coverage.) As noted previously, private insurers view flood insurance as generally uninsurable.

At first, relatively little insurance was purchased. In 1972, following a $3 billion flood loss from Hurricane Agnes on the eastern seaboard of the United States, only $98 million was paid out in damages under flood policies, although federal flood insurance was available in the affected communities. The publicity brought about by this event apparently increased sales somewhat. In the next year or two flood coverage increased from about $1.5 billion to $4 billion. However, after 1973 when the element of compulsion was introduced, a larger growth in the program occurred. Coverage increased until by 1977 over $35.2 billion of insurance was in force on about 1,156,481 policies. It is estimated that by 1979 coverage will grow to $54 billion on 1,605,000 policies in 16,500 communities. There are 20,000 locations in the United States which are flood prone. By 1977 over 15,678 communities had qualified for flood insurance, representing about 75 percent of the total number of areas which could benefit from the program. Over 90 percent of all flood policies are on residential property.[26]

Initially, the Federal Insurance Administration operated as a partnership with private industry. The National Flood Insurance Association (NFIA), a pool of private insurers, was utilized to underwrite the cov-

25. *A Unified National Program for Managing Flood Losses* (Washington, DC: USGPO, August, 1966), House Doc. No. 465, 89th Congress, 2nd session.

26. *Insurance Facts, 1976,* p. 25; and *Budget of the U.S. Government,* Fiscal 1979, p. 506.

erage, with the government bearing the cost of subsidized rates. Private insurance agents and brokers are utilized to distribute the coverage. However, in 1978 the partnership with N.F.I.A. was terminated, for various reasons, and a separate government corporation was set up to operate the program for the Federal Insurance Administration.[27]

The flood insurance program is one in which government control and participation is increasing instead of decreasing, as is true in the programs of riot insurance and nuclear energy liability. The rationale for the flood insurance program seems to include much of the discussion in Section II of this paper.

SWINE FLU VACCINATION PROGRAM

Swine flu broke out in 1976 on a military post at Fort Dix, New Jersey, affecting some 21 men. One died. Then President Gerald Ford announced to reporters that the last outbreak of flu in 1918–19 in the United States caused the death of 548,000 Americans, and that he was recommending to Congress a $135 million national vaccination program to combat it. Most of the government's health experts believed that the probability of a swine flu outbreak on a large scale was very small, perhaps two percent. Yet officials believed that the chance of no outbreak of flu should not be accepted, and ultimately the vaccination program was undertaken. It developed that no outbreak occurred and that the vaccination pro-

gram proved later to be largely unnecessary.[28]

Before the vaccination program could be carried out, manufacturers required adequate liability insurance as protection against legal suits which might arise because of bodily injury or death arising from the vaccine. Courts have held that manufacturers may be liable for such loss under the "strict liability doctrine" even though all due care is taken in its manufacture.[29] Because the scale of the vaccination program was unprecedented, private insurers were unwilling to offer complete liability coverage to manufacturers without government guarantees and ultimate acceptance of most of the risk.

There were several causes of unacceptable high risk levels perceived by manufacturers. Leslie Cheek, of the American Insurance Association, testified that there could be between 3.8 million and 10 million adverse reactions to the vaccine in a population of 200 million, resulting in plausible claims against manufacturers. If it costs an average of $2500 to defend one claim, defense costs alone could cost between $9.5 billion and $25 billion, in addition to actual damage awards.[30] Albert B. Sabin testified that one vaccine for all age groups was not adequate, that knowledge was lacking as to how

27. Samuel H. Weese and J. W. Doms, "The National Flood Insurance Program— Did the Insurance Industry Drop Out?," *CPCU Journal*, vol. 31, no. 4 (December 1978), pp. 186–204.

28. Philip M. Boffey, "Anatomy of a Decision: How the Nation Declared War on Swine Flu," hearings before the Subcommittee on Health and the Environment, of the Committee on Interstate and Foreign Commerce, House of Representatives, 94th Congress, 2d Session, 1976, pp. 438–39.

29. *Davis* v. *Wyeth Laboratories, Inc.* 399 F. 2d 121 (2nd Cir., 1968) and *Reyes* v. *Wyeth Laboratories, Inc.* 498 F. 2d 1264 (5th Cir.) cert. denied 419 U.S. 1096 (1974).

30. Leslie Cheek, *Swine Flu Hearings* (Table 1), pp. 85–86.

long vaccines could be stored without loss of potency, how long they would be effective, once administered, and how long it would take to train people to administer the vaccine.[31]

In the final insurance arrangements which were worked out, private insurers and drug manufacturers agreed to accept up to stated levels of loss due to contaminated vaccine. Four drug manufacturers were each required to accept a retention of $2.5 million of initial liability. About 48 private insurers accepted an additional $55 million of liability in the aggregate in two layers, one for $5 million and the second for $50 million, premiums for which totalled $2.4 million and $6.25 million, respectively. The insured liability limits totalled $220 million for all four manufacturers. Total potential liability of the government was probably much greater than these amounts, as illustrated by the size of suits already settled by the government on cases of paralysis and deaths from "Guillain-Barre syndrome" which allegedly resulted from the vaccination program. Thus, the major risks of the program fell upon the government.

EVALUATION AND CONCLUSIONS

The purpose here was to evaluate the impact upon society of increasing government responsibility for selected types of risks: the risks from perils of riots in certain areas, crime, nuclear liability, flood, crop failure, and product liability of manufacturers of flu vaccine. The analysis proceeds from the basic axiom that risk is a burden upon society and upon its members individually. More attention to efficient ways of risk management are being sought and greater effort is being made to reduce the total burden of risk. Transfer of specified risks to the government is seen by some as one way to reduce this burden and to manage risks at less cost and with greater effectiveness than would otherwise be possible. All of the risks discussed are residual in the sense that they were unacceptable under normal underwriting conditions and at normal rates by private insurers. Also, these risks were deemed too high to be assumed by the individuals affected. Subjectively at least, the risks presented appeared formidable, and people sought governmental assistance.

If risks are too great to be assumed individually or by private insurers, then it may be reasoned that the government should assume or otherwise handle the risk, if it can. However, government enterprise is not necessarily always the best or the most efficient. Furthermore, various surveys show that people prefer private management of risks to government management, if they have a choice.

Evaluation criteria

The question of private vs. public risk management may be answered in part by looking at: the importance of the burden imposed by given risks, the apparent success of the government's management of the risk, and whether or not private insurers, or individuals, should handle the risk, or whether the risk is a burden which reasonably should be shared by all taxpayers as a group rather than by people individually. All but one of the six areas of risk examined in this article are handled by the government at a cost greater than the revenues produced by those benefitted;

31. Albert B. Sabin, M.D., *Swine Flu Hearings*, p. 62.

that is, at a subsidy from general taxpayers. The sole exception is the riot reinsurance program where the government has made a "profit." With these criteria in mind, let us examine each of the six areas serially:

Riot reinsurance

From the discussion of FAIR programs above, one may reasonably conclude that at first the risk seemed, subjectively at least, to be a burden too large for insurers to accept under normal rates and underwriting conditions, and certainly too great for individuals to accept. The FAIR plan program was adopted in half the states, and the reinsurance mechanism provided the incentive for private insurers again to accept marginal physical damage risks in areas where riots seemed imminent. After the initial period, however, private insurers apparently no longer wished to utilize the reinsurance program in significant volume. The normal private insurance mechanisms seem able to handle the risk, and should be given the encouragement to continue. The government's reinsurance mechanism performed its task when a crisis was perceived, but is now no longer really necessary. The reinsurance mechanism, therefore, should be phased out.

Crime insurance

Although crime loss is great and the risk is substantial, for various reasons the insurance mechanism does not work particularly well as a way to handle this risk. Federal crime insurance has not been eagerly accepted on a voluntary basis. Although it has been made available in nearly half the states, the volume of business has been minimal and is concentrated in only a few states. There seems to be little justification for imposing upon taxpayers generally the burden of crime insurance subsidies. (This is not to criticize other ways of dealing with the crime risk through government, such as police protection, safety activities, education, and other programs.) Private insurers have been able to offer crime insurance on reasonable terms in most areas and have been able to demonstrate the ability to service what markets exist for this type of insurance.

Nuclear energy liability risk

It would appear that the nuclear liability risk seemed to be great enough initially that some type of government guarantee was necessary in order to persuade private investors to build nuclear power reactors. Government expenditures on safety activities, inspection, research, and development of standards seem to be justified as a governmental function to protect members of the public from potential damage from nuclear accidents. Now, however, private insurance and the assessment liability plan show promise of eliminating the need for government insurance. As in the case of riot reinsurance, government involvement in the risk assumption should be dropped, since the private sector can handle it effectively.

Crop insurance

The risks of unavoidable losses in farming lend themselves well to the insurance mechanism. These risks are sufficiently burdensome that crop insurance has been well accepted, both subsidized governmental all-risk coverage and private crop-hail coverage. Because of government subsidies, the rates applicable to all-risk crop insurance might be too low to permit effective competition by private insurers. Although government-operated crop insurance seems to operate well, the question arises as to why taxpayers as a group should be required (through their federal taxes) to reimburse farmers for crop insurance, since these risks could be privately insured. The free market pricing mechanism should be allowed to operate where possible. An attempt should be made to determine the terms and conditions necessary to attract private insurer interest in their field. Continuance of government insurance seems justified only if private insurers will not provide coverage on reasonable terms.

Flood insurance

There seems to be little doubt that the risk of flood seriously affects large numbers of persons throughout the United States. Private insurance of the flood risk is difficult at best, since several of the requirements of insurability are not met. This is a risk, furthermore, which seems to justify governmental treatment, since taxpayers who are not directly affected by flood are affected negatively nonetheless as a result of the annual flood losses which can disrupt entire regions of the country. The governmental flood insurance mechanism provides a way to require those who are affected directly to bear some of their own costs of risk transfer and at the same time allows a contribution by the general taxpayers toward a program which is for the general welfare. The flood program shows signs of being operated reasonably well and being

accepted by significant numbers of persons.

Swine flu liability risk

Undoubtedly, the liability risk involved in the flu vaccination program was substantial, both for the government as well as for private manufacturers of the vaccine. Courts have increasingly tended to impose the strict liability on the manufacturers of defective products. The size and scope of the program were unprecedented, and there were many unknowns. Willingness by the federal government to accept most of the risk undoubtedly was a factor in enabling private insurers and individual manufacturers of the product to cover the remaining risk of contaminated vaccine. The program was undertaken for the benefit of the general public, and it seems proper that the risk and its cost of transfer should also fall upon the general public through the governmental mechanism.

SUMMARY

When they were first reviewed by Congress, all of the six areas of risk examined here seemed to present serious problems on which the Congress decided to take action by authorizing government-sponsored risk transfer programs. It is the author's conclusion that three of the areas should now be eliminated or phased out for the following main reasons: riot reinsurance, because the risk is no longer perceived as "great"; crime insurance, because not only is the government program being accepted minimally by purchasers, but also because private insurance is generally available; nuclear energy liability insurance, because private coverage and assessment liability programs are adequate for foreseeable needs. The government's all-risk crop insurance program, while enjoying market acceptance, is able to exist because of subsidized rates. Private insurers should be given an opportunity to compete on equal footing. The flood insurance program and swine flu vaccination liability immunity appear to be two government programs that are justified by the scope and size of the risks involved, the social purposes that are achieved, and by the present inability or unwillingness of the private insurance mechanism to cope with these risks.

Book Department

INTERNATIONAL RELATIONS AND POLITICS

REINHARD BENDIX. *Kings or People: Power and the Mandate to Rule.* Pp. xii, 692. Berkeley: The University of California Press, 1978. $20.00.

The chief focus of this ambitious work is an inquiry into the transformation of authority and its legitimation from the medieval period to the present. Specifically, Bendix examines the means by which secular autocracy was legitimated and ultimately, if slowly, transformed through the centuries into "the mandate of the people"—a mandate which has been subject to different interpretations across the societies whose histories he details.

Bendix proceeds by comparing the roots of secular authority in Japan, Russia, France, and England and then turns in reverse order to an examination of the transformation of the mandate to rule from secular kings and oligarchs to "the people" in these countries and in Germany. Among the key tensions that Bendix identifies in the evolution of these societies and, especially, in the evolution of state authority are those between: (1) sacred and secular sources of authority and the overlap between, or distinctiveness of, them; (2) centralizing tendencies and peripheral (village and rural) sources of authority; (3) monarchical and aristocratic sources of authority and later elitist and pop-ulist doctrines of authority; and (4) universalistic (national community) and particularistic (parochial) loyalties. In the societies examined by Bendix, these tensions have varied both in their importance and, particularly, in the forms they have assumed.

Bendix suggests that the ability of a society to absorb knowledge about other societies is related to these tensions—to the intensity and form of their occurrence. He sees intellectual mobilization ("the growth of a reading public and an educated secular elite dependent upon learned occupations") as an independent cause of change. As they develop, societies become more receptive to the examples of more "advanced" states, economies, and cultures. England and France provided the earliest models because of their progress in constitutionalism, democratization, and industrialization. How such ideas are interpreted, however, depends on how the crucial issues of legitimation have been resolved in the recipient societies. Before a society is itself intellectually mobilized, the resolution of these issues shapes a "genetic code" which governs the assimilation of ideas and developments from the outside.

Historians, Bendix believes, have underestimated the impact of such intellectual diffusion and the importance of the intellectual mobilization which makes it possible. They have done so, Bendix implies, because they adhere to a structural (implicitly Marxian) framework which tends to treat societies in isolation and sees the division of labor as the key force in social change. In any event, Bendix's interpretation invites comparison with the historical interpretation of political development advanced by Barrington Moore in his *Social Origins of Dictatorship and Democracy*.

According to Bendix, the role of exemplar has now been assumed for developing countries by the U.S., the U.S.S.R., and China. But he believes that intellectual mobilization in the Third World has vastly outpaced the development of stable political institutions. Although the tensions from which state authority has evolved in the industrialized societies, especially those between national and parochial loyalties, have never been fully resolved, they are most severe in the third world where rapid intellectual mobilization strains fragile political institutions.

Quite clearly, this is a book of prodigious scholarship and vast ambition. Yet, its organization requires much of the reader. For while the author claims to have asked similar questions in different contexts, it is not abundantly clear that he has succeeded in doing this in a way that explicitly organizes the comparative dimensions of his analysis. Despite the grand scale of this book, therefore, there is little theoretical integration and the task of drawing and organizing inferences falls heavily upon the reader. Most chapters, in fact, dwell in graphic detail on historical developments in the societies the author chooses to examine. The few chapters which purport to be theoretical, of which Chapter 7 and the final chapter are particularly central, largely contain rather broad-gauged assertions about the propelling forces behind social change and their implications for the contemporary world. Following upon the voluminous effort that precedes the final chapter, some of the assertions contained in it seem remarkably pedestrian. On the other hand, a good many more of Bendix's assertions, especially those in Chapter 7, are, at a minimum, stimulating and persuasively argued. But Bendix

has neither provided an empirical test of alternative theories of development nor, more importantly, has he specified the structure of a multicausal theory. The reader who is interested in parsing a structure of explanation from this book will find instead an intellectual posture rather than a specified theory. In short, Bendix deals with his material at two distinctive levels, one very general and the other very detailed, without really explicating a theoretical structure that binds the two levels together. Nonetheless, he has addressed some grand questions, inspired a number of provocative insights, and produced a monumental research effort. For these qualities, this is a book to which the appelation "significant" is rightfully attached.

BERT A. ROCKMAN
University of Pittsburgh

JULIAN CRITCHLEY. *Warning and Response: A Study of Surprise Attack in The 20th Century and an Analysis of Its Lessons for the Future.* Pp. viii, 123. New York: Crane, Russak, 1978. $14.

This book is a prime example of the prophet-of-doom school of foreign policy analysis, represented in the United States by the Committee on the Present Danger, the Coalition for Peace through Strength, and the latter's seventy-nine affiliated organizations now mobilized to defeat SALT II. The author is a Tory M.P. from Aldershot, and appropriately serves on his party's Defense Committee. He views with alarm the recent increases in Soviet military strength and deplores the state of NATO's defenses, which he finds parlous.

He characterizes President Carter as providing "the erratic leadership of an innocent at large." Britain suffers under "a minority Socialist government" faced with "a vocally anti-military and Russophile section of its own Party." France and Italy are "split in half" with the Communist Party in the ascendant, and the Netherlands, Norway, and Denmark are much the same. Indeed, Belgium and Germany seem to him the only reliable members of NATO.

The basic theme of the book is simplistic. Historical sketches summarize the major surprise attacks since Hitler's first blitzkrieg: the German attacks on Poland, Denmark, Norway, the Low Countries, and Russia; the Japanese attack on Pearl Harbor; the Korean War; and the Israeli-Arab wars of 1956, 1967, and 1973. On this basis the author concludes that NATO must expect a surprise attack by the Warsaw Pact armies. To avoid the appalling choice of war or surrender, he feels the West must improve its defense capability with every weapons system available, and should deploy at once the cruise missile, the neutron bomb, a nuclear minefield along the Iron Curtain, and much greater armies, navies, and air forces.

Critchley blames "the academics of the Rand Corporation" for deserting the strategic concept of massive retaliation in favor of the doctrine that we must do all possible "to make the world safe from all nuclear explosions." He deplores the substitute strategies of mutual deterrence and flexible response as insufficiently deterring.

The difficulty with this kind of argument, which can be neither proved nor disproved, is that exactly the same case can be made by Soviet hawks: NATO military expenditures and armed forces are greater than those of the Warsaw Pact nations, not to mention China's 4.3 million armed forces which alone almost match either NATO or WARSAW. U.S. bombers can now deliver 11,000 warheads, twice as many as a decade ago. By selective statistics, either side's threat may be made awesome, precisely because that is the actual situation under the "balance of terror" of the nuclear age.

An example of the author's selectivity is a quote from the International Institute of Strategic Studies' *The Military Balance 1978*, saying that the military balance in the European Theater has recently been moving "steadily against the West." But he fails to note the next paragraph, in which the IISS details the ten points of the Long Term Defense Program adopted by NATO in 1978 (under the "erratic leadership" of President Carter) for improving the Alliance's readiness to respond to surprise attack. In brief, there is indeed a case for NATO preparedness, but the author both overstates it and leaves the reader with the mistaken impression that nothing is being done about it.

OLIVER BENSON
University of Oklahoma
Norman

MARTIN HILL. *The United Nations System: Coordinating Its Economic and Social Work.* Pp. xv, 252. New York: Cambridge University Press, 1978. $31.50.

International organizations are no less subject to Parkinsonian imperatives than other bureaucracies. Indeed, they tend to become even less tractable. The easy way for diplomats who disagree on approaches to problems as awesome as global poverty, is to sidestep tough administrative decisions by creating new agencies, rather than consolidating old ones. The proliferation of units and programs exacerbates redundancy, confusion, and inefficiency within the UN system: Approximately 167 different agencies and organs are now involved in social and economic activities.

Proliferation is but one of the dangerous tendencies which international administrators confront. There is increasing fragmentation and geographic dispersal of semi-autonomous agencies. Their programs are increasingly dependent upon voluntary rather than regularly assessed funding arrangements. (Already over half of the UN's social and economic activities are financed not by the regular budget approved by the General Assembly, but out of extra budgetary resources.) Even the UN's most important source of support, the United States, encourages the latter development.

Considering these tendencies, to what extent is it possible to coordinate the myriad of UN social and economic activities? In one sense coordination is simply not possible. It cannot be imposed, ordered or directed by authorities in such a decentralized, bureaucratic system. In another sense coordination is possible, albeit incredibly difficult. Coordination involves on-going efforts to influence change by indirect means as well as through established mechanisms, and to persuade elites who bargain for resources such as influence, information and funds. With that conceptualization at the core of this analysis, the argument for reform rather than a radical restructuring of the UN system makes much sense.

Martin Hill's thoughtful and exhaustive UNITAR study asserts that necessary changes are possible within the framework of the existing Charter. They must begin with attitudinal changes. In Hill's words "The silence about many critical issues of organization and structure . . . must be broken." Although they are only short steps in the right direction, resolutions by the 32nd General Assembly attest to the contributions of the author and his colleagues in helping to break that silence. The author died after completing all but the last draft of the book's postscript (which updates developments since 1974). Several of his recommendations, such as the creation of a high ranking Director-General's post in the Secretariat, responsible for coordination and coherence in the entire UN system, have already been adopted.

The book delineates the problems of coordination within the UN setting. It identifies priorities and prescribes solutions to many of administrative problems. It offers no easy answers, rather it provides a balanced overview of a very complex topic. This study is no light reading for generalists or even scholars who are mildly interested in international administration. The prose is dry and the wit is sparse. (One example of the latter is a reference to the ACC's "somewhat imprudent claims to competence" rebuffed by CPC and ECOSOC in 1969.) The author was careful not to downgrade any of the major organs or committees responsible for coordination. Even the present Secretary-General is dealt with impersonally. Although the latter writes a fulsome introduction, Hill did not include him in his evaluation of top UN officials.

Of the first three Secretaries-General, only Dag Hammerskjöld was determined to innovate administrative reforms that might revitalize and better coordinate disparate UN programs. Trygve Lie had little inclination to engage in interagency disputes. U Thant was a moderator but no innovator in administration. Hammerskjölds initiatives were squelched, causing him to give them up in frustration. Given that background, the limited time available to Secretaries-General, and their inevitable preoccupation with crises, it is no wonder that a consensus about the need for a new high level position responsible for coordination (using the Administrative Committee on Coordination and otherwise) came about.

The organs responsible for coordinating social and economic activities are carefully scrutinized beginning with the Assembly, but especially the Economic & Social Council (ECOSOC—which has never functioned as it was intended to), the Administration Committee on Coordination (ACC) (which has often functioned to merely legitimize predetermined agency positions), and the Secretariat's Department of Economic and Social Affairs (ESA). None of the other coordinating organs are neglected. Much is also said about UNCTAD's challenge to the Council, UNDP's relationship to the latter and the (World) Bank group, and other tenuous organizational relationships. The need for the Council and the Assembly to involve (specialized) agency representatives at a much earlier stage in their overall policymaking is also underlined.

Hill described the abortive effort in 1969 to integrate UN regional economic commissions and FAO programs in Africa. His constructive purpose was to suggest how similar efforts might be pursued differently in the future. The postscript also explains why actions such as the creation of the World Food Council in 1974 and the following year's UNIDO (United Nations Industrial Development Organization) Conference, which set exorbitant goals and severed that organ from the General Assembly, created administrative problems beyond those that are addressed.

This book is clearly a major contribution to those interested in international administration. The author's lucid prose, careful documentation, and detailed appendices provide a rich body of data and ideas.

PAUL CONWAY
State University College
Oneonta
New York

ANDRZEJ KARKOSZKA (for the Stockholm International Peace Research Institute). *Strategic Disarmament, Verification and National Security.* Pp. 174. New York: Crane, Russak and Company, 1977.

WILLIAM R. VAN CLEAVE and S. T. COHEN. *Tactical Nuclear Weapons: An Examination of the Issues.* Pp. 119. New York: Crane, Russak and Company, 1978.

Many analysts of national security affairs have pointed out that the edifice of nuclear deterrence is built upon theories and concepts that were developed in the late 1950s and early 1960s, and it is important to consider how valid these constructs are in the contemporary international system.

The research and writing of *Strategic Disarmament, Verification and National Security* was sponsored by the Stockholm International Peace Research Institute (SIPRI). One has to read the fine print of the preface to discover that the author of the study is Andrzej Karkosza, who was a research fellow at SIPRI from 1973 through 1975 and who is now affiliated with the Polish Institute of International Affairs in Warsaw. (It would be nice if SIPRI would publish the names of the authors of its publications on the title pages of the studies rather than hiding them in the prefaces.)

The title of the study leads one to expect an analysis of the technical and political aspects of that vitally important necessity of contemporary arms control, verification. The book is, however, an overview of the subject of strategic nuclear arms control and there is little discussion of recent issues of verification. In fact, the author primarily synthesizes the academic writings on arms control and disarmament of the 1950s and 1960s. The major weakness of the study derives from the overly ambitious goal of the author, for he valiantly attempts to cover the relationship between politics, disarmament (which he considers synonomous with arms control), and verification. But the scope is too broad and, given the relatively short length of the study, the theoretical contributions are limited.

The fact that the author of this book is from an Eastern European state is in itself reason enough to read the book, for he has a very different perspective on the subject than either his Western or Soviet colleagues. He argues, for instance, that the "military-industrial-scientific complex" is "the main driving force behind decisions on the military and security policy of capitalist states" and that "in socialist states, on the other hand, the main feature of the decision-making process is that political considerations are always the dominant feature . . ." (p. 45). One can argue with this proposition, but it is refreshing to read an analysis of strategic arms control by a non-Soviet, non-American author.

Tactical Nuclear Weapons is an examination of the current thinking in the United States and the Soviet Union concerning nuclear weapons designed to be used for battlefield operations. The book was coauthored by two analysts eminently qualified to analyze their subject: William R. Van Cleave, a defense strategist at the University of Southern California and former member of the U.S. SALT delegation, and S. T. Cohen, a nuclear physicist who played a central role in the development of the enhanced radiation warhead (the so-called neutron bomb). The authors' thesis is that "neither a viable posture nor a viable doctrine exist in NATO for the defense of Europe or more particularly for the employment of tactical nuclear weapons" (p. 101). They argue that American defense planners have not thought about the strategy for employing tactical nuclear weapons since the mid-fifties and that defense planners should focus on this issue immediately. As the authors note, the reason that American strategists have not focused on this subject is the belief that any use of nuclear weapons would quickly escalate to general nuclear war. As President Kennedy put it, "Inevitably the use of small nuclear armaments will lead to larger and larger nuclear armaments on both sides, until the worldwide holocaust has begun." Every president since Kennedy has expressed his belief in this proposition. Van Cleave and Cohen do not believe it and, furthermore, believe that it is wrong. The evidence that they present, however, is not convincing. They do not indicate how the "great divide" between nuclear and conventional war can be maintained if tactical nuclear weapons are used.

A central problem concerning tactical nuclear weapons is the problem of communications, command, and control (or in the lexicon of strategists, C³). If NATO were to deploy a new generation of sophisticated tactical nuclear weapons, how would they be controlled: by the President, the NATO commander, or local battlefield commanders? If the President were to control these weapons, the C³ problems involved with such control are enormous, perhaps even insurmountable. If the local battlefield commanders had control of the weapons, unauthorized use would be a distinct possibility.

Van Cleave and Cohen briefly mention, but do not consider seriously enough, the problems involved within the NATO alliance for developing a new doctrine of tactical and theater nuclear warfare. The Europeans, understandably, do not want to fight a nuclear war on their territory and are therefore hesitant to support the development and deployment of a new generation of tactical nuclear weapons (hence the furor over the "neutron bomb"). It is highly improbable that the United States and its NATO allies could work out a commonly accepted doctrine of tactical nuclear warfare.

These two books are valuable analyses of two aspects of contemporary security issues: strategic nuclear arms control and tactical nuclear weapons. While the first largely reflects the views of the pioneer analysts of the fifties and sixties, the Van Cleave and Cohen book challenges these views.

DAN CALDWELL
Pepperdine University
Malibu
California

ØYSTEIN NORENG. *Oil Politics in the 1980's: Patterns of International Cooperation.* Pp. xvi, 171. New York: McGraw-Hill, 1978. $5.95.

This is a highly readable, well-documented, original analysis of the world petroleum situation as it now stands, and of alternatives for OECD-OPEC cooperation and confrontation during the 1980's. The volume is part of a number of recently released and forthcoming studies commissioned by the Council on Foreign Relations dealing with issues likely to be of major international concern during the coming decade. The author is a specialist on energy policy issues and international affairs, currently on the faculty of the Oslo Institute of Business Administration. He was formerly associated with the Norwegian Ministry of Finance and with Statoil, Norway's government-owned petroleum company.

The first two-thirds of the book constitute an incisive review of the principal facts and trends that underlie today's, and will shape tomorrow's, world petroleum situation: the present oil reserves picture and the outlook for additional oil discoveries; patterns of and prospects for energy consumption in the OECD countries; the politics and economics of the dominant country groupings within OPEC; and the main factors behind past and likely future oil pricing developments.

It is in the last third of the book that Noreng makes use of the relevant facts laid out earlier to make a case for some sort of scheme that will foster OECD-OPEC cooperation in the decades ahead. His argument runs as follows. The present oil regime is a relatively stable one because the United States and Saudi Arabia play a dominant moderating role. But this political balance will probably be eroded in the future by the dynamics of the world oil market. Specifically: (1) slowly-rising petroleum prices will not stimulate an all-out search for alternative energy sources, and thus the oil reserves/demand relationship will deteriorate irreversibly with eventual disastrous price and supply consequences for the OECD countries; (2) the burden of meeting the growth in OECD demand for petroleum will fall increasingly on the countries with small populations and large oil reserves, which will eventually refuse to pump more oil in exchange for financial assets and will impose production ceilings that will cause prices to increase sharply; and (3) the OPEC countries with ambitious industrialization programs (namely, the ones with large populations and relatively small oil reserves) can be expected to insist on high petroleum prices as a means of paying their rapidly-rising import bills, and this will give the oil pricing system an upward bias.

What we have, says Noreng, is a structurally deficient oil regime that will not stand the test of time, and if we are to move to a new one in the years ahead it better include strong links of OECD-OPEC cooperation to counter the potentially-disastrous above-described trends. His suggestion is to start thinking about four possible agreements. The first and most difficult one would be on oil prices and supplies, and it would acknowledge that petroleum prices must rise in real terms whenever OECD demand for oil rises because that is the only way to stimulate the search for alternative energy sources and to prevent abrupt OPEC-mandated price increases.

The second agreement would open the door to joint OECD-OPEC ventures in the field of alternative energy sources, mainly by setting up financial incentives for the international oil companies to plunge into energy research. The third agreement would create new financial instruments (for example, indexed oil bonds issues by the OECD countries)

that would guarantee oil producers a real return and would diminish their reluctance to pump more oil. The final proposed agreement would be on technology and trade, with the purpose of aiding the oil producers to industrialize their economies and modernize their societies.

Seldom does one get the opportunity to read a book with a more important message and with more stimulating suggestions.

ARTURO C. PORZECANSKI
Morgan Guaranty Trust Company
New York

MORTON SCHWARTZ. *Soviet Perceptions of the United States.* Pp. 224. Berkeley: University of California Press, 1978. $12.50.

This book examines Soviet perceptions of the United States, chiefly as reflected in the publications of the USA Institute of the Soviet Academy of Sciences. Soviety policymakers, limited by Marxist-Leninist ideology, initially viewed the United States as a typical capitalist state—exploitative, oppressive, decadent, and crisis-ridden. Recently, Soviet scholars have been better informed and more sophisticated. They still have difficulty in comprehending our political and economic system; they can understand a strong President but not limited government, majority rule, or rule of law. It is not surprising, then, that they have had great difficulty in understanding how we make foreign policy and conduct diplomatic relations. As Georgi Arbatov, director of the USA Institute, says, "competition with the United States is an extremely complex matter" (p. 12).

The dogmatic assumptions of the Stalin period are no longer accepted in the Soviet Union, partly because of change in Moscow, partly because of change in Washington (military defeat in Viet Nam and the anti-war movement in the United States). The nature and expense of an arms race have altered thinking on who would benefit more from such a race. Perhaps equality—balance—might be better for both sides. Much of this changed thinking is traceable to the period when Nixon was President and Kissinger Secretary of State, despite the fact that both were noted for their opposition to the Soviet system.

This development of a "new realism" coincided with Moscow's stress on "detente." The Soviet Americanists developed a "particularly acute appreciation" of the advantages which a relaxed international atmosphere holds for Soviet diplomacy. In the process, they became the defenders and advocates of detente; they have a vested interest in it, they lobby for it. This, in turn, has meant improved relations between the two countries.

In both Moscow and Washington tension and cold war have bolstered party militants and ideological fundamentalists. Each government has its hawks and its doves, and it is logical to conclude that a period of military equality—emphasized in the SALT talks—would provide the political parity—balance—which might make peaceful relations possible.

There are some in Moscow, however, who see the United States as increasingly impotent, lacking in the national will necessary to be stronger than the Soviet Union or even equal to it. Should such belief come to the fore, Moscow might well be emboldened to take an adventurous course. The United States, therefore, must maintain a military capability which will stay Moscow's hawks.

With the departure of Brezhnev presumably near, it is in America's interest to reinforce the idea of the advantages of a continuing detente. Perhaps the present concentration on "spheres of common interest" will "demonstrate that the cold war policy of seeking to harm the other side has indeed been jettisoned" and that ". . . the United States should strive to use detente to further diminish the Soviet fear of American hostility and neutralize Soviet leadership opinion which inclines toward a policy of confrontation and antagonism" (168–9).

The research on this book has been done most carefully, the documentation is very complete, and we are greatly indebted to Professor Schwartz for his timely analysis and interesting and hopeful conclusions.

DONALD G. BISHOP
Sun City Center
Florida

RICHARD SMOKE. *War: Controlling Escalation.* Pp. xvi, 419. Cambridge: MA: Harvard University Press, 1978. $18.50.

This book's 419 pages cover a subject of vital interest to every world inhabitant: escalation of war and what to do about it. The author, a student of escalation's literature, analyzes in depth eight historical war situations, to try to arrive at generalizations on how escalation should be handled. The book, he states, is intended for decisionmakers, working level civilians, and military officers; and for scholars specializing in international relations, foreign policy, and related fields.

This book represents a praiseworthy scholarly pioneering undertaking. Harvard University Press deserves credit for publishing such a potentially helpful volume to prevent the escalation of war.

As a result of his studies, Mr. Smoke expresses concern about the possibility of wars in the 1980's and 1990's. He sees the necessity for controlling war escalation as timely for study. He presents his studies of escalation and its causes in eight historical situations: the Spanish Civil war, the wars of German unification, the Austro-Prussian war, the Franco-Prussian war, the Crimean war, and the Seven Years war. In each case he analyzes the sequences of escalation and their results. He attempts to draw conclusions from these cases and tries to get at the heart of causes of escalation and their possible control.

He comes to the conclusion that decisionmakers need "a new and richer kind of assistance from analysts and researchers" to control escalation in future wars. All this is to the good. But the study regretably is written in gobbledegook jargon, and is difficult to decipher and understand. I know few decisionmakers, working level civilians, or military officers who would have the disposition to wade through the volume.

To accomplish the announced purpose of this volume and appeal to those for whom it was written, the Harvard University Press might have had the good sense to run it through the typewriter, as they say, so that those for whom it was intended might read and understand it.

EDWARD L. BERNAYS
Cambridge
Massachusetts

BURTAN A. WEISBROD, JOEL F. HANDLER, and NEIL K. KOMESAR. *Public Interest Law: An Economic and Institutional Analysis.* Pp. x, 580. Berkeley: University of California Press, 1978. $27.50.

The term public interest law (PIL) is new to the language, as is the institution known as the public interest law firm. This book introduces the reader to the structure, resources, and activities of this "nonprofit industry." And it answers a number of important questions. What is public interest law? How effective is it? What are the limits of litigation as a mechanism for conflict resolution? What are the variables determining choice of cases and methods of handling them? What is the impact of PIL advocacy of under-represented interests on resource reallocation? And what are the circumstances under which non-law advocacy may be more useful than law advocacy?

This is an unusually well-integrated volume. Though the various chapters are written by many different economists, sociologists, and lawyers, the outline for the volume was developed after a year-long seminar directed by Professor Weisbrod in which the contributors participated. Each chapter was presented and critiqued in at least one seminar. The result is a cohesive study in which the eight case-study chapters in Part Two (on the environment, consumerism, housing, employment discrimination, medical care, occupational health and safety, education finance, and taxation) reflect the concepts developed in the six predominantly theoretical chapters which comprise Part One.

The framework is constructed around economic analysis and evaluation. Specifically, the authors point out that studies of the public sector (or at least the few that there are) have concentrated on government intervention as a correction for private market failure. This book deals with a parallel concept to that of private market failure, namely, public interest activity essentially seeking to repair government's own deficiencies. In short, these essays deal with one example of the "voluntary public sector," public interest law firms, as "intermediaries between individuals seeking redress and the bureaucratic agencies." The result is very satisfying. There is an excellent analytical treatment of the meaning of public interest generally (and an appendix comparing concepts of public interest). There is a careful coverage of the "behavior" of public interest lawyers (selection of cases, strategies, tactics) and the "tools" they use (litigation, lobbying, and dissemination of information). An "ideal" PIL behavior is set forth and a capacity to predict the probable behavior of PIL groups is created by comparing their structure and participants with those found in two other groups: the private law sector and the non-law public interest sector.

The conclusions are sympathetic to but also critical of public interest law. The bias of PIL groups towards test-case litigation is described, as is their propensity to focus on judicial victories rather than on real social change. Concern is also expressed about funding problems and the legal restrictions on "nonprofit" organizations. All in all, a systematic and balanced study, this book is a major step forward in law and society research.

WILLIAM C. LOUTHAN
Ohio Wesleyan University
Delaware

AFRICA, ASIA, AND LATIN AMERICA

GORDON BENNETT, KEN KIEKE, and KEN YOFFY. *Huadong: The Story of a Chinese People's Commune.* Pp. xxxiii, 197. Boulder: Westview Press, 1978. $15.00. Paper $6.95.

In the basic strategy for China's revolutionary modernization, which Mao Tse-tung shaped in the 1950s and remolded in the 1960s, the rural people's commune plays a most significant role. What we know about this working and living grass-roots environment that encompasses economic, political, administrative, military, educational, cultural, and other daily activity for 650 million Chinese peasants, comes principally from official Chinese sources with bits and pieces added by foreign visitors. Huadong, a commune about 30 miles or so north of Guangzhou (Canton), is one which many foreigners (including this reviewer) have visited and gotten data about over the years since the ping pong diplomacy breakthrough. Professor Bennett and his two student collaborators have taken advantage of the extensive data, photographs, interpretations, and experiences of these visitors to put together a most useful descriptive analysis of Huadong which contributes much to our understanding of the Chinese commune and through it the revolutionary process that has been reshaping Chinese society.

Bennett's study, a joint project of the China Council of the Asia Society and the Texas China Council (affiliated with the Center for Asian Studies at the University of Texas), is aimed at providing authoritative information on the commune for wide use in adult public education. The result is a tight work that succeeds in presenting China's major innovative institution in a comprehensive, readable fashion without sacrificing technical standards. The book is a useful adjunct to other works on China that can be used effectively in adult education programs as well as at the college level.

Professor Bennett's organization helps the reader to comprehend the day-to-day living and working patterns of the Chinese peasant in the context of China's strategy for development—to fashion a modern socialist industrial society with sustained growth, efficiency, and equity. After an introductory chapter puts Huadong and communes in historical and social perspective, four chapters

in succession deal with major aspects of the commune: government and politics; economy; society; and culture. The ultimate chapter deals briefly with future prospects. Appendices provide a summary chronology and activities occurring at the commune's three operational levels; readers are also introduced to the pinyin romanization system that is superseding familiar spellings (for example, Beijing for Peking). The result is a clear sense of the hard yet ordered and purposeful lives commune members lead and the ways open to them to pursue their self-interest within the framework of a collectivist organization.

CHARLES HOFFMAN
State University of New York
Stony Brook

JAMES JUPP. *Sri Lanka: Third World Democracy.* Pp. xxi, 423. Totowa, NJ: Frank Cass, 1978. $29.50.

James Jupp has written an informative account of Sri Lankan politics from independence to 1977, with an epilogue covering the results of the general election held that year. The first chapter surveys the political scene from the colonial period to the 1970s. Then there are chapters dealing with such topics as the social setting, political parties and their organization, minority politics, electoral politics, institutions, and the revolutionary challenge of 1971.

The framework is descriptive rather than conceptual. This is not to say that Jupp is not analytical; in fact, this book is full of interesting interpretations. Rather, he eschews the approach of "modernization theory" as being inappropriate, for political developments in Sri Lanka in the last three decades do not fit the model of a transition from "tradition" to "modernity". On the contrary, Jupps argues that the movement *away* from Western attitudes and practices in Ceylon has been a necessary step towards modernization and socialization. For example, British attitudes had stressed values considered desirable for a governing elite, had been contemptuous of trade and commerce, and had encouraged a system which emphasized status and hierarchy. A break with this system and these values was necessary in order to achieve economic modernization in the framework of a more egalitarian society. As Jupp puts it: " 'Modernization' is a difficult term to apply to the progress of independent Sri Lanka, and 'Westernization' is clearly inappropriate. 'Indigenization' too, has its difficulties." (p. 352). Instead, Jupp's main argument is that the dominant political force in Sri Lanka has been Sinhala Buddhist revivalism which wished to create a system which was both modern and indigenous.

A principal theme of the book is that in recent years, politics in Sri Lanka have led to a consensus between the two major forces in the country's politics, one mildly reformist (represented by the United National Party) and the other radically socialist (represented by the Sri Lanka Freedom Party). The basis of the consensus is commitment to a program of democratic socialism within the framework of a state that is fully within the tradition of the Sinhala Buddhist revival. Only the Ceylon Tamils remain outside the consensus.

Jupp has covered his ground thoroughly. His bibliography is extensive, he has carried out numerous interviews to reinforce his written sources, his writing is commendably clear, and there are a number of useful features such as a glossary (at the beginning, for a welcome change), a chronology of events, and a number of maps, charts, and tables. I suspect the book may be less favorably received by social scientists committed to such analytical categories as "modernization," "system maintainance," "functional specificity," and "institutional autonomy," at which Jupp takes a few swipes in his concluding chapter. But I heartily recommend it as an excellent study of the politics of a neglected corner of the third world.

PETER HARNETTY
University of British Columbia

MAJID KHADDURI. *Socialist Iraq: A Study in Iraqi Politics Since 1968.* Pp. vii, 260. Washington, DC: The Middle East Institute, 1978. $12.95.

Inter and intra factionalism, alike in civil and military circles, in postindependent Iraq prevented any particular group from consolidating power; and no regime was able to secure legitimacy and implement socioeconomic reforms. Majid Khadduri, a leading scholar of Iraqi affairs and now a retired academician, has attempted to identify systematically this shifting milieu of Iraqi politics through three separate volumes covering a span of almost half a century. The first volume *Independent Iraq* (1951, 1960) dealt with Iraqi politics under the Monarchy. The second volume *Republican Iraq* (1969) studied the Revolution of 1958 and its aftermath. The current volume *Socialist Iraq* is a sequel to the earlier two volumes and is essentially a study of the Revolution of 1968 with a special emphasis on political and economic development under Arab Socialist rule. Khadduri's study makes three major observations about the Iraqi Socialist movement and the Ba'thist regime.

The Iraqi Socialist movement is part of a larger socialist movement spread in Arab lands after World War II. While its theoretical framework may not be different from the other Arab socialist movements, its scope and direction have acquired a local coloring, for the Iraqi leading personalities stamped the movement with their own imprint and identified it with their own local interests and conditions. The movement essentially sought progress, social justice, political participation, and prosperity—a new social order considered unattainable under either the royalist or republican regimes. Failure of the 1958 Revolution to remove socioeconomic inequalities and establish political democracy prompted an alliance between the Ba'thist leaders, such as Hassan al-Bakr and Abd al-Qadri, and the dissident army officers, Colonels Abd al-Rahman al-Dawud and Abd al-Razzeq al-Nayif, to end republican rule and bring about the Ba'thist regime.

Under the Ba'thist rule, a series of drastic changes have to date been designed to define the framework of Iraqi's evolving political structure. Based on socialist teachings and experiences, two temporary constitutions promulgated the machinery of the government into four principal branches: the Revolutionary Command Council (RCC), the National Assembly, the Presidency, and the Judiciary. The Ba'th Party functions as a separate entity, never to merge or to become part of the state. It merely intends to influence and direct men and organizations towards Ba'thist principles and guidelines. The state, in Ba'thist eyes, is only a means toward an end, while the Party provides leadership and direction for action. Despite commitment to collective leadership, factionalism and dissension between and within competing groups led to a struggle for power resulting in the rise of two Ba'thist leading personalities, Hassan al-Bakr, President of the Republic and Saddam Husayn, Vice President of the RCC. Other political parties and groups including the Kurds, Independent Democrats, Progressive Nationalists, and the Communists exist today only in name within the framework of the Progressive National Front.

Following a period of relative stability, the Ba'thist regime initiated a chain of development schemes indicating a significant departure from the social and economic policies of previous regimes. New policies of national economic plans, agrarian reforms, nationalization of the oil industry, industrialization, and social, educational, and cultural development aimed to establish a socialist society in which all citizens enjoy the benefits of progress and prosperity. The country's foreign policy was redirected in favor of closer alliance with the Soviet Union in light of strong support for Israel in the West, and the regime's commitment to socialist goals. Soviet cooperation was pursued not only for ideological reasons but also for military, technical, and economic assistance. Soviet support for Iraq's foreign and domestic policies coupled with the Ba'thist concilliatory policies towards its Arab and non-Arab neighbors have enabled the regime to pursue an independent policy in such issues as nationalization of the oil industry and the settlement of the Kurdish question.

Apart from the absence of a theoretical treatise, Khadduri presents an informative account of the origins, drives, and aims of the Arab Socialist movement and the Ba'thist regime. The author's personal interviews with the leading political leaders and his diligent attention to the names and synopses of important personalities as well as public documents and proclamations clearly reflect Khadduri's scholarly commitment. Khadduri's analysis of the Ba'thist regime is, however, confined to the Iraqi setting alone. The successes or failures of the 1968 revolution could have been better evaluated had they been compared with similar revolutions in Algeria or other Arab countries. Similarly, Khadduri's careful analysis of the Ba'thist elites leaves unanswered questions relating to congruity of Ba'thist teachings with the Iraqi public or, for that matter, with Islamic beliefs. A detailed critique of the popular reaction to the Ba'thist policies is absent. In light of the recent religious uprisings in Iran, Turkey, and other Moslem countries, Ba'thist teachings and elitist orientation may prove to be incompatible with the aspirations of the Sunnite and Shiite population of Iraq.

AMIR H. AHANCHIAN
The Institute For International
   Political and Economic Studies
Tehran

ALI A. MAZRUI. *Africa's International Relations: The Diplomacy of Dependency and Change.* Pp. 310. Boulder, CO: Westview Press, 1977. $23.75.

Ali Mazrui has a habit of forcing his readers to reconsider the familiar and the habitual. The starting points we so often take for granted Mazrui holds up for reexamination. His most recent book— *Africa's International Relations The Diplomacy of Dependency and Change* —is no exception.

This volume will be most useful to readers with a basic literacy and competency in African affairs, and who want an intelligent and highly personal exposition of Africa's position in a highly interdependent world. The phenomenon of interdependency is by its nature complex and unwieldy, a difficult animal to capture in any analytic net. Mazrui organizes his material on this subject along geographic lines: Africa and Western Europe, Africa and Asia, Africa and the United States, Africa and the Diaspora; and thematic lines: Race and Dignity, Population and Politics, Africa and International Ideologies. To each one of these areas, thematic and geographic, he applies his wide-ranging and synthesizing mind in order to identify what he sees as its major substantive issues. For Africa and the Middle East the major issues turn on the ability of the actors to overcome and resolve their historic assymetrical political and commercial relations and the cultural attitudes that sometimes reinforced these relations. Conversely, between the United States and Africa the principal issues are the absence of a sustained historical relationship. Mazrui writes that "the most important sins committed by the USA in Africa have so far been the sins of omission—of indifference and caution, of insensitivity and moral distance." In the face of rising nationalism, international resource and financial crises, and the appearance of new state and business actors these are the major issues which in these areas may bind nations together and push them apart.

Herein lies the strength, and the weakness, of Mazrui's approach. The breadth, the confrontation of issues in an illuminating and sometimes idiosyncratic fashion is his hallmark here and in other works. One leaves the work with new insights into many of the time-honored political dilemmas that confront men and women in Africa and the world beyond—the problems of caste and class, of the possibility of leadership in a constrained environment. On the other hand the absence of a central compelling argument to link these insights and tie them together in a logical structure means that one finishes the book without a feeling for the central dynamic that drives or sustains the separate substantive issues within each geographic or thematic area. What emerges are clusters of images and arguments. In this respect it differs from much of the "dependency" literature.

There are certain consistencies however. One is his implicit insistence on the duality of all phenomenon, which may bring opportunity or constraint, and usually a bit of both. This view seems informed as much by a certain non-Western philosophical perspective as it is by a self-consciously Hegelian dialectic one. An outgrowth perhaps is his recognition of the multidirectionality of change. Europe and the United States affect Africa, *and* Africa's behavior has consequences for those areas as well. Thirdly, Mazrui regularly includes the black Diaspora in his political analyses of Africa's international relations.

The book is recommended for those with an interest in Africa and those who care about the position of the LDCs in a world of rapid change within an international hierarchy of sometimes surprising longevity and strength. Yet within that hierarchy there is room for constructive change at the margin. Recasting the familiar Swahili maxim frequently applied to small African states in world affairs (When elephants fight it is the grass which is trampled), the author gives us a not untypical Mazruian turn of phrase which captures something of Africa's position in a nuclear stalemated Cold War: "When two elephants are confronting each other in petrified stillness . . . it is the neutral grass in between which *benefits.*"

ERNEST J. WILSON III
University of Pennsylvania

E. WAYNE NAFZIGER. *Class, Caste, and Entrepreneurship: A Study of Indian Industrialists.* Pp. x, 188. Honolulu, Hawaii: The University Press of Hawaii, 1978. $12.00.

This work is a short, meticulous and thorough study of fifty-four manufacturing entrepreneurs in Visakhapatnam, a newly industrializing city in the Indian state of Andhra Pradesh. It attempts to study entrepreneurship, not only from the perspective of economic growth, but from that of a more equitable distribution of income, wealth, and economic opportunity. Specifically, it seeks to provide "an insight into the extent to which official objectives, that the 'backward classes' and 'weaker sections' of the country share in India's economic growth, have been realized."

Nafziger executes the study by analyzing the caste, educational background, training, work experience, access to capital, paternal economic status, and occupation of his fifty-four entrepreneurs. He is fortunate in having access to data concerning the caste composition of the entire city of Visakhapatnam, even though the census has not carried data on caste since 1931. Thus, unlike many other empirical studies on Indian entrepreneurship, he is able to compare the caste composition of his sample with that of the population of the city as a whole. However, census data does carry information on migration, occupational background, education, literacy, and religion which he also uses to compare the characteristics of his group with that of the entire city.

Moreover, by correlating caste, paternal economic status, education, prior work experience, sources and amounts of capital, and degree of access to governmental assistance, to the entrepreneurs' income class and the gross value added of their firms, the author is able to uncover the factors related to success in business.

Nafziger examines a number of definitions of the term "entrepreneur." He chooses to opt for one close to that of Frank Knight's: "The entrepreneur is the ultimate decision-maker in the enterprise. It is he, and not the hired manager, who commits the (ownership) capital and bears the risks." Where more than one person owns capital within the firm, "the entrepreneur is identified as the person with the largest initial capital share in the enterprise."

For those who know India, the study's major conclusions cause little surprise. The median education of the entrepreneurs is much higher than that of Visakhapatnam's population. High paternal economic status leads to "more prior management experience, more technical and management training, more education, and more initial capital." These factors, in turn, lead to much greater access to governmental assistance and success in business. An extremely high proportion of the successful entrepreneurs come from wealthy, dominant, and high caste families. This enables them to "avert the threat of democratization and industrialization to their economic standing."

But isn't it also true that the very spread of industrialization creates opportunities for better employment, higher wages, and social mobility for the "backward classes" and weaker sections of the country, thus aiding their economic welfare and the spread of democratization. The author himself honestly admits: "This study has not analyzed the indirect effect of the development of entrepreneurs on persons with low income or low status."

MINOO ADENWALLA
Lawrence University
Appleton
Wisconsin

ROBERT NORTON. *Race and Politics in Fiji*. Pp. xv, 210. New York: St. Martin's Press, 1978. $17.95.

This handsome volume is an illuminating analysis of a complex political economy in which expressions of sharply articulated racial and ethnic differences (between Europeans, Fijians and Indians)—cleavages which might have been expected to plunge a new nation into chaos—have instead become "a regularized feature of structured relationships in which the political opponents meet and cooperate." As Norton's manuscript went to press a major political crisis in Fiji arose from the unexpected success in the general elections of March 1977 of an extreme nationalist Fijian whose party split the Fijian vote and nearly put the Indian-led opposition into power. Such an outcome, averted by the decision of the Fijian Governor-General to commission the outgoing prime minister to form a caretaker government pending new elections, threatened the tacit consensus that Fijians must be prominent if not preeminent in government. The reader, left up in the air by the author's preliminary analysis of these events (in a postscript dated May 1977), should note that new elections later in the year triumphantly reasserted the Fijian political hegemony and perhaps most of the "architecture of inter-racial accommodation" skillfully delineated in this valuable monograph.

The 1977 crisis also bears out the wisdom of following R. Bendix's injunction in *Nation-Building and Citizenship* to encompass within an analysis a whole range of events that are compatible with "the conflicting tendencies inherent in any complex society." In Fiji, Norton sees the relation between politics and society as responsive to the assertion of both racial divisions and class divisions: "though racial loyalties have usually prevailed . . . they have sometimes been most strongly affirmed when possibilities arise that organization will proceed according to other principles."

Norton's thesis should command wide attention, for it expounds the "conditions under which a profound racial division in economy, society and culture may be circumscribed in political organization." While most of the book necessarily examines the components of both conflict and equilibrium in Fiji, well-chosen contrasts with Guyana and Malaysia point up the unusual lesson Fiji offers students of multiracial societies: "It may be the development of a culture that admits racial contention, allowing it to be acted out in regularized ways rather than repressing it or denying it, which facilitates control of conflict and the achievement of integration." The author, a lecturer in anthropology at Macquarie University, Sydney, is much too cautious a scholar to push his hypothesis further afield—to Quebec, New Caledonia or the West Indies, for example—but it does have most interesting ramifications; at very least it will draw the attention of more of his North American peers to the relevance of one of the sophisticated dramas now playing in the new nations of the South Pacific.

The success of Fiji in heading off or rather institutionalizing the explosive potential of racial differences owes much, the author admits, to the conventions of compromise fostered among opposing groups under British rule. Similarly, the predominance of Fijians since independence is rooted in the greater cohesiveness of the unitary "protectionist" institutions unique to them in the earlier period and maintained in modified form ever since as the Fijian administration. Though the author explains this in detail, he still writes disparagingly of the "decades of confinement to subsistence communities." I will argue from my own research that these same decades gave Fijians the sense of proprietorship, loyalty, unity, and dignity that underpins the political games they now play with such poise and skill. The colonial period bequeathed Fijians not only real power but the self-confidence and grace to make nation-saving compromises between sectional interests and the need for a more just social order. There is a very dubious implication on p. 53 and elsewhere that a more rapid propulsion of village Fijians into dependence on the colonial economy and the elimination of "protectionist" legislation would have decreased inequalities as well as the opposition between races: it might also have eliminated Fijians as a political force in much the same way as the Melanesians have been reduced to impotence in New Caledonia.

There are one or two irritating errors such as a guide to the pronunciation of Fijian words that does not discriminate between voiced and unvoiced sounds, but nothing to mar the originality of the central argument and the importance of this book to students of race relations and Third World societies.

TIMOTHY J. MACNAUGHT
University of Hawaii
Honolulu

S. N. NWABARA. *Iboland: A Century of Contact with Britain 1860–1960.* Pp. 251. Atlantic Highlands, NJ: Humanities Press, 1978. $11.00 (paper).

VICTOR AZARYA. *Aristocrats Facing Change: The Fulbe in Guinea, Nigeria, and Cameroon.* Pp. xvi, 293. Chicago: University of Chicago Press, 1978. $19.00.

These works both are excellent examples of the ongoing revolution in African studies which has seen a marked shift in the last two decades from a predominantly Eurocentric perspective to one in which Africans figure as the most prominent human factor in shaping the continent's destiny. Indicative of this is the fact that the authors both strive, and for the most part with success, to utilize methodologies which enable them to delve beneath the veneer of colonialism in order to gain a real appreciation of how two West African peoples have reacted to the changes wrought by European overrule and, more recently, political independence and nationalism. Nwabara's sources, to be sure, are those traditionally used by imperial historians (manuscript materials from the colonial secretariat and the Public Record Office —not "Records Office" as Nwabara lists it—together with Blue Books, other official reports, and printed sources of predominantly European origin), but he utilizes these to delineate the Ibo side of interaction with their colonial rulers. He also makes some use, particularly for the period 1930 to 1960, of oral data. Azarya, however, relies much more extensively on oral information in presenting a sociological perspective on Fulbe reaction to ongoing political change.

The basic thrust of *Iboland* is an examination of the respective roles that religion, commerce, and colonial rule played in shaping attitudinal interchange and reaction between Ibo and Briton. Nwabara opens with the initial British attempts to create a formal political presence in the region and closes with the onset of independence as what Harold Macmillan called the "winds of change" swept Africa. Considerable attention is devoted to the missionary presence and their impact in areas such as education, cultural development, and what might well be styled (although the author chooses not to do so) the process of Europeanization. The more negative sides of the British presence such as military conflict—notably the Aba Revolt—imposition of alien customs in the face of widespread opposition, and occasionally myopic administrative approaches also receive careful consideration. On the whole Nwabara's is a well-argued and tightly reasoned presentation; but at times, thanks in large measure to the limitations imposed by his sources, the process of interaction weighs rather heavily towards the British side of the picture. Another shortcoming, this one glaring in nature, is the failure to provide an index. Such points aside, this is a work of substantial scholarship which adds appreciably to our understanding of one segment of the European impact on Africa.

Azarya's study covers much the same period as *Iboland*, and at first glance the approach he adopts might seem quite similar. However, *Aristocrats Facing Change* deals with the European presence only to the extent of its effect on the Fulbe, an important ruling group in wide areas of West Africa for roughly the last two centuries. The analysis is a comparative one which carefully documents Fulbe adjustment to various forces (both internal and external) as this ruling elite struggled to maintain their political preponderance. Regions of modern Guinea, Nigeria, and Cameroon are used for comparative analytical purposes, and the result is a balanced assessment of the relative importance of various factors involved in adjustment. His central thesis is that social change, far from being a determinant of internal adjustment capabilities, frequently is the product of outside influences over which the Fulbe (or by logical extension, others) exercised little control. This is a solid work of scholarship which, despite certain limitations imposed by overuse of sociological jargon, has important interdisciplinary ramifications. Specifically, it illustrates the need for greater cooperation and interchange of ideas between historians and sociologists of Africa, and it raises new concepts which are certain to stir further debate. Both works attest to the present vitality of African studies and are useful additions to our understanding of the West African past and the actuating elements which helped shape present realities in the region.

JAMES A. CASADA

Winthrop College
Rock Hill
South Carolina

WILLIAM L. PARISH and MARTIN KING WHYTE. *Village and Family in Contemporary China.* Pp. xiii, 419. Chicago: University of Chicago Press, 1978. $23.00.

Sociological and anthropological field studies of China, which had a promising future in the two decades before 1949, became ideological casualties of the Communist revolution. Eminent native scholars such as Fei Hsiao-t'ung found their work severely curtailed, while foreign researchers perforce devoted their attention to accessible Chinese communities in Hong Kong, Taiwan, and Southeast Asia. As of this writing, the situation remains essentially unchanged. Thus one of the major social transformations of contemporary history has had to be vicariously, and often precariously, documented from the periphery of the Chinese mainland. No study has done this better than the present work, which, although confined to data from one province, is perhaps the most iconoclastic analysis of modern rural China yet to appear in print.

Parish and White employ systematic interviews with their Hong Kong informants, former residents of a selected sampling of sixty-three villages in adjacent Kwangtung province, to construct a multifaceted portrait of the South Chinese countryside over the period 1969–1974. Concentrating on obvious but fundamental issues—which aspects of pre-1949 village and family life have been altered and which have not, what factors promote or oppose change, and why change occurs in some villages but not others—the authors delineate a rural society strikingly at variance with both Maoist egalitarian dreams and Orwellian conformist nightmares. Kwangtung peasants appear as neither stereotyped "new socialist men" nor "ardent Confucianists," but as shrewdly "flexible, family-oriented individuals" effectively coping with unique sets of local problems and opportunities. In a word, they are humanized.

The value of this book is apparent even in a cursory listing of its principal findings. Collectivization of agriculture has not leveled economic inequalities between city and countryside, or disparities among villages and families. While state health, education, and welfare programs have redistributed rural resources more equitably, primary reliance upon kin and neighbors for social services is still essential (the more so because collectivization has reinforced rather than diminished village solidarity). Peasants still maintain stem families and prefer male offspring, though mass birth control campaigns have won qualified acceptance. Marriages continue to be arranged and divorces are rare, but obtaining a bride is more costly than before the revolution, since a potential wife's labor will now constitute a greater share of family income.

Traditional relationships between spouses and child rearing practices have not been substantially modified, and women's liberation as known in the West largely remains empty talk. Although ritual specialists have been suppressed, the celebration of weddings, funerals, and hoary annual festivals such as the New Year far overshadows official holidays in significance. The authors' most provocative general conclusion is that the social ties of Kwangtung villagers have narrowed rather than widened since the 1950's. Rural communities have become more autarchic, endogamous, and cohesive because of, rather than despite China's socialist metamorphosis of the past quarter-century.

ROBERT P. GARDELLA
United States Merchant Marine
  Academy
Kings Point
New York

ALFRED STEPAN. *The State and Society: Peru in Comparative Perspective.* Pp. xix, 348. Princeton, NJ: Princeton University Press, 1978. $18.50. Paperbound, $4.95.

Primarily a work in political philosophy, this also is a valuable study in comparative politics, as well as in recent Latin American history. Crammed with ideas, extensively documented, dispassionate, it likely will play a significant role in stimulating reflection, analysis, and field research.

The objective is twofold: to help understand certain political processes in Latin America; and, as an aid to that end, to "demonstrate the viability" of a type of analysis that, it is believed, considering the present stage of comparative politics offers "the greatest potential" for developing political theory and cumulative research (pp. 290–91).

Critically surveyed in the course of the analysis is an immense amount of pertinent literature; in fact, one finds here perhaps the most extensive sifting of publications on political processes in several Latin American countries to be found anywhere. Appended is a 22-page bibliography, principally in English, to a considerable extent in Spanish, occasionally in Portuguese or French, including monographs, books, articles, dissertations and other unpublished manuscripts, government or other public and private reports. To these sources were added, during four trips to Peru between 1972 and 1976, direct observation and interviews with participants in the formulation and execution of government policies.

Finding limitations to the "classic-liberal" (or what the author sometimes also calls the "liberal-pluralist") approach to political theory, as well as limitations to the "classic Marxist" approach, in that neither gives adequate consideration to the impact of state policies and structures on the social system in an era when the role of the state clearly has been expanding worldwide for many years, the author compares and contrasts these two approaches with "an important but neglected" one which he calls "organic-statist," the consideration of which is imperative, it is insisted, when analyzing the action of any regime in Latin America.

By elaborating this and other concepts, an analytical framework is built up in Part I to use when comparing attempts in Latin America to set up and "institutionalize" new regimes. In Part II attention is then focused on Peru, since the action of the political elite that took power there in 1968 approximates the organic-statist model by reason of its leaders' conception of "a participatory, solidaristic society," with a "state-forged

yet decentralized economy" in which self-managing groups were to play an important part (p. 230); since also Phase I of this regime's action, or up until about the mid-1970s, along with the reforms launched by the Cardenas government in Mexico, the first Peronist government in Argentina and "perhaps one or two other(s)," represent "the more important reformist, incorporating periods in modern Latin American history" (p. 291); and since, finally, an analysis of the initial successes and subsequent failures of this attempt will help provide "empirical and theoretical rigor to key concepts concerning the capacities and limits of the modern state" (p. xiv).

Thus, questions are raised regarding the ways in which this Peruvian strategic elite employed inclusionary policies to integrate into the new political order the "weakly organized," like urban squatters (ch. 5); the "strongly organized," like working-class and upper-class groups, and the sugar, petroleum, and manufacturing industries (ch. 6), plus the local activities of multinational firms (ch. 7). Why, although firmly established initially, did this organic-statist regime subsequently failed to "institutionalize itself?" What hypotheses are particularly useful for predicting success or failure by way of either inclusionary (as in this case) or exclusionary policies; and in what ways, as revealed by this Peruvian case, is the organic-statist model a fruitful or deficient tool.

In addition to Peru, considerable empirical evidence to support the analysis is mobilized from Mexico, Brazil, Argentina, Chile, and, more briefly, Bolivia, Ecuador, Colombia, Venezuela, Spain, Portugal, and Italy.

For the general reader the addition of a glossary of concepts not generally known, or defined only by inference when first employed, would have been helpful. It is obvious that not everything can be included in any account. However, it is noted that four sets of forces create, maintain, or alter the character of the political world; namely, the ecological, economic, political and cultural. The approximation to reality, therefore, in any account like this—as well as the permanence of impact of any political regime over the long run—depends upon the degree to which all four sets of forces are integrated into an organic whole. This undoubtedly perceptive account deals almost (but not quite) exclusively with only two: the political (predominantly) and the economic. In a real world both sets are influenced, and to some extent even circumscribed, by the ecological and, far more than is often realized, by the cultural as well.

DONALD PIERSON

Leesburg
Florida

EUROPE

DAVID IRVING. *The War Path: Hitler's Germany 1933–1939.* Pp. xvii, 301. New York: Viking Press, 1978. $14.95.

JAMES P. O'DONNELL. *The Bunker: The History of the Reich Chancellery Group.* Pp. 399. New York: Viking Press, 1978, $13.95.

The subjects of these volumes are the polar periods in the history of Nazism. Irving deals with the days of triumph: the achievement by Hitler of supreme leadership in Germany and of a dominant position in European politics which enabled him to annex Austria and incorporate Czechoslovakia into the Reich. At the other pole, O'Donnell deals with the last phases of the collapse of Hitler's plan to build a thousand year Reich by conquering and enslaving the rest of Europe, and with his end, by suicide, in a bomb shelter.

The War Path is a detailed account of the planning, intrigues and manipulation that enabled Hitler to get the upper hand in dealing with his reluctant generals, and the inept diplomacy of the Western Powers. The book leaves no doubt that Hitler bears the sole responsibility for instigating the attack on Poland and planning the conquest of France and Russia. His chief military and political advisers dared not interfere with his decisions and, although apprehensive about the outcome, stood by him obediently and supportively. The ambivalent atti-

tude of his entourage is epitomized by von Ribbentrop's reaction when Hitler surprised his foreign minister with the announcement that he had that morning decided to order the march on Poland. The shaken Ribbentrop replied: "I wish *you* luck, my Fuehrer" (emphasis mine). Neither he nor the generals raised any objections when Hitler in arrogant self-assurance promised, "I will see to it that this Polish conflict will never, never, never result in a European war." Two other revealing anecdotes woven into Irving's absorbing narrative are worth singling out in this connection. After one of his successful diplomatic coups, an exuberant Hitler exclaimed to his secretaries: "I will go down (in history) as the greatest German of all time." And in a conversation with Walther Hewel, an ambassador on his staff, he confided that "as a private person I would never break my word, but if it is necessary for Germany—then a thousand times." These traits of Hitler, his egomania and his capacity for perfidy were the chief props of the legend which surrounded him and effectively blocked any opposition to his will.

The War Path is well written and offers new and valuable material. It is a worthy and welcome companion to Irving's previous venture into the history of Nazism, his book on *Hitler's War*: 1939–1945. In the course of his extensive researches in preparation for this volume, Irving has accumulated a vast assortment of records. The material he used for the scholarly documentation of his narrative is now on deposit in the Irving Collection of the Institute of Contemporary History in Munich.

O'Donnell, like Irving a journalist cum historian, also has done extensive research and assembled a vast amount of first-hand material to provide a comprehensive and detailed account of the final days of Hitler's life. The events and circumstances connected with this tragedy have been previously discussed by Trevor-Roper in his accurate story of the *Last Days of Hitler* (Oxford, 1947). The story was incomplete, however, because Trevor-Roper was unable to interview several hundred eye-witnesses who were with Hitler in the bunker; they were at the time imprisoned in Russia. O'Donnell spent five years locating and interviewing about one hundred and fifty of the survivors of the debacle. They proved to be a rich source of information and he was then enabled to provide a virtual day by day account of events in the bunker and the physical and mental states of its inhabitants. Among his chief informants were SS Major-General Wilhelm Mohnke, the bunker troop commandant; Dr. Ernst Schenk, in charge of the bunker hospital, the switchboard operators, and the valet, Sergeant Rochus Misch.

Historically, the most valuable part is the little known story of the break out of the men and women who did not follow Hitler in committing suicide, as did Goebbels, ambassador Hewel, General Krebs, and a few others. Of interest are also the numerous accounts of Hitler's conversations with various members of his staff. There is, for example, this startling pronouncement of Hitler when General Mohnke reported to him that his troops defending the perimeter of the bunker could not hold out for more than one more day. This was April 30, a few hours before Hitler shot himself. Hitler replied to Mohnke: "Too bad really. I have sincerely hoped to make it until May fifth. Beyond that date, I have no desire to live. . . . May fifth was the day Napoleon died on St. Helena—another great career that ended in total disappointment, disillusion, betrayal and despair."

On Hitler's mental state in these last days, Dr. Schenk recollects an illuminating report made to him by ambassador Hewel, who was with Hitler every day and almost every night. When Dr. Schenk asked the ambassador if Hitler had become insane, Hewel replied: "Never to my knowledge. Long fits of silence, yes. Volcanic explosions, yes. Hitler was a consummate actor, not a rug-chewer . . . Hitler became more morbidly suspicious than ever, more erratic, more murderously vindictive. Toward the end he was less the leader than a man flinching from reality, the blithely ignored, the chaotic destruction, may even have reveled in it; for at times he would discuss it or a

trifling episode in his great mission . . . During our final talks, he shrilly insisted that the war had been forced on him by Bolshevism, international Jewry and Anglo-Saxon plutocracy. . . . At the end he had lost all confidence in his old clique and in the last days he wanted to hang his generals. As I look back at those long briefing sessions, it strikes me that Hitler was hopelessly engulfed in the grandeur of his mission, a sense that was not disintegrating into self-pity. When the Goddess Nemesis began to avenge his hubris, he lost his nerve."

Neither Irving's nor O'Donnell's book is analytical oriented. They therefore contribute little to a better understanding of the Nazi period. However, they do provide new and illuminating anecdotal material and historically valuable data which are genuine contributions to the literature on the Nazi period.

Theodore Abel
University of New Mexico
Albuquerque

William A. Jenks. *Francis Joseph and the Italians, 1849–1859.* Pp. 206. Charlottesville, VA: The University Press of Virginia, 1978. $12.95.

In the decade between 1849 and 1859 the Habsburg Monarchy was increasingly hard pressed to maintain its power and influence in Italy. In particular, the growing movements for constitutionalism and nationalism challenged the monarchy's legal position in the north and its dynastic and political interests throughout the peninsula. This challenge is the subject of a new study by William Jenks, whose narrative suggests that by 1859 the Austrians had been defeated by a combination of mistaken policies, their own ineptitude, Piedmontese *Realpolitik*, and French and Russian revisionism. Jenks misses the high drama of this conflict between two competing sets of political and moral values, but his narrative has the virtue of avoiding the characteristic partisanship of much writing on Italian unification. His title does, however, raise false expectations, Francis Joseph is only one of the book's several Austrian protagonists, while the only Italians to earn the author's sustained interest are rulers, governmental officials, and diplomats. Nevertheless, Jenks has written a useful book that rescues the Habsburg Monarchy's Italian policy from the secondary role to which most English-language accounts of the Risorgimento have relegated it.

Jenks focuses attention upon Austrian administration of the Kingdom of Lombardy-Venetia and upon Vienna's relations with each of the governments of the Italian peninsula. From his discussion, at least two major themes emerge. The first concerns the decisive role played by the Crimean War in the history of Italian unification. Jenks is hardly the first historian to show how the Crimean War isolated the Habsburgs diplomatically and provided Piedmont with favorable conditions for a policy of territorial aggrandizement, yet by drawing upon published and unpublished primary sources he succeeds in shedding new light on the desperate international situation into which the Habsburgs maneuvered themselves during the 1850s.

Jenks' second theme concerns the degree to which the Austrians pursued policies that actually undermined the position in Italy they were determined to uphold. By enforcing political absolutism and administrative centralism throughout the empire, for example, Francis Joseph and his advisors lost whatever chance they might have had of gaining the allegiance of the Lombard and Venetian upper classes. Furthermore, the military and diplomatic support given the various conservative courts of Italy only caused the monarchy to share in the opprobrium heaped upon the Pope and the rulers of Naples, Modena, Parma, and Tuscany by liberals in Italy and abroad. It could, of course, be argued that a financial strong and ably led Austria might still have maintained itself in Italy despite diplomatic isolation, hostile European opinion, and Piedmontese provocation. Jenks demonstrates, however, that the Habsburgs lacked both the financial strength and the wise leadership necessary to sustain the status quo. While Jenks does not deny the real achievement of the Piedmontese under Count Cavour's leadership in driving the Austrians from Lombardy in 1859, his discussion helps place that accomplishment in perspective.

Because of the good sense Jenks brings to his topic, it is unfortunate that he has not given greater care to the preparation of his manuscript. It is unfair to blame him for his publisher's disturbingly inaccurate promotional summary of his book, but it is the author who must bear responsibility for a prose style deficient in topical and transitional sentences. Student readers will wish for better guidance through a wealth of factual information. Professional historians, on the other hand, will regret that Jenks has not taken the history of Austria's Italian policy through to the loss of Venetia in 1866; the narrative trails off unconvincingly after Austria's defeat at Solferino in June 1859. Within the chronological limits Jenks sets for himself, moreover, inadequate attention is given such important topics as the ties that existed between Italian and Magyar nationalism and the degree to which Austro-Prussian rivalry in Germany aided the cause of Italian unification. Finally, the bibliography fails to mention such titles as Charles Hallberg's *Franz Joseph and Napoleon III*, Augusto Sandonà's *Il Regno Lombardo-Veneto 1814–1859*, and Hans Kramer's *Österreich und das Risorgimento*. Their omission leads to the conclusion that Jenks has not sought to write the definitive work he could have written on his topic.

RONALD E. COONS
The University of Connecticut
Storrs

JOHN R. LOW-BEER. *Protest and Participation: The New Working Class in Italy.* Pp. xviii, 285. New York: Cambridge University Press, 1978.

Among the various forms taken by the political euphoria of the late sixties and early seventies was the notion that a new historic agent of the socialist revolution had emerged: "the new working class." French activist theorists, such as Serge Mallet and André Gorz, argued that technological and organizational changes in advanced sectors of capitalist economies had brought into existence a new worker vanguard comprised of engineers and highly skilled technical workers. The stake of these workers in professional autonomy and in an unrestricted development of technology was presumed to clash with the criterion of profitability governing the use and development of productive forces under capitalism. The new working class interest in greater and greater worker control over the work process would eventually blossom into a movement for the overall transformation of society in the direction of participatory socialism.

Whereas the writings of Gorz and Mallet took the plant or an entire industry as their unit of analysis, John Low-Beer has sought to examine the question of the revolutionary potential of the new working class through an indepth analysis of the attitudes of individual Italian workers. His sample includes a group of eighty-eight technical workers from the Milan area, interviewed in 1970–71 during the "hot" years of Italian labor struggles. In order to test a variety of hypotheses about the relationship between work place organization, on the one hand, and labor militancy and general political attitudes, on the other, Low-Beer divided his sample between two different factories: one organized along hierarchical and centralized lines, the other along lines which gave greater leeway for worker autonomy and participation in the structuring of the work process.

In support of the new working class thesis, he found that the dissatisfaction of workers with their firm was related to the congruence between the nature of their work and the organizational framework within which the work was carried out: dissatisfaction was high where the work was involving and perceived in positive terms but the supervision was close and little or no attempt was made to enlist the participation of workers in the structuring of the work process. On the other hand, Low-Beer's findings also support the position of those theorists, such as Goldthorpe and Lockwood, who reject any notion of a "technological determinism" governing worker behavior, and instead insist on the importance of orientations derived from conditions outside the immediate place of work. Low-Beer found, for example, that strike participation and labor militancy in general were more closely correlated with the inheritance of a working-class political culture hostile to the "bosses" than with discontent with the organization of the firm. Similarly, Low-Beer's Italian workers had a greater propensity than Goldthorpe and Lockwood's English counterparts to view class relations in power terms and to identify themselves as members of the "working class" rather than as members of the "middle class." This difference was related to political attitudes and solidaristic aspirations for mobility which originated outside of the work place.

John Low-Beer demonstrates an admirable mastery of the literature in the area of the sociology of work. Unfortunately, he has attempted to tackle an epochal question (the revolutionary potential of the new working class) with methods which raise doubts about the generality of his findings beyond the narrow numerical, temporal, and geographic confines of the study. He himself is aware of the problem, especially in discussing some of the discrepancies between his findings and those of similar studies done at different times and different places. The study is further dated by the fact that debate over the new working class (qua revolutionary vanguard) has faded away in Europe as capital has reasserted its prerogatives. More to the point these days is the question whether a class with a revolutionary vocation will ever match up with a revolutionary situation.

LARRY GARNER
DePaul University
Chicago

WILLIAM O. MCCAGG, Jr. *Stalin Embattled 1943–1948*. Pp. 423. Detroit, MI: Wayne State University Press, 1978. $18.95.

A quarter of a century has passed since the death of Stalin. Soviet society and contemporary international relations are still influenced by his legacy, although the judgment of his brutal regime is still unresolved. In the Western world, we have seen the rise of Stalinology, insep- arable from Kreminology. In the USSR, amid the silence of official history, the Soviet citizens can appreciate his impor- tance only by finding clues in the party's changing views and policies. But in the western countries we have been flooded with numerous works whose number has been surpassed only by those about an- other dictator—Hitler.

McCagg's survey of Stalin's foreign policy and the politics of communism in the postwar years is probably the best one available to us today. Its massive citation of numerous sources in various languages in "Notes" (pp. 331–404) is really overwhelming; and the same praise can be heaped upon the extensive "Selected Bibliography" (pp. 317–321), "General Sources" (pp. 319–320), "The Radio and the Press" (pp. 320–321), and "Documentary Collections and Official Histories" (p. 321). Especially valuable is McCagg's use of a mass of fascinating archival work by Soviet, Czechoslovak, Hungarian, Polish, and Yugoslav his- torians; recent studies of American and British policy; and the public documents of the Soviet, European, and Asian Com- munist parties.

Applying modern research methods to the study of communism in the 1943– 1948 period, McCagg propounds that Stalin, who was a Marxist-Leninist, sensed the potential for insurrection at the end of the war and recognized that revolutionaries might attack his imperi- alist allies. Accordingly, from 1944 through the confrontation with Tito in 1948, Stalin did everything in his power to in- hibit revolutionary activity abroad which he could not directly control. Stalin's for- eign policy after the war opposed the containment policies pursued by the Western Powers. During 1945 his will- ingness to encourage the peaceful spread of revolution abroad enabled the Soviet Communist Party to resume moral lead- ership on the domestic political scene, subtly and unexpectedly usurping his authority. To meet this challenge, and to dissolve the expectations that the vic- tory had aroused, Stalin resorted to for-

eign policy probings of Western solidar- ity which have confused all historians of the era. (McCagg, interestingly enough, challenges the Cold War notion that his trouble with Tito and Mao Tse-tung in 1945 was atypical and that at home, in the Kremlin, his control was complete).

At no point does the author lose his grasp of the details involved in his theme. The result is a serious and impor- tant book which is also quite fascinating.

JOSEPH S. ROUCEK
City University of New York

WILLIAM L. MILLER. *Electoral Dy- namics in Britain Since 1918.* Pp. xiv, 242. New York: St. Martin's Press, 1978. $18.95.

GRAHAM WOOTTON. *Pressure Policitcs in Contemporary Britain.* Pp. 256. Lexington, MA Lexington Books, 1978. $19.95.

Very often voting behavior is the sub- ject of detailed short-term studies con- centrating on the events and outcome of individual elections. This is notably so in the area of British electoral politics, where the Nuffield series dealing with general elections since 1945 provides an invaluable historical source on cam- paigns, issues, and results. One excep- tion to this approach is *Political Change in Britain* by Butler and Stokes, origi- nally published in 1969, which intro- duced the student of British politics to the prospect of cycles of party strength and the complexity of factors of social change in determining partisan commit- ment.

William Miller's new book is welcome for two reasons. It breaks new ground in elaborating further a systematic and long-term approach to electoral behav- ior, reanalysing the survey data used by Butler and Stokes as well as drawing on much new census material; also, it gives attention to the need for a sophisticated level of differentiation between a wide range of voting determinants, and thereby focuses on some factors which have gen- erally been regarded as negligible.

As Miller himself notes, the angle of his study is deliberately narrow in that he chooses to concentrate on examining "the social patterns in constituency voting and relate them to the appeals parties made to the electorates of different kinds." The reason for this choice relates directly to the British form of electoral system; the major hypothesis of this study is that "how people voted depended significantly more on where they lived than on their occupations" (p. xiii). Miller looks closely at environmental effects within constituencies, drawing similar conclusions to those presented by Putnam on American voting. The results of this section offer some interesting insights into the different pressures operating in favor of political consensus according to the social structures of constituencies as well as a range of different issues. Of the many indicators selected, one of the more novel is religion, where the author finds that although political parties have avoided exploiting this during the past 60 years (in England), it has nevertheless helped to condition reactions to the three main parties.

The only major reservation about this useful work concerns style and presentation. While based on extensive computerized data, it rests content with presenting the results in a technical form which is likely to inhibit the nonspecialist reader. Only too rarely does the author spell out his findings in interpretative and conceptual language. More of this would have enhanced the cohesion of the study.

Wootton's examination of pressure group politics in Britain is a less distinguished work. It is a very detailed survey of a vast range of pressure groups without any serious attempt to categorize or evaluate their real importance. At the beginning Wootton mentions his typology briefly and eventually returns to it at the end; but it is not a helpful one and in any case is forgotten throughout the book itself. The aim of this study seems to be to cover as many possible cases of pressure group activity, instead of concentrating in depth on selected representative examples, but the end result is inadequate. Invariably, discussion is restricted to a blow-by-blow account of parliamentary mechanics, and

the social forces which might impel pressure groups are generally ignored. The author's last chapter speculating on possible trends towards a corporate-state situation in Britain is the only occasion when he frees himself from his material, but altogether this book does not make any significant contribution to the literature already available on the subject.

GEOFFREY PRIDHAM

University of Bristol
England

N. EDWINA MORETON. *East Germany and the Warsaw Alliance: The Politics of Deténte.* Pp. xv, 267. Boulder, CO: Westview Press, 1979. $18.00.

Just before the Prussian-Danish War of 1864 Lord Palmerston described the complicated problem of Schleswig-Holstein in an acerbic conclusion: "Only three men have ever understood it. One was Prince Albert, who is dead. The second was a German professor, who became mad. I am the third, and I have forgotten all about it."

Were Lord Palmerston alive today, he would in all probability be equally as fascinated with the triple current German problem of East Germany, West Germany, and Berlin. This post-World War II problem is suffused with ambiguity and confusion and it desperately needs clarification. Anything which helps to explain it is welcome to historians and political scientists.

The author of the present study teaches Soviet Politics and Foreign Policy and Comparative Communism at the University College of Wales. Specializing in German and Soviet security problems, she worked on this study at the Center for International Studies, Massachusetts Institute of Technology, as a Harkness Fellow of the Commonwealth Fund of New York.

This is a valiant attempt to throw light on the intertwining politics of East Germany, West Germany, the Soviet Union, and the Warsaw Alliance. Dr. Moreton is dissatisfied with the almost universal acceptance by Western historians that East Germany has been a "pliant Soviet satellite" and that its leader until 1971,

Walther Ulbricht, was a colorless, malleable *apparatchik*. Prior to the invasion of Czechoslovakia, this assessment of East Germany, she says, was almost universally accepted, explicitly in the West, tacitly even in the East. She opposes the presumption that East Germany, and also Eastern Europe in general, were too closely bound to the Soviet policy for any meaningful differentiation of policy preferences. She sets her goal: "There have been numerous analyses of the German problem in the Western sense but only recently has attention been directed toward its implications for East Germany and the possible repercussions within Eastern Europe. This study will hopefully redress this imbalance."

With this aim in mind, the author examines the role and influence of the GDR in Eastern Europe, emphasizing the changing nature of the German problem and the impact of East Germany on the pattern of relations with the Warsaw alliance from 1967 to the present. After treating the origins and development of the German problem, she analyzes the differing responses of the Warsaw pact states to successive West German initiatives toward the Soviet Union, the relationship between the GDR and Eastern Europe, the Grand Coalition Government of 1966–1969, Willy Brandt's new Ostpolitik in 1969–1972, and the post-Ostpolitik era.

The author also treats the relative strength and weaknesses of the East German position in the Warsaw Alliance, the role of Ulbricht in the Czechoslovak crisis in 1968, the relationship of East Germany to the Soviet Union, and the transfer of power in East Germany from Ulbricht to Honecker.

What emerges is a brilliant tour de force, a painstaking examination of the shifting relationships in a critical European area. The scholarship is commendable and deserves praise. The writing style is clear-cut and to the point.

Yet the reader is left with a curious sense of dissatisfaction. In her zealous search for the details of policy change, Dr. Moreton loses sight of the one overwhelming fact in the East German-Soviet Union relationship. East Ger-

many remains Moscow's buffer state against the West and the Russians have no more intention of allowing that situation to change than they have of releasing Rudolf Hess from Spandau. East Germany has not gone the way of Yugoslavia in 1948 and Albania in 1961. The author admits that East German-Soviet relations have been and remain "remarkably close." That does not quite tell the story of Moscow's hegemony and domination.

LOUIS L. SNYDER
City University of New York

PETER H. SOLOMON, JR. *Soviet Criminologists Policy.* Pp. x, 253, New York: Columbia University Press, 1978. $15.00.

This work is a concise scientific text and an abridged reference aid on Soviet criminologists and criminal policy with emphasis on the Stalin (1928–1953) and Khrushchev (1956–1964) periods. Much of the research for this book was conducted in the USSR during 1968–1969, followed by a short research trip to Moscow in the spring of 1974.

Based in part upon firsthand interviews with Soviet scholars and upon materials available only in the USSR, Peter Solomon analyzes a series of decisions on such issues as alcoholism, crime, and the prevention of juvenile delinquency. However, the most valuable contribution in this work is to be found in the sections dealing with parole and recidivism.

Parole (conditional early release) was introduced into Soviet criminal law in 1954, then "consolidated and expanded" in the 1958 Fundamental Principles of Criminal Legislation. The only condition attached to parole was that the commission of a new crime of the same seriousness as the original one would send the parolee back to confinement to complete the original term as well as his new sentence. "Specially dangerous" recidivists were excluded entirely from parole privileges.

The result was that during 1961 and 1962 two other categories of offender were excluded from parole eligibility—

persons who violated the parole conditions and persons guilty of a short list of the most serious crimes (p. 91). It was also discovered that during the years 1962–1965 almost half of all offenders in confinement had been released on parole. During the Stalin regime (the 1940s) there was no parole at all.

A careful examination, based on this work, of the participation of Soviet criminal law scholars in the parole and recidivism decisions leads us to the conclusion that it was of good quality. However, no mention is made of the criminologists who were forced to pay "homage" to Stalin in their works in order to emerge unscathed. Are those contributions included in this book or are they still in vogue?

This reviewer was also surprised at the absence of any reference in this work to Dostoyevsky and Solzhenitsyn. Fyodor Dostoyevsky, who was a Russian version of a recidivist and a parolee, published his book *Memoirs from a Dead House* a century ago (1861–62), shortly after his return from Siberia—a book which, as a fictionalized chronicle of his experiences under the frightful regime of the Siberian prison camp, was received with loud acclaim even by Lev Tolstoy. The Siberian ordeal—a time of living burial —served to aggravate an epileptic condition from which Dostoyevsky suffered for the rest of his life, and which he described vividly in *The Idiot* (1869).

Alexander Solzhenitsyn's *One Day in the Life of Ivan Denisovich* first appeared in the Soviet periodical *Novyi Mir* in November 1962. This novel, the publication of which was authorized by Khrushchev in person, was an immediate literary and political sensation. It revealed the predicament of a simple Red Army soldier who escaped from the Germans only to find himself falsely accused of high treason and incarcerated in one of Stalin's notorious slave-labor camps.

I heartily recommend this work especially to any graduate student in the Russian field.

IVAR SPECTOR
University of Washington
Seattle

UNITED STATES

RICHARD CARWARDINE. *Trans-atlantic Revivalism: Popular Evangelicalism in Britain and America, 1790–1865.* Pp. xviii, 248. Westport, CT: Greenwood Press, 1978. $18.95.

An outgrowth of his doctoral thesis, *American Religious Revivalism in Great Britain, c. 1826–1863*, Richard Carwardine's *Trans-atlantic Revivalism* has been thoroughly researched on both sides of the Atlantic. It explores the powerful and intricate interrelationship of revivalists in Britain and America, pointing out with particular clarity the development of the evangelical movement in the United States and the effect of American evangelical leaders on the development of the British revivalist movement.

Focusing on the material on the American evangelists in terms of their effect specifically in England, Wales, and Scotland, the author illustrates the influence of outstanding American revivalist leaders, such as Charles G. Finney, Edward N. Kirk, and the Irish born American, James Caughey, first in the United States and later in Britain. Where many ministers of an evangelical turn of mind came originally from Britain to the United States in the late eighteenth and early nineteenth century, by the 1830's the power of American revivalism was reaching from its original frontier habitat, first to the American urban scene, and then abroad to Britain. Carwardine points out the significant difference of approach in the areas affected by revivals.

To handle the complexity and scope of material at his command, the author necessarily faces the almost insuperable task of presenting a consistent view, reasonably free of generalizations. While he is for the most part successful, there are occasional difficulties. For instance, he points out that in adapting to urban needs, revivalists were faced with a foreign and a highly mobile population which required a more agressive approach than had been necessary on the frontier. A few pages later the reader is reminded of the need of city revivals to tone down their approach in order to attract the respectable middle class. Again, John Kirk is described as a radical who "attacked church establishments, denounced the Corn Laws and American slavery, and suffered for his undeviating teetotalism." Following is the statement that "Fergus Ferguson, Sr. and Henry Wight were of a similar liberal mold." No doubt the label of "liberal" is quite clear within this context, but one might wish for a construct more suited to the present connotation of the conceptual meaning of terms used.

On the whole, the book presents a thought-provoking analysis of the waves of revivalism that swept America and Britain in the first sixty-five years of the nineteenth century. The history of individuals is well documented and the transcultural effects are carefully explored. The volume should prove useful to students of nineteenth century Anglo-American church history and should be equally of note to those readers whose interests lie in the field of American Civilization and/or Anglo-American relations during this period. An excellent bibliography, clearly presented graphs illustrating the numerical aspects of revivals, and several excellent photographs of evangelical leaders of the period are to be found in *Trans-atlantic Revivalism*.

DOROTHY RUDY
Montclair State College
Upper Montclair
New Jersey

DAVID CAUTE. *The Great Fear: The Anti-Communist Purge Under Truman and Eisenhower*. Pp. 697. New York: Simon and Schuster, 1978. $14.95.

In 1973 David Caute (almost the stereotype of the British intellectual, including intolerance for the ways of the American colonials) published *The Fellow Travellers*, an account of "me-too communists," that is, persons who in nine times out of ten decline to join the local Party. He then observed, "During the years 1928–56 some of the most distinguished writers, philosophers, critics, scientists and publicists of the West became communists or fellow-travellers."

In the present book the focus is intended to be on the "purge" under two American presidents (see title). In this respect the effort is a failure, for neither presidential library was even visited and neither president is linked with much evidence to the hated crusade. But there has been a dedicated and successful effort to expose the foibles, crudities, and outright failures of due process in the nation during the years when we had the atomic and hydrogen weapons and the Soviets sought both. We must grant that the land of Jefferson, Hamilton, and Madison chased and hounded apparent communists with sometimes fiendish excess. Of course, there is the caveat that we sought to guarantee our security as a nation against spies; and the overwhelming majority completely agreed that we wanted no part of a dictatorship of the proletariat here in America.

Caute has presented us an appendix, a 46 page index, and a name-filled text with a truly astonishing who's who of American communists and fellow travellers. Not since I reviewed Max Kampelman's *The Communist Party vs. the C.I.O.* has this observer been so convinced that the effort to subvert our media, unions, professions, and civil service was a deadly serious business —and that it had its successes. (Ergo, a bit more charity for the "witch hunters" is in order when we fulminate against "red scares" in our textbooks.)

A few numbers: from 1948 to 1955 the Army discharged 776 draftees as security risks; 1947–56 the federal government fired 2,700 risks and 12,000 persons resigned during or after investigation; 283 State Department personnel had to "pack their bags," 1945–46; by 1956 about 500 AEC scientists had been dismissed or denied clearance when applying for promotion; from the thirties to the fifties "some three hundred film directors, actors, writers and designers joined the CP."

Yes, Virginia, there were communists, and, yes, we laboriously and too often ineptly or even illegally or unconstitutionally uncovered and persecuted many. When passing judgment, however, we might bear in mind that even the always judgment-passing author does concede that we in the United States fell short of "a genuine head-bashing and blood-letting." Our concentration camps were only on paper. The purge "was not on the whole a killer;" the repression "never reached the frontiers of fascism." So: in an era when millions were tortured and died because of their political beliefs (Hungary, Czechoslovakia, Moscow) we behaved considerably less badly than some peoples—if the thought offers any comfort to those who so often express great personal or vicarious guilt over our "purge."

In this awful century, so full of incalculable misery and woe, the present reviewer is of the opinion that we should tone down somewhat the overkill of sympathy for the travails of those who knowingly or stupidly embraced Stalin-of-the-Gulag and sought to transplant the communism of the Comintern and the Cominform to the United States.

VAUGHN D. BORNET
Southern Oregon State College
Ashland

ROBERT M. GOOLRICK. *Public Policy Toward Corporate Growth: The ITT Merger Cases.* Pp. xii, 212. Port Washington, NY: Kennikat Press, 1978. $15.00.

Mr. Goolrick has written a Watergate thriller in the form of a tract on political economy. The assessment by John Tunney in the Foreward is apt: "He writes like a scholarly Agatha Christie as he unfolds the details of the machinations of all parties to the ITT drama." It is the ITT affair (=Watergate) which is the main concern of this work and the state's policy toward corporate concentration is a necessary backdrop for the discussion. Truth in advertising then points toward the transposition of the title and subtitle of the book.

The logic at work here is impeccable: the 'Dita Beard memorandum'—smacking of antitrust policy for sale—was a crucial factor in Nixon's precipitous presidential demise and, hence, for a better understanding of this phenomenon it is necessary to place the matter within the wider context of antitrust policy. In particular, how could the obviously pro-business Nixon administration find itself an adversary of ITT—a pillar of international capital concentration?

As a preliminary, the legal and economic basis of antitrust policy are explained. Of particular relevance on this score is the failure of orthodox economics to provide theoretical warrant for opposing the divergent form of corporate concentration known as the conglomerate. Accordingly, neither the Kennedy nor Johnson administrations filed suit against this type of merger activity, Yet, it was exactly this type of merger that was involved in the ITT affair. And the reason for prosecuting ITT is to be found in the strong-willed personage of Richard McClaren who served as Nixon's assistant attorney general in charge of antitrust. McClaren, a former corporate lawyer, set out to constrain the congomerate behemoth under the banner that big is bad, and the ITT mergers were convenient instances. Thus the reader is left with a mismanagement theory of Watergate; the ITT affair occurred because Nixon was unable to control his assistant attorney general. This is Nixon's own mismanagement theory on its head; Watergate was the result of his inability to prevent his staff from doing the right thing!

This book will certainly not be the last word on either the political economy of antitrust or the Watergate debacle. The lacunae are glaring. Moreover, the paucity of references is annoying at best. But the currency of the ITT affair as well as the author's 'mysterious' style breathes life into the too frequently dreary subject of antitrust.

ROBERT M. LARSEN
University of Utah
Salt Lake City

JOHN HOHENBERG. *A Crisis for the American Press.* Pp. xii, 316. New York: Columbia University Press, 1978. $14.95.

Mr. John Hohenberg is a long time journalist and has been Professor of

Journalism at several universities. He received the Pulitzer Prize Special Award for his services to journalism, and the dust jacket of this book makes the claim that this, his tenth book, is his most important. One hopes that this claim is erroneous.

The arguments of the book are simple: the American public is becoming disenchanted with the American press and is beginning to feel that the press needs some measure of control. At the same time, the character of the press is changing because family owned newspapers have by-and-large disappeared due to confiscatory inheritance taxes. In their place, most newspapers have become parts of giant chains or even conglomerates.

The reason the public has become disenchanted with the press is because the press is in an adversary relationship with government. The adversary relation with government is a role forced on the press by actions of the government over the last thirty years. In particular, the national government has used the plea of "national security" to hide a variety of misdeeds and the press has reluctantly been forced to ignore these claims to expose these governmental violations of the public interest. Big business is also anti-press. The government has begun to attack freedom of the press in a number of ways. For example, a number of investigations have been proposed by members of Congress as well as laws to regulate the press. So far, these have failed, but attacks by the courts have had some measure of success.

In particular, the courts are expanding the meaning of libel so the press must beware of what it prints. The courts have restricted what can be printed before a trial about a pending case, and the courts have ruled "community standards" apply to define what is pornographic, an obvious infringement of the rights of a free press. Moreover, the fact that terrorists have often successfully demanded that newspapers print their propaganda as a price of the lives of hostages has led to a public demand that terrorist acts not be published.

Mr. Hohenberg admits the press is not perfect and that some injustice some-times results from the act of the press, but essentially he argues any injustices committed by the press are less important than the potential harm to the public interest from regulation of the press.

The author writes well, as could be expected of a professional journalist. His account puts together a good summary of news and events that have been widely reported, statistics that may not be widely known, and occassional anecdotes and inside stories about the press. He uses no argument that John S. Mill didn't use in *On Liberty*, but his illustrations are very timely.

My real quarrel with Mr. Hohenberg is that this work is so parochial. For example, he decries the fact that newspaper ownership is becoming concentrated in the hands of a very few people. He fails to see and associate the process with the disappearance of the family farm or the family grocery store. The author does see that public perception of government, business, and many traditional institutions is much more negative today than in times past, but somehow this gets dismissed. Only the press is important.

One could also point out that much of the argument he makes could be placed in the context of society's rights vs. individual rights. For example, the court cases he cites are usually seen as upholding individual rights while the counter-argument of Mr. Hohenberg usually are supportive of society's rights.

In summary, there is little here of interest to social scientists though the subject merits treatment.

O. ZELLER ROBERTSON, JR.
Saginaw Valley State College
Michigan

STEPHEN D. KRASNER. *Defending the National Interest: Raw Materials Investments and U.S. Foreign Policy.* Pp. xiii, 404. Princeton, NJ: Princeton University Press, 1978. $20.00. Paperbound $5.95.

In contrast to Marxists and pluralists, who perceive United States foreign policy as the result of societal pressures, Krasner analyzes seventy years of American policy toward raw material investments abroad by focussing on the state as an autonomous entity which seeks to implement the national interest against resistance from other international and domestic actors.

In his empirical-inductive search for the United States national interest, Krasner looks at those acts and statements of the central decisionmakers (primarily the White House and the State Department) that aim to improve the general welfare and show persistent rank-ordering over time. What emerges from this study as the American national interest in the international commodity markets has three components, ranked here in order of increasing importance: (1) stimulating economic competition, (2) insuring security of supply, and (3) promoting broader foreign policy goals, such as general material interests and ideological objectives.

While weaker countries concentrate on preserving their territorial and political integrity and looking out for their economic interests, only nations with power to spare will try to remake the world in their own image. Since 1945 the United States has been in such a powerful position, and the key to its foreign policy was ideology—(anti-communist) Lockean liberalism. This policy was generally conducive to the growth of American-based multinational corporations, but it cannot be fully explained as "long-term preservation of capitalism." Krasner asks the Marxian "structuralists": What was to be gained for capitalism in Vietnam to warrant the social disruption that intervention caused at home? The author generalizes from his case studies that United States central decisionmakers were willing to use economic and diplomatic pressure to protect the interests of American corporations, but they reserved the use of force for ideological objectives. Not even the oil crisis of 1973/74, which threatened the energy supply of the entire capitalist world, prompted direct military action.

So far so good, but Krasner runs into difficulties when he presents his "statist paradigm" as superior to the liberal and Marxist alternatives. He relegates too readily such traditional concepts as "sov-

ereignty" and *raison d'état* to the logical-deductive approach of the "realist" school and explicitly denies a normative component of his empirically derived national interest (footnote 33, page 54). This reviewer finds it difficult to perceive the state's interest as qualitatively different from other interests without some normative criterion. Lacking such a distinction, however, Krasner's statist approach does not seem irreconcilable with Arthur Bentley's pluralist view that the state is "an interest group in itself."

KARL H. KAHRS
California State University
Fullerton

GARY ORFIELD. *Must We Bus? Segregated Schools and National Policy.* Pp. xiv, 470. Washington, DC: The Brookings Institution, 1978. $16.95.

Most Americans, if they think about the matter, probably believe that the school desegregation battles are behind us. On TV we see each fall a few demonstrations, last ditch stands against court ordered busing. Occasionally we read of a new court case initiated in a large urban area to end racial segregation.

There are some who, aware of the limited progress since *Brown* v. *Board of Education*, are nonetheless impressed with the achievements since 1954. Orfield's well-documented analysis shows that even the latter view is unjustified, especially if equal progress is anticipated in the future. The statistics do not warrant optimism.

For example: there are high levels of school segregation in large cities outside the southern and border states. And in most of these there are no desegregation plans and no litigation pending. Segregation is worsening in the northeast, at a standstill in the midwest, and lessening in the South. Blacks in the North actually have fewer white classmates typically than do blacks in the South. The core of the segregation problem is to be found in the older cities whose schools are surrounded by the populous school districts of the largely white suburbs. Most of the 33 states outside the southern and border states have, however, negligible or easily manageable problems of segregation.

School integration is no longer a matter of bringing together black and white children. The issue is becoming more intractable because of the rapidly increasing, often non-English speaking, Latino population. Hispanics are also divided on integration. Many wish it while others favor Latino schools with English as a second language. Fortunately the courts to date do not consider bilingual education to be a constitutional right.

The greatest hurdle in the desegregation struggle is, of course, attitudes prevailing among the public, politicians, and the courts. In short they say integration "yes," busing "no." But busing Orfield makes clear is the only feasible method to carry out desegregation. His conclusion derives from a thorough consideration of other aspects of this still urgent problem: the national versus the state role in desegregation; prospects for integrated housing, school finance, integration across district lines, and the politics of enforcement. This work is indispensable to any serious study of school desegregation.

JAMES R. BELL
California State University
Sacramento

NORMAN K. RISJORD. *Chesapeake Politics, 1781–1800.* Pp. ix, 715. New York: Columbia University Press, 1978. $27.50.

This engrossing and informative work is so good that readers may forget their suspicion that its title was intended to exploit the success of James Michener's novel. Professor Risjord, already highly regarded in the field, has crafted a remarkable history of partisan politics in those early years. He studied three states: Virginia and Maryland very closely and, less thoroughly, North Carolina— no Chesapeake state by either his definition or the dust jacket map. Also included are Kentucky and Tennessee, both before and after partition. Neither justifies the title, but both support the central theme.

The work focuses on state and local issues in the 1780s: debtor relief, paper money, judicial systems, and the like. While some readers may find some of these items obscure, they are important to our understanding of growing partisan politics in the Confederation era. Risjord lucidly depicts how these controversies were resolved and how they contributed to that growth. The 1790s array is better known: Hamilton's economic program, Federalist foreign policies, and the Alien and Sedition Acts, among others. Here, the camera pans back and forth from Congress to state governments, as Risjord skillfully demonstrates how these issues and the growing partisanship of this period mutually affected each other.

Throughout both decades, political parties increased in coherence and importance. By computer analysis of roll-call votes in Virginia and Maryland, Risjord shows that the process began before the Philadelphia Convention. Later, the parties solidified until by the mid-1790s party identification was the most important element in elections and in legislative voting. The author's cliometric proof of considerable correlation between the Antifederalists and the later Jeffersonians, and between the pro-Constitution party of 1787–88 and the Federalists of 1791–1800 is a significant contribution to the debate begun in 1913 by Charles Beard. Many will applaud finding that the new data supports the old Progressive.

Risjord anticipated that occasional tedium might be caused by so much data; and personal glimpses of the Founding Fathers provide relief. An elderly and partisan Washington is seen through a 1799 keyhole, in one poignant example, making political tests of officer candidates.

Lavishly documented from start to finish, the book is full of valuable conclusions and portraits. Its footnotes and bibliography themselves are arresting. No serious historian will be disappointed by this work, although many may have to wait for the paperback to afford it.

W. T. GENEROUS, JR.
Choate Rosemary Hall
Wallingford
Connecticut

MICHAEL SCHUDSON. *Discovering the News: A Social History of American*

Newspapers. Pp. 228. New York, Basic Books, 1978. $10.95.

Professor Schudson's book is the freshest approach to a rut-bound subject within my recollection. As a sociologist, he started out with the proposition that if there could be a history of ideas and a sociology of knowledge, then there could also be a history of ideals and a sociology of values. He fixed upon the origin and ramifications of objectivity in journalism, and broadened his quest by seeking an understanding of the interrelationships between journalism and the economic, political, social, and cultural influences of given periods. None of the other histories of journalism has attempted to find such interrelationships, certainly not at this depth.

Straight as a laser beam, he pursues his twin inquiries through three stages of New York City newspapering: the penny press, the 1880's (roughly), and the *World* vs. *Journal* thing alongside the Chattanooga-bred approach of Ochs' *New York Times*. This exclusive focus upon New York does not set well, for "A Social History of American Newspapers" must come from Kokoma, Keokuk, and Yakima as well as New York. It also is unsettling as a generalization from the unique, and is warped by the nonrecognition of other localities as the point of origin of techniques, procedures, assumptions, and ideals which then were placed in the big showcase of New York.

Small matter, for the book is a delight. It sparkles with ideas, from the naive to the exhilarating to the eyebrow-raising. He presents a continuous series of provocative explanations for the several changes in New York journalism. The explanations are speculative only in the sense that they generally are not demonstrable, but most are too sinewy to be brushed aside. His chapter on American (New York) journalism as a vocation after 1880 is an assay that enriches the literature by itself, while begging to be nationalized beyond the recollections of New York newspapermen. To add to the enjoyment, Professor Schudson is a literate sociologist. Never once does he

terrify the reader with an expression that has the sound of a rubber boot being sucked up out of six inches of mud.

Something seems to go wrong with his laser beam, though, when he analyzes the 1920s and 1930s as the seedbed of newspaper "objectivity." Sweeping in an armful of the contradictions of the 1920s, he seems to be saying that Walter Lippman is to be credited— or blamed—more than anyone else for rationalizing the concept of newspaper objectivity. It is a probing chapter but not immediately convincing.

His fifth and final chapter is an essay centered on the convulsions of the 1960s and the responses of the news media to them. Those troublous years may be too green of memory to permit a judicious historical appraisal, but the essay probably is the best-balanced overview that could be written as of now.

This book must be read by all who are interested in the history of journalism. Despite its shortcomings, we at least know that a keen, new mind has engaged the subject from an unexpected quarter. If his future work will carry the inquiry to a national level, he could be the person to show us the beauty of the whole forest, which none who has gone before him has even attempted.

OLIVER KNIGHT

The University of Texas
El Paso

TAD SZULC. *The Illusion of Peace: Foreign Policy in the Nixon Years.* Pp. vii, 822. New York: The Viking Press. 1978. $20.00.

This massive volume is a remarkable book. The author, one of our best known and most reputable journalists, evidently scorns, as journalists commonly do, all academic paraphernalia: there are no footnotes, no citations, no bibliography, no explanation of his sources. He does, in the Prologue, mention the various kinds of experiences and materials that are the basis for his "information and impressions" about the Nixon policies; this includes secret and confidential material, from which he quotes freely in the book, but which is not more exactly identified anywhere in the text. The reader is bound to wonder how Mr. Szulc got access to such documents not generally available and perhaps about the appropriateness of their use. Some quotations can, of course, be identified by the alert reader because of proximity to an event or for other obvious reasons, but in general the reader is compelled to rely on the journalist's word for the authenticity of his material. This reviewer does not doubt Mr. Szulc, but the book is such a biting attack upon both President Nixon and Mr. Kissinger that his sources should have been more clearly revealed.

The account is chronological throughout. There is a Book for each year of Nixon's Presidency, with rather apt titles: for example, "1969: The Year of Promise"; "1971: the Year of Shocks"; "1974: The Year of the End"; each Book is divided into Chapters, each one chronological within itself. This means that the different subjects are treated in a hop-skip-and-jump manner, Viet Nam to Middle East to Detente to China, back and forth. Although somewhat confusing to the reader, this does have the advantage of relating these policies realistically to other current situations and problems. The account is detailed but fascinating, with special emphasis on the secretiveness and other devious methods employed by both Nixon and Kissinger. For example, the story of the preparations for Kissinger's secret visit to Communist China requires more than five pages, and reveals how the secret became known to the London *Daily Telegraph*—which refused to believe its own correspondent—and to the Joint Chiefs through the navy yeoman who was brought along as Kissinger's clerk-secretary in order to preserve secrecy. Mr. Szulc comments at this point: "Nearly everybody high in the Nixon administration, it seems, was spying on everybody else."

According to Szulc, foreign policy was "theater" to Nixon, which may in part account for his addiction to secrecy. The policy "had to be protected in its diplomatic secrecy from the prying eyes of bureaucrats, congressmen, news-

men, and the public at large . . . had to be swathed in secrecy until the architects themselves were ready to reveal the results." Beyond that, however, and presumably in further protection of the policy, Nixon is in each case directly accused of distortion and deliberate falsification. To bolster his public case, Nixon next plunged into an outright lie"; "The President engaged in further untruths"; "his administration policies were characterized by extraordinary immorality." This harsh indictment is easy to believe, in view of Watergate and all the rest, and in every case Mr. Szulc submits detailed evidence.

The same charge is also made against Mr. Kissinger, particularly with regard to the way in which he took over the State Department, even before he became Secretary, and made himself at least the President's equal in the making of foreign policy. Mr. Szulc believes that Nixon "must have hated" Kissinger because of the Nobel Peace Prize and his attitude, "proud and alone," with respect to the impeachment proceedings; and that Kissinger had not only expressed "intellectual contempt" for Nixon from the outset, but became "increasingly hostile to the President—in private." He was "hoping for Nixon's impeachment." In view of all this, it is easy to understand the title of the book. Mr. Szulc concludes with this sentence: "Having promised the 'structure of peace', Richard Nixon exacted an immense price from Americans—and from the world—for giving only the illusion of peace."

CLARENCE A. BERDAHL
University of Illinois
Urbana-Champaign

SOCIOLOGY

JUDITH A. BAER. *The Chains of Protection: The Judicial Response to Women's Labor Legislation.* Pp. x, 238. Westport, CT: Greenwood Press, 1978. $16.95.

The Chains of Protection is a vital and thorough examination of a complex and often haltingly enunciated area of law: the judicial interpretation of special labor legislation for American women. Beginning with 1872—when an Indiana statute that prohibited females and nonwhites from becoming licensed bartenders became the first piece of women's labor legislation to be challenged in an American appellate court—her analysis continues for roughly one hundred years of judicial handling and mishandling, and concludes with the adjudication of the Equal Pay Act of 1963 and Title VII of the Civil Rights Act of 1964 in various legal actions up to 1976.

This book succeeds at several levels. First, it has no peer as a carefully researched, insightfully analyzed, and lucidly penned examination of a narrow field of law that nevertheless has affected millions of Americans—both female and male—and has enormous economic, political, and social inter-relationships. But *Chains of Protection* spills over these analytic boundaries and by way of analyzing special labor legislation for women addresses a broader question: can legislation protect a class of persons without simultaneously chaining them in a disadvantaged position. Obviously this is an important question for all public policy analysts, even more so as government increasingly seeks to protect new groups of Americans.

Finally, *The Chains of Protection* succeeds in uniting two partners that often are quarrelsome to the point of destruction—commitment and scholarship. Baer's motivation for writing this book is made clear in her very first words:

This book is an effort to unite feminism and scholarship. It arose from my conviction that passionate commitment is compatible with dispassionate inquiry, and from my determination to explore the moral issue of sexual equality. (p. IX)

While passion may commonly subvert scholarship into a fact distorting and analytically strait-jacketed diatribe, *The Chains of Protection* provides convincing evidence that scholarship can coexist with passion, at least in the hands of a competent and ethical scholar. In-

deed, *The Chains of Protection* suggests that under favorable circumstances commitment can enhance scholarship, making the search for facts more aggressive, helping to frame the issues more precisely, making its analysis more full, and giving life to otherwise formless facts. For all these reasons, then, *The Chains of Protection* should be read not only by those interested in the subject matter that it examines, but also be those who appreciate sound scholarship for its own sake.

GEORGE R. SHARWELL
University of South Carolina
Columbia

JOHN BAKER. *The Neighborhood Advice Centre: A Community Project in Camden.* Pp. ix, 310. Boston, MA: Routledge and Kegan Paul, 1978. $16.75.

This book describes and seeks to evaluate an experiment in local governmental administration. It focuses on the establishment and operation of a citizen-based and citizen-operated agency in the Camden borough of greater London. The book's significance lies in the uniqueness of this kind of administrative mechanism—a notable departure from the legislatively-created administrative machinery made subject to direction by a chief executive, and charged with fulfillment of specific tasks for a specific clientele. It is common, under these arrangements, for the administrative agency over time to heed only its more vocal and influential clients, and to fall into a pedestrian manner of performance respecting the less visible claimants upon its services. An agency's sense of mission, indeed, eventually becomes one of locked-in responsiveness to only a few.

As a corrective, units of government in England and America are increasingly turning to administrative entities made accountable to some portion of the public directly, possibly a client group, rather than to a legislature and/or a chief executive. Tasks, priorities, and personnel are decided upon under broad grants of authority by a governing board drawn from the sponsoring group; current examples in this country include the community-level action programs fostered by Lyndon Johnson's War on Poverty, and the neighborhood-level system of public school governance set up in New York City and other places. Funds derive from specially granted powers or through earmarked monies from a higher level.

The Camden venture, and the case for this book, rests on this perspective. Several chapters early in the study document the demographic, ecological, and economic characteristics of Camden; the area, while diverse, contains many lower income renters, some in public housing. The heart of the study is the problem encountered by this group in making an impression on Camden borough hall. The elected borough council had no formal channel for communicating with these constituents; (political party discipline restricts efforts at establishing direct access to the council, except through the various party leaders). Unofficial channels thus had only limited clout; the borough's housing, health, planning, and recreational agencies chose to be attentive to the council, a few commercial groups, and the mandated requirements of their respective professions. Haggling led to an experimental-type solution—a neighborhood advice center, set up for a brief period and charged with (1) alerting borough residents, especially the poor, about various public services; (2) advising them on how they might pursue solutions to their problems through public channels; and (3) helping neighborhood residents articulate their aspirations, be aware of what was involved in pursuing them, and form priorities accordingly. New groups with new demands would be encouraged. Leadership and staffing were arranged through social action agencies, with borough council concurrence. Money came from the council, but much help was volunteer; so the sums involved were relatively small.

Four chapter's detail the center's work, and four assess its impacts. Giving information proved easier than raising a

neighborhood's consciousness (#3, supra). This difficulty had many roots; the poor's well-known passivity towards political action was one. The Center's relations with the borough executive and council were ambivalent; conflicts with executive departments were frequent inasmuch as the Center often suggested direct approaches to dealing with problems which bureaucrats found impractical. The Center had few qualms, for example, about advising constituents to disregard lines of command and "go to the top" with requests, or pursue grievances in wider public forums. The borough council viewed the Center more favorably; at least the poor's problems were still kept off councillor's desks. No grandiose schemes were proposed. As before, the council had time and means to treat with the poor only from afar. To the poor per se, the Center was most successful (according to surveys) as a vehicle for expediting tenant-landlord (public and private) problems. It was the council's busyness with other things that gave the Center its autonomy. Its autonomy underlay its successes; its brief life accounts for its inexperience and thus its difficulties. In all, viewed by results, the Center was successful. Reasons for non-renewal are not thoroughly explained, but the study's worth is commendable for a wide audience notwithstanding, on both sides of the Atlantic.

HARRY W. REYNOLDS, JR.
University of Nebraska
Omaha

AUDREY BORENSTEIN. *Redeeming the Sin: Social Science and Literature*. Pp. xxv, 269. New York: Columbia University Press, 215 pp. $15.00.

Audrey Borenstein wrote this book after she had finished a book of short stories. A teacher of sociology—with a background in anthropology—and a novelist, she felt that literature and the social sciences, as represented by sociology and cultural anthropology, had much to offer one another.

Though not original, her criticisms of the limitations of sociology and cultural anthropology in understanding the people who make up society are well-taken and I have no argument with her here. Sociological theory, unlike theory in the physical sciences, can hardly be used as foundation stones to create a better understanding of why we behave as we do in our many varieties of societies and cultures. And quantitative sociology depends largely upon its premises rather than upon its mathematical methodology. Public opinion polls and questionnaires can also disguise leading questions as well as biases, despite the rejoinders of pollsters.

For a novelist, Mrs. Borenstein has done an ineffective job in organizing her material. I found it difficult to pick up the book and read it through. The name-dropping in the first half of the book was a bit too much for my taste. I would disagree with her that George Peter Murdock is one of the "masters" of anthropology. And why, if she wishes to call herself a "humanist sociologist," does she not mention Alfred McClung Lee as one of the "humanist" sociologists?

After over fifty years of experience in sociology and anthropology (as well as being the author of an as yet unpublished fictional memoir), I would disagree that literature—with a few exceptions, many of which are not listed here—has much to offer sociology. At the same time, however, it is possible that most books on sociology, sociological journals, and papers at sociological meetings have little to offer the literary field. Personally, I have gained more insights from knowledgeable journalists, perceptive historians, and those few rare economists who can be eclectic among the choices to be found in economic theologies.

DAVID RODNICK

Lubbock
Texas

KENNETH E. BOULDING. *Ecodynamics: A New Theory of Societal Evolution.* Pp. 368. Beverly Hills, CA: Sage Publications, 1978. $15.00.

Kenneth Boulding is one of the great synthesizers, and *Ecodynamics* appears to be intended as his *summa*. All Boulding's familiar themes are evident: the importance of the scientific revolution from *The Meaning of the Twentieth Century*; the unity of all knowledge from *The Image*; the superiority of cooperation to competition from *Conflict and Defense*; and so on. Moreover, Boulding draws his themes together in a comprehensive "evolutionary" theory. The conceptual blocks are Teilhard's, but the shape is Boulding's. Teilhard's providentially ordered geosphere, biosphere, and noösphere are modified by Boulding to accommodate Modern Man and his chief work, the scientific revolution. The pattern is not biological, as in Teilhard, but social: the universe is a "stereo movie," with creative humanity providing the most affecting images though cultural evolution. Space and time are provided, but the image of what was, is, and ever will be has been left to the Man of Knowledge. "Ecodynamics," the pattern of evolution, is now more the work of Man than of God. Of all the animals, Man alone can "expand the niche" through the knowledge which forwards cultural evolution or destroy the niche through such stupidities as war and waste.

Boulding thus answers the economy vs. ecology question with the word economists and ecologists have in common—"equilibrium." His is a rubber-band world which can be stretched, but only so far. He acknowledges the danger of "overshoot systems" such as those outlined by the Club of Rome and Garrett Hardin. There are limits to "avoiding overshoot by niche expansion," namely, the have–have not gap, pollution, resource shortages, overpopulation, and the other evils associated with the "superculture." Economists and other social scientists have erred in assuming the easy equilibrium of celestial mechanics. But what interests Boulding most is stretching, flexing, testing, transcending: "It is important to realize, however, that no limits are absolute. The evolutionary process is one in which existing limits have constantly been transcended. . . . The classical economist saw economic development as the race between capital and population. We might broaden this to see it as a race between increasing knowledge and increasing scarcity." A "trinity of trinities" carries us forward or backward, although the principles of "noögenetics" are only similar, not like, those of "biogenetics." The trinity of Things, Organizations, and People (TOP) leaves a spawn of human artifacts with which to work; the trinity of Knowledge, Energy, and Materials (KEM) provides the motive force; and the trinity of Threat, Integration, and Exchange (TIE) gives direction and purpose through an inner structure of habits and behaviors. Nevertheless, equilibrium is the key concept: overshoot of the Threat System could produce nuclear holocaust; of the Exchange System, chronic Third World poverty; of the Integration System, too-great deference to authority with consequent tyranny and stagnation. Undershoot is, by implication, equally unwelcome. Man is the origin of social evil, be it a Brave New World or a World of Want.

Man is also the origin of social good, so *Ecodynamics* is the sequel to Boulding's non-Communist manifesto, *A Primer on Social Dynamics*, which was inspired by his encounter with Japanese radicals during a lecture tour in the mid 1960s. No solution to the crisis of the superculture can be found within the Threat System—that is, through class conflict. Nor can one be found within the Exchange System—that is, on the basis of classical capitalist self-interest. The solution must lie somewhere within the Integration System—that is, in collective, rational, moral, purposeful human effort. Thus Boulding claims his creed would, and should, lead "toward a realistic radicalism"; "Suppose one were to ask what changes in the noösphere in say the next 100 years or so, that is, in the totality of images of the world and the values placed on them, are most desirable from the point of view of the human race? In my own view the answer would be a transformation of radical ideologies to realistic visions. There is no hope in a stand-pat conservatism and in blind resistance to all

change, [but] it is the radical illusions, not the conservative coldness, that are the greatest enemies of the radical passion. If the radical passion is to be fulfilled, if we are indeed to move into a world that is better than what we have now, the radical illusions must be discarded and a realistic appraisal of the dynamic effects of human action must be widespread."

Boulding contends that today's sources of conservative threats to dynamic equilibrium are traditional religion, fixed ideologies, materialism, scientific reductionism, and technophilism. The radical illusions include, besides class interest and group welfare, the assumption that the rich must get poor for the poor to get rich, the notion that revolution is a kind of magic which creates progress out of ardor and ignorance, and the illusion "that it is easy to set up institutions in which things go from bad to better rather than from bad to worse." *Ecodynamics* is therefore quite unlike Rostow's *Stages of Economic Growth* on one extreme and Schumacher's *Small is Beautiful* on the other, because, in a sense, it attempts to marry the notions of getting what you want and wanting what you can get. Boulding is the Burke of the post-industrial revolution, a *philosophe* with his head in the future and his heart in the past, an economist with an ecological bent and a determination to map the "goodness function," a realistic radical seeking a revolution consistent with prudence and traditional ethics.

THOMAS J. KNIGHT
The Pennsylvania State University
University Park

DEVEREUX BOWLY, JR. *The Poorhouse: Subsidized Housing in Chicago, 1895–1976.* Pp. 254. Carbondale: Southern Illinois University Press, 1978. $15.00.

The author's role should have led to a revealing story. He is supervising attorney in charge of the office of the Legal Aid Foundation serving slum dwellers. He has produced a pedestrian account of the succession of architectural designs of public housing across forty years, showing that earlier philanthropic projects, like those sponsored by Julius Rosenwald and Marshall Field, did not point the way to sound public policy. "There is no evidence . . . that the housing has helped to make the residents more self-sufficient or contented, in fact the opposite may well be the case" (p. 221).

Bowley speaks in passing of the importance of good management, but he does not make clear that the management of public housing involves sensitive understanding of tenants' problems and readiness to devote time to dealing with them.

When I was the first director of the (then) National Association of Housing Officials in Chicago in 1934 I brought to the U.S.A. Miss Alice Samuel, a representative of the British society of public housing managers, to show that there was a career here that combined ability to read oil gauges with skill in dealing with the social and personal problems of the tenants and readiness to invest time in applying it.

Mr. Bowly does not set the housing program in its broader setting. The government of Chicago was dominated by the aldermen, whose posture was that they wanted no public housing in their ward. They also controlled the sanitation equipment, which bore the number of a ward and could not be used in another ward without the approval of the alderman.

Bowly reports the work of Miss Elizabeth Wood, the first director of the Chicago Housing Authority, who had a fine perception of the role that CHA should play. She reached understandings with Mayor Kelly that permitted her to refuse to make patronage appointments. She did not achieve similar rapport with Mayor Kennelly. When the political pressures became unmanageable she left. She had two young men on her staff as researchers: Martin Meyerson, now president of the University of Pennsylvania, and Edward C. Banfield. They sought to make the basic studies that an inert city planning department should have made. They voiced their frustration in a book, *Politics, Planning and the Public Interest*. Mr. Bowly identifies

them as teachers at the University of Chicago. They may have been asked to lecture there, but this characterization masks their role. The Chicago Housing Authority was simply not the base for city planning.

Mr. Bowly notes in passing that the social reformers who spearheaded the housing movement in the expectation that it would meet the needs of the depressed turned against it when they saw that better shelter alone did not cure their problems.

The title of the book seems patronizing. Indeed, the author's attitude toward the slum dwellers seems patronizing.

CHARLES S. ASCHER
Institute of Public Administration
New York

PHILIP J. FUNIGIELLO. *The Challenge to Urban Liberalism.* Pp. 273. Knoxville, TN: The University of Tennessee Press, 1978. $13.50.

The history of urban revitalization efforts in America has only recently been subject to serious scholarly review. Historians have in the past few decades, often in response to the growing urban crisis, begun to examine our national efforts at policy making and program implementation. Yet, there are still serious gaps in our knowledge.

One of those gaps is filled in admirable fashion by Philip J. Funigiello, an historian at the College of William and Mary. In *The Challenge to Urban Liberalism,* covering federal-city relations in World War II, Funigiello presents a thorough account of a period that augurs much of the urban problems of our own time.

The extensive migration from small towns and suburbs into the cities gave urban activists a seemingly perfect opportunity to work toward improving city life. There were, however, numerous obstacles that blocked revitalization efforts.

As is still the case, many mayors waited for direction and money from Washington before making needed improvements in their communities. Congress was wary of moving too quickly into uncharted territory. Important public groups felt that urban change could lead to undesireable disruptions of the existing social status. Furthermore, the public had generally adopted an attitude that it was best to deal with first things first: win the war and then take on social change.

And the President was none too helpful. Funigiello writes that Franklin Roosevelt "strongly believed that the future of American society lay in maintaining the strength of the countryside." Ironically, Eleanor Roosevelt is presented as a most prescient observer. She argued that urban needs in the future would demand a democratization of decisionmaking so that it would become more effective and responsive to the needs of all the people, not merely the privileged.

Funigiello writes about patterns of migration during the war, civilian defense, housing and community action plans, urban conservation concepts, federal redevelopment legislation; and he contrasts British and American postwar planning.

FRED ROTONDARO
National Center for Urban
    Ethnic Affairs
Washington

BARBARA J. HARRIS. *Beyond Her Sphere: Women and the Professions in American History.* Pp. x, 212. Westport, CT: Greenwood Press, 1978. $15.95.

The coming of age of women's historical studies is brilliantly exemplified in this work by Barbara J. Harris, professor of history at Pace University in New York City. In this collection of essays, originally presented as a series of lectures in the Pace Career Management Program for Women, she presents not only a historical account of the position of American women in regard to professional involvement, but also illuminates the European historical underpinnings of attitudes towards women. Harris' book constitutes an outstanding synthesis of the contemporary research into women's historical studies being conducted in America and abroad, and her venture is most successful.

Harris' careful analytical account begins with a thorough description of

the impact made on European attitudes towards the role of women by such phenomena as the acceptance of the ideas on the subject postulated by Aristotle and St. Paul, as well as by the widespread adoption of the cult of the Virgin Mary, and the antifeminist views embodied in the thought of the Protestant Reformation. These ideas and concepts were, to one extent or another, included in the intellectual baggage carried by Europeans to America, where they rapidly formed an intellectual foundation for what Harris terms an "ideology of inferiority" held by the male dominated society toward women.

By the late eighteenth and early nineteenth centuries, theories concerning women's place in a "cult of domesticity" were rampant on the American scene; a conceptual framework in which women were relegated to the home and to marriage while being arbitrarily imbued with supervirtues that they were expected to expend on their male spouses and offspring. Backed up by women's idealistic support, the men of America would be strongly bolstered in their efforts to successfully cope with nineteenth century society.

The author vividly depicts the efforts on the part of numerically small numbers of American women to offset the "cult of domesticity" through forcing entry into male dominated professions such as medicine, college teaching, and the law. In these efforts, which wreaked considerable psychological pain on the women involved, the pioneers of female engagement in the professions were not only opposed by almost all of the men of the society but by many highly articulate women as well. Those few individuals managing to gain entry into schools of professional preparation, and to obtain degrees, found that employment possibilities were almost nil in other than female run institutions and schools.

Harris continues her narrative through Victorian days and into the twentieth century, with an especially sharp focus on the disappointing environment for women following the adoption of women's suffrage; a reform which pushed all other women's issues to the side and which resulted in little of tangible worth to the feminist movement. The professions remained closed to all but a scattering of determined women until after World War II. The "cake of custom" was finally broken in the 1960s as a new and determined feminist cadre came to the fore in American society. Still, as Harris stresses, much remains to be done before a state of true equity exists insofar as women professionals are concerned.

Harris' volume is solidly based on exhaustive and intensive research into contemporary scholarship on women. Throughout her analysis she carefully examines historical theories regarding the position of women, as well as taking a critical look at recent historiographical explanations of these theories. In the process the author provides necessary correctives to the work of others and offers stimulating alternative explanations. Her book deserves to be widely read by those concerned with the historical and contemporary status of American women.

NORMAN LEDERER
Washtenaw Community College
Ann Arbor
Michigan

SHEILA M. ROTHMAN. *Woman's Proper Place: A History of Changing Ideals and Practices, 1870 to Present.* Pp. xiv, 322. New York: Basic Books, 1978. $12.50.

In this historically accurate and thorough work, Rothman delineates four distinct characterizations of women by society over the last one hundred years and examines the tremendous impact that each had in shaping public policy. "Virtuous womanhood" of the late 1800s developed into "educated motherhood" which was replaced in the 1920s by the move to "wife-companion" and finally was superseded by "woman as person" in the 1970s.

Tremendous technological advances in the late 1800s held the potential of liberating women from the drudgery of the home and menial labor and enabling her to use her energies in more constructive areas. However, increased leisure time for middle class American women did not result in educational pursuits or concentration on careers, but rather in an infatuation with consumption, which limited women's aspirations to the realm of the home as surely as the wooden scrubbing board had narrowed the outlook of their mothers. A virtuous woman, the ideal to which most women of the time aspired, was urged to develop appropriate skills corresponding to her natural endowments; caretaking, nurturing, teaching in order to become better wives, mothers, and social reformers.

Despite strong resistance from the medical community, women began to enter colleges. Physical education programs were especially designed for women to enable them to become 'fit to learn.' Since it was assumed that intellectual activities continually put women in a risk situation, intellectual accomplishments were relegated to a second place status. The role of a college education for women was to prepare them for the difficult task of child rearing and the concept of educated motherhood served to perpetuate the belief that women were the ideal teachers of the young. Although increasing numbers of women were entering the work force at this time, they were seen as temporary workers who were just "killing time" until marriage. Jobs with potential for advancement were not available to women and when women entered fields formerly dominated by men, such as elementary school teaching, salaries were cut in half. It was during this period that a sex stereotyping of occupations emerged which persists even today.

In the 1920s a shift occurred which resulted in a new role for women and a move, as Rothman says, from the nursery to the bedroom. Women were now primarily wives and companions to their husbands and thus responsible for making the marriage exciting to ensure their husband's happiness. Training for this new role came largely from college sororities. It was here that women learned the art of makeup, fashion, charm, and seduction. The dissemination of birth control devices initiated by Margaret Sanger strengthened the wife-companion ideology. Now sex was for fun and women knew that to be successful wives they must continue to be stimulating in the bedroom.

The emergence of woman as person came when America moved to the suburbs. Women, who had spent their lives dreaming of being a wife-companion, found the reality they lived in to be unbearable isolation. The move to woman as person was characterized by an emphasis on individuality and the belief that if the woman first made herself happy, the happiness of her husband and children would probably follow.

Throughout *Woman's Proper Place*, Rothman makes the important point that from the early suffrage groups such as the National Woman's Party, to the women's movement of today, women "have not been able to unite in a movement that would allow the identity of sex to override the differences in class."

In addition to being interesting and informative reading, the notes and index make *Woman's Proper Place* a valuable source book.

LES LEANNE HOYT
Arizona State University
Tempe

ECONOMICS

FREDERICK W. BELL. *Food From the Sea: The Economics and Politics of Ocean Fisheries*. Pp. xxiii, 380. Boulder, CO: Westview Press, 1978. $25.00. Paperbound $12.00.

Currently professor of economics, Bell has served as Chief of Economic Research for the National Marine Fisheries Services where he was responsible for all economic analysis and policy evaluation concerning the U.S. fishing industry. Noting that fish are sought for food, recreation, serve as a basis for animal feed and fertilizer, and are derived from a multiple-use environment, he attempts to answer, "What forces determine the present supply and demand for fishery products? More importantly, what steps are needed to utilize the full potential of the sea. . . ?"

A review of the situation and several answers to his questions are presented in the ten chapters which follow: Trends in World Fisheries; The Food Crisis, The Demand for Fishery Products; The Resource Crisis, The Supply of Fishery Products; Why Manage the Fisheries?; Environmental Deterioration and Fishery Resources; Fisheries for Recreation Use, The Sleeping Giant; Aquaculture, A Food Panacea?; Underutilized Fishery Resources; The Economic Plight of the Fishing Firm and Industry; and The Role of Government in the Fisheries.

The book is copiously annotated but, unfortunately, somewhat dated (e.g., the Appendix carries 'Current Fishery Statistics' which cover the years 1974-76). Given the dramatic changes which have and are occurring in the fisheries, those whose focus is *not* in maritime affairs would be misled. This is especially true for countries like the United States which have extended control over the continental shelf waters and/or their resources. Still, the 63 figures and 83 tables (primarily drawn from the last decade) are invaluable—and one must allow for publishing time lag.

Bell states that, "The purpose of this book is to provide the reader with the foundations of the economics of the fisheries" (p. 3). The readers he envisaged are ". . . two groups in particular: those who want a comprehensive treatment of fishery economics, or more precisely the political economy of food from the sea . . . and those who can use the book for courses. . . . Written for both the general reader and the student, this book requires no previous training in either biology or economics" (xxi).

And there's the rub. For the scholar the book becomes annoyingly simplistic and repetitious in many places, obviously stressing the emphasis on student readers (which is also marked in the summary which concludes each chapter and by the inclusion of a half dozen or so 'study questions' for each chapter). However, for those who are naive or in the dark completely concerning the growing importance of this 'stepchild' (politically, economically, socioculturally, and even in the natural sciences), this overview will present a great deal of very useful data and commentary—

which, hopefully, will encourage more attention to maritime matters before the pessimistic future which Bell foresees (p. 357) is upon us.

M. ESTELLIE SMITH
State University of New York
Oswego

CHARLES D. BRIGHT. *The Jet Makers: The American Aerospace Industry from 1945 to 1972.* Pps. 228. Lawrence, KS: The Regents Press of Kansas, 1978. $14.00.

Introductory works about the American aerospace industry often fail mainly because the admixture of scholarly interests in this field is so broad. Political scientists descend on the industry as part of the much acclaimed "military-industrial complex"; historians dig through the issues of aerospace development per se; economists find fascination with the hybrid form represented by corporate giants that depend for survival on specialized government markets; management scholars focus directly on issues of private research and development (R&D) management that exist within public sector accountability rules; and sociologists burrow into the industry by virtue of broader interests in power elites, often joined for part of the journey by policy analysts curious about American defense policy politics. The list looms endless.

Diversity of scholarly interest, congressional hearings and government reports notwithstanding, the uninitiated can get a solid foundation knowledge about the American aerospace industry by reading relatively few books. John Rae's *Climb to Greatness* offers first rate historical treatment of the industry. *The American Military Establishment* by Yarmolinsky and Neiburg's *In the Name of Science* are good explorations of the military-industrial complex. Weidenbaum, in *The Modern Public Sector*, writes lucidly about the institutional form represented by aerospace "primes." Excellent coverage of the salient managerial issues involved in aerospace programs appears in Sayles and Chandler, *Managing Large Systems*. Pace's *Negotiation and Management of Defense Contracts* is a fine technical introduction to federal procurement processes, and Fitzgerald's *High Priests of Waste* is an equally fine introduction to the seamier sides of those processes.

First and foremost, *The Jet Makers* is a highly readable update of Rae's *Climb to Greatness.* As such, it is very useful. Bright's nutshell portrayal of major forces that have shaped large aerospace "primes" over the last twenty-five years extends Rae's work in important ways. Bright also provides excellent insight into: (1) linkages between Air Force strategic preferences and consequent industrial development among its chief suppliers; and, (2) intricate interrelationships that have developed between corporate vitality, weapon system development/production, Federal procurement processes, and commercial activity in this industrial sector.

Bright's major problem is that he is not content to offer descriptive history. Rather, he sets out to determine, "How did the United States, which was behind in the race [for a balanced mixture of technological and quantitative superiority over the Soviet Union] in the forties, leap to the fore by the early sixties?" (pg. xv). Bright does not plausibly demonstrate that the United States was either militarily behind the U.S.S.R. in the forties or in the "fore" by the early sixties. Further, he puts narrow overemphasis on the jet engine and the U.S. Air Force as major shapers of industrial development, glossing over such highly important factors as electronics/avionics and the roles of other federal agencies as industry stimulator/customers. Finally, *The Jet Makers* fails as a scholarly work because Bright shuns argumentation and citation, even when making controversial points. Consequently, the neophyte reader has no way of knowing which points are controversial and of these, which are minor.

RANDOLPH KUCERA
Sangamon State University
Springfield
Illinois

BOOK DEPARTMENT

187

DAVID COLLARD. *Altruism & Economy: A Study in Non-Selfish Economics.* Pp. x, 221. New York: Oxford University Press, 1978. $15.95.

The recent literature challenging the philosophical and psychological assumptions regarding economic behavior utilized in neoclassical economic theory has been enlightening, but this book is a superb synthesis of prior attempts to separate rationality and self-interest. The theoretical basis of the work is to develop a theory of exchange based on rational nonselfishness.

The author utilizes the Edgeworth Box to show how consumption externalities provide a relevant altruistic model and the need for collective action. This brief excursion through welfare theory and public goods theory provides the theoretical structure to challenge the optimality of self-interest. The use of basic game theory and the "prisoner's dilemma" show the advantages of cooperation given a positive assurance by each player. This strategy brings a confluence of ethical systems that lead to cooperative behavior, including Bentham, Rousseau, Kant, Pareto, Rawls, and the Christian ethic of turning the other cheek.

The application of the theory of altruism shows how political strategies and public policy can influence a cooperative payoff in an assurance game. A brief discussion of the forces that have historically made consumers successful implies that only those small in size and bound by ethical, charismatic, or religious motives were long-lived. The discussion of voluntary contributions and taxation shows that the introduction of nonselfishness and moral forces does increase the redistribution via voluntary as well as political action.

The chapter on blood donors rests heavily on the previous research of Richard Titmuss. This discussion shows that the introduction of price, in fact, does not bring a better social result but ironically reduces the Kantian spirit of duty as well as reducing the contagion effect of altruistic action. This conclusion shows what can be termed a "moral Gresham's Law" and the author argues

that the contagion effect makes altruism like sexual potency—an act that is strengthened and developed by use.

Altruism and economics are best utilized in the discussion of future generations with respect to the depletion of scarce resources and environmental pollution. The central argument is that acts of collective investment are essential if the discounting rate or the technologies do not fairly protect future generations. The more altruistic the current generation, the greater the planned earnings and investment.

The goals of egalitarianism, efficiency, economic freedom, and democracy can best be achieved by an increase in altruism by example and exercise. The social dynamics of altruism can best be gained by understanding the relationship between action and human nature and by having political entrepreneurs act with moral force and not just from self-interest, enlightened or otherwise.

This volume is an excellent treatise. The only weakness is the brevity with which the author attempts to capture the history of thought on sympathy and the economic man. This book would be of great interest to scholars in ethics, philosophy, political science, sociology, and most importantly economics. The topic and treatment give the the book wide appeal. The ideas and theories in the book should stimulate exciting responses from a number of fields. This is an excellent treatment of a most important interdisciplinary topic of public choice and action.

W. E. SPELLMAN

Coe College
Cedar Rapids
Iowa

IRWIN GARFINKEL and ROBERT H. HAVEMAN. *Earnings Capacity, Poverty, and Inequality.* Pp. xvii, 118. New York: Academic Press, 1977. $12.00.

This monograph represents one of a series sponsored by the Institute for Research on Poverty at the University of Wisconsin. This highly empirical study is based on the judgment that measurement of economic status based on current income is probably misleading for policy purposes. The heart of the study centers around the concept of "earnings capacity" which is an index of economic status for a household unit designed to measure the potential rather than current income. It is defined ". . . as the income stream that would be generated if a household unit employed its human and physical assets to capacity." This analysis thus lies near the concept of "permanent" or "full" income developed by Dusenberry, Friedman, Ando, and Modigliani.

The book attempts to analyze the issue of the "worthiness" of the beneficiaries of public transfer payments. Opposition to income transfers in the past has centered around the assumption that the poor are in that state because they have failed to use their full capabilities. The authors conclude that low utilization of earnings capacity plays a relatively minor role in explaining poverty. This implies that neither laziness nor reliance upon transfer payments is responsible for low earnings of the poor. Only one-fifth of the observed income inequality can be attributed to differences in capacity utilization. Thus 80 percent of the variation in income is caused by factors other than differences in the application of a person's potential in the labor market. This particular conclusion may be subject to some debate if the statistical procedures employed by the authors are critically analyzed. The authors, however, have been careful to present any drawbacks or limitations in their statistical techniques.

One of the most interesting findings of the book deals with labor market discrimination in the United States. While discrimination in the labor market accounts for a small portion (3% to 6%) of overall inequality in the United States, it accounts for 43% to 60% of the total earnings gap between black and white males. It was found, based on the earnings capacity, that blacks who live in large families, and who live in large families with strong attachments to the labor market are more likely to be poor, than if the current income definition were used.

Furthermore, blacks of a given economic status have slightly higher capacity utilization rates than do whites of similar economic status. While many feel that poor families and blacks fail to take as much advantage of economic opportunities as whites, according to this study these groups utilize as much of their earnings potential as do rich and white households.

Although some of the analysis made for tedious reading and could have been moved to additional appendices, overall the study is a pioneering attempt to provide an empirical and conceptual framework for the examination of poverty in the United States. It breaks new ground in an effort to deal with a problem whose solution continues to elude policymakers. This monograph is a useful tool for government bureaucrats and serious students of the poverty problem.

RUSSELL BELLICO
Westfield State College
Massachusetts

BRUCE HEADEY. *Housing Policy in the Developed Economy.* Pp. 276. New York: St. Martin's Press, 1978. $21.95.

Is political science a science? If it is, then there should be discoverable principles by which a national policymaker could select the best program to meet a particular situation. *Housing Policy in the Developed Economy* is an effort to validate that proposition.

Bruce Headey teaches Political Science at the University of Melbourne. Having lived in England, having spent a year at the University of Michigan's Institute of Public Policy Studies, and having given some lectures at the University of Stockholm, he has put together a short treatise on the manner in which the governments of three advanced, stable societies responded to an issue which is abiding but not quite life-or-death, namely housing. The time frame is from 1932 to the mid seventies for Sweden and the U.S.; for the U.K. it stretches back to 1919.

Headey first defines the criterion for effective performance as equity—the degree to which households, despite differences in income, enjoy equally desirable housing or at least are benefitted to the same degree by government subsidies and authority. He appears to assume that all three governments genuinely espouse this goal. The book proceeds to sketch the political process of moving toward this goal in each country, involving the interaction of special interest groups—landlords, bankers, tenant unions, homeowners, local housing bureaucrats—and the emergence of innovative programs which sometimes don't. The plan of the book almost suggests a board game, some variation on Monopoly, perhaps.

The range of policy instruments available in the three countries are quite similar: rent subsidies, mortgage subsidies, mortgage insurance, income tax deductions for mortgage interest, tax treatment of homeowners' imputed rental income, public construction and ownership, and rent control. Overlooked are depreciation allowances, financing of municipal infrastructure, and antidiscrimination measures, which are significant in the United States at least.

Once into his historical accounts, Headey tends to lose sight of his equity criterion for the simple reason that all three nations, during most of the period examined, were mainly concerned with simply getting more houses built. Construction was at a low ebb during the thirties and through World War II when the inventories actually deteriorated; after the war unprecedented increases in family formation occurred. The problem and the catchword, then, was "shortage," not equity.

In Sweden it seems clear from this account that the government attempted to address the housing shortage in a manner calculated to produce equitable results as well, by concentrating upon large rental apartment block projects in planned settings for the two-thirds of all construction which was public or cooperatively controlled. Since government gave itself a virtual monopoly on land development and came to control most capital funds for house construction, the form and pace of building lived up to official expectations. However, rapid household formation had not been expected, so young couples still faced a ten-year wait for housing in the mid-1960s. A conservative shift in 1967 led to decontrol of rents and other changes which stimulated output and eased the shortage. Headey gives Sweden high marks for achieving substantial equity while ultimately accommodating sheer quantitative pressures.

In Britain the effect of government programs was to increase the role of council housing—owned by local government and assisted by national subsidies—at the expense of private rental housing; privately financed owner-occupied dwellings increased largely of their own accord, helped by indirect tax subsidies. Political shifts were far more frequent in Britain than in Sweden, and the housing spigot got turned on and off quite often. Successive fiscal and balance-of-payments crises also made housing efforts discontinuous, but progress was made toward expanding the inventory. As for equity, council housing is generally a step up for families renting in the private market, yet the public inventory is not homogeneous; applicant households are assigned to new, obsolescent, or undesirable council dwellings according to whether they are "respectable," "moderately respectable," or "problem" families in the eyes of the local housing inspector. Even the best council housing projects are not wanted in homeowner suburbs because a stigma is attached to public tenancy.

The housing policy of the United States, Headey observes, has been to stimulate private enterprise, or more precisely, homeownership. Mortgage lending for this purpose has been reformed and beefed up by risk-reducing programs such as mortgage insurance, the Home Loan Bank system, secondary market agencies, and in the depression the Home Owners Loan Corporation. The direct public cost of such programs is very small, but homeownership entails indirect fiscal costs because interest and property tax payments by owners are income tax deductions; imputed rent is not taxed at all. The effect of all these benefits is skewed toward the upper end of the income distribution. Publicly owned housing exists in very limited quantities and is politically unpopular. Programs aimed at subsidizing homeownership for low-income families have been tried but discontinued because of the direct public cost and also because of "horizontal" inequity—some families enjoying ownership under such programs while others with the same or even lower income fend for themselves in the obsolete private inventory.

Headey's interesting survey is burdened with a bias against homeownership. In all three countries, he concedes, the overwhelming preference is for this form of housing, and this makes one wonder why it is inequitable for governments to foster ownership. He suggests that part of the reason for the preference is that the public does not know that homeownership involves some public cost, but his cost-benefit argument is incomplete at best. The book provides food for thought, leaving more to be said on the subject of governments and the housing problem.

WALLACE F. SMITH
University of California
Berkeley

JAMES E. KRIER and EDMUND URSIN. *Pollution and Policy: A Case Essay on California and Federal Experience with Motor Vehicle Air Pollution.* Pp. vii, 401. Berkeley: The University of California Press, 1977, $15.95.

In many ways the environmental movement of the seventies has replaced the concern that was evident in the sixties over the United States' policies in Southeast Asia. Today on college campuses instead of hearing anti-war slogans we see posters of the earth with the words "Love Your Mother." This volume is a reflection of the changing priorities in the American culture. It focuses on attempts by both federal and state agencies to control air pollution in California during the years 1940–1975.

Pollution and Policy is more an histori-cal account of the area of the United States (i.e. Southern California) that first developed serious problems with air pollution resulting primarily from motor vehicle emissions. More than two-thirds of the text is an attempt to put the air pollution problem in California into historical perspective. The authors write in the preface that "A good grasp of the present required more than a glimpse of the past." True to their word the volume is substantially more than a "glimpse" of the past. While this analysis may be exciting to the historian, it may well be disappointing to the social scientist who had hoped for some type of rigorous analysis of contemporary pollution problems in California. The historical narrative contains an account of the early attempts to deal with the problems, state "experimentation" in the field of pollution control, and the beginning of federal domination of this public policy. Part IV deals with the years 1970–1975 and is an analysis of the Clean Air Amendments of 1970 and the problems confronted when officials attempted to implement many of the new anti-pollution provisions.

The most original, analytic, and best portion of the volume is found in the last section of the book where the authors identify five general "themes" discovered in their research. These are: 1) the policy process has been one of reaction rather than initiative and the reactions taken have usually been the minimum necessary down the path of least resistance; 2) those who wished to change the status quo were given the tasks of overcoming inertia and uncertainty; 3) the early policies adopted insured that the pollution problem would grow to "crisis" proportions; 4) many times policymakers limited their visions of possible solutions to technological innovations; and 5) the authorities authorized many studies which also resulted in the policymakers doing something about the problem which was not disruptive to anyone. Lastly the authors offer a valuable analysis of the federal air pollution program in which they claim that the ". . . reliance on uniform standards set without regard to costs is inefficient and inequitable. . . ."

The volume suffers from the drawback of being a "case essay" and thus does not offer the reader any comparative analysis. It is speculative, impressionistic, and lacks the rigor found in most contemporary public policy works. However, the volume is well written, contains a useful index, and concludes with some original and innovative analyses about one of the crucial problems of this decade.

J. A. RAFFAELE
New Mexico State University
Las Cruces

ERVIN MILLER and ALASDAIR LONIE. *Micro-Economic Effects of Monetary Policy: The Fall-Out of Severe Monetary Restraint.* Pp. viii, 228. New York: St. Martin's Press, 1978. $17.50.

This book launches a strong attack against the monetarist and/or laissez-faire views which guide the advocates of severely restrictive monetary policy as a tool to fight inflation. The first assault, in Chapter 2, is against the conventional wisdom which asserts that, since a sustained inflation cannot be supported without continual monetary expansion, rapidly and permanently reducing inflation necessarily requires severe monetary restraint. On the contrary, argues the author, by raising interest rates and, thereby, business costs, restrictive monetary policy is, in fact, inflationary! This is a well-worn argument: since interest payments are a business cost, rising interest rates act as a cost-push factor, just like rising wages, in pushing up prices. Moreover, he argues, this cost-push factor has become increasingly more important with the unprecedented levels of interest rates appearing since 1965.

The flaws in this argument are well-known. As well as increasing costs, rising interest rates—quite unlike rising wages—also directly reduce aggregate demand, particularly for construction, inventories, and consumer and producer durables. Moreover, they reduce capital values and, therefore, wealth while, quite apart from interest effects, monetary restraint reduces general

liquidity. Both these effects will tend further to depress demand. The critical question is whether the inflationary effect of increased interest costs is outweighed by the deflationary effect of reduced demand. In the conventional wisdom, supported by virtually all econometric evidence, the net effect of monetary restraint is deflationary. This does not mean, of course, that such effect is immediate or that it does not have serious consequences for unemployment or income distribution.

Chapter 2 is largely devoted to argument and evidence regarding the increasing importance of interest payments as a business cost and, therefore, as a cost-push factor in inflation. The major damning indictment of severe monetary restraint lies in Chapter 3 where the author considers the impacts on unemployment and output. There are serious and socially unacceptable distributional effects attached to this inflation cure. First, restrictive monetary policy (or for that matter, any contraction in aggregate demand) necessarily generates a recession and an accompanying rise in unemployment. Moreover, the rise in unemployment will be quite unevenly distributed across the labor force, falling most heavily on teenagers, blacks, Chicanos, and females; that is, on the already poor. The author details many of the well and not-so-well-known costs of unemployment; these costs are both private and social as well as monetary and psychological.

In Chapter 4, the author shows how new innovations in banking and money markets in the 1960s and 1970s have severely undercut the effectiveness of monetary policy while, it is already well-known, such policy may act with quite a long lag. This has led to the necessity for increasingly severe monetary restraint to produce any given outcome. Given lags in the effect of monetary policy, the net short-run impact of severe monetary restraint is simply further to jack up interest rates and unemployment with little effect on inflation. The anti-inflation effects will not result for some time in the future.

In short, the author concludes that

society cannot afford severe monetary restraint as a solution to inflation. It represents "bad economics and bad social policy and, ultimately, is immoral." (p. 123) That it is bad economics is clearly false; however, it is undeniably bad social policy.

The author's solution lies in "indicative planning," perhaps in the French mold. Chapter 4 presents a general overview of the considerations involved in such a plan. His view is quite Galbraithian. There already exists an enormous degree of planning in both the corporate and government sectors of the U.S. economy. Many of the elements of the author's indicative planning model are already in place. Nonetheless, such planning as exists is not coordinated, often is directed toward conflicting goals and does not necessarily operate in the public and social interest. The author's plea is, essentially, for extension and centralization of the planning mechanisms which already exist so as to operate the economy in a manner consistent with attainment of socially-desirable goals. Whether attainment of such goals (such as price stability and high employment) requires the elaborate planning mechanism envisioned by the author is arguable. Nonetheless, the point remains that any attempts to reduce inflation through severe monetary restraint or other restrictive demand policies will be in serious conflict with most other social goals. Greater coordination in the government's use of the various macro policy and planning tools at its disposal is certainly called for.

The last two chapters of the book, written by Alasdair Lonie, present a more detailed empirical analysis of the effects of rising interest rates on the company, housing and personal sectors of the United Kingdom economy over the past decade.

JON HARKNESS

McMaster University
Hamilton
Ontario

RICHARD SAUNDERS. *The Railroad Mergers and the Coming of Conrail.*

Pp. xiii, 375. Westport, CT: Greenwood Press, 1978. $25.00.

This is one of the best fact-and-map-packed books published to date on the history of the rise and fiasco of the American railroad industry, written from the standpoint of merger movement and Washington bureaucratic ineptitude. Professor Saunders has lucidly illustrated the cutthroat upheavals of the railroad consolidation movements, the heroes and villains, the Supreme Court landmark decisions, ICC's inertia, the Transportation Acts of 1920 and 1940, the rise and fall of Penn Central, and the birth of Conrail in 1976. If history were lessons for redressing errors made in the obstreperous mismanagement of today's railroads, this book would be a student's manual.

These events began with the Supreme Court's "narrowest-of-margins" decision, March 14, 1904, which ordered the dissolution of Hill's railroad empire-Northern Securities Company because it was judged in restraint of trade under the terms of the Sherman Antitrust Act of 1890. This spelled doomsday for railroad consolidation as a panacea for the ills of the enterprise. Subsequent prosecutions under the Clayton Act of 1914 and the Transportation Act of 1920 signalled government intent to regulate the industry for the public good. The former tightened nuts-and-bolts in the Sherman Act while the latter set rates for the enterprise and arrested the robber-baron acquisitive "binge" for a railroading empire. In 1917 the USRRA was created to meet the dire circumstances in the industry that were begging for action. Two years later, Glenn Plumb, of the militant wing of the Brotherhood, proposed a socialist plan as remedy.

The Transportation Act of 1940 and the Supreme Court decision in the McLean case of 1944 rubber-stamped consolidation in the public interest. The dieselization of the railroads in the years 1946–54 brought dramatic savings, capital, and prosperity to the industry. This, however, was short-lived because of the resurgence of truck competition which engendered a "crying-towel-syndrome" in the industry.

The 1960s produced the merger of Erie and Lackawanna and eight years of merged existence that accomplished none of the goals intended. In the East, West, North, and South mergers sprawled creating cartels and stifling competition. Penn Central rose in 1961 and fell in 1966. On April 1, 1976, the government came to the rescue by creating Consolidated Rail Corporation.

Despite overlapping chapters, the book is a tremendously valuable reference work.

JOHN B. ADESALU
Loyola College
Baltimore

JOSEPH H. SPENGLER. *Facing Zero Population Growth: Reactions and Interpretations, Past and Present.* Pp. xiv, 288. Durham, N.C.: Duke University Press, 1978. $18.75.

In the 1930s and 1940s, demographers forecast that the population of the United States would level off in this century. Although the population totals that were predicted turned out to be much too low, the post-World War II baby boom did not last. In recent years, fertility has again dropped sharply. It is now estimated that the aggregate population of the United States will peak sometime later than forecasted earlier, probably in 2015–2020 at 250 million. One would expect that shifting from conditions of rapid to zero population growth would have significant economic consequences. This book includes a review of the opinions of economists on the effects of population growth and its possible cessation. There is also a detailed analysis of the factors affecting population growth and the relationship of changes in population growth to age composition.

Before World War II, the Keynesian point of view that output would be adversely affected by slower population growth was generally held by economists. Primarily through its effect on expectations, slower population growth was thought to reduce total investment, to exacerbate the expected excess of saving over investment and, as a result of this imbalance, to create high levels of unemployment. The theory that economic fluctuations are caused by changes in investment is no longer as widely accepted as it used to be. If economic instability is instead caused by variations in the rate of expansion of the money supply (the conclusion of the more recent monetarist theories), no reduction in output would be expected to result from zero population growth.

The author believes that the most significant results of a change to a stationary population are related to its effect on age composition. The percentage of the total population aged 65 and over is expected to rise from 9.8 percent in 1970 to between 19 and 21 percent in 2030. Meanwhile, the male population aged 65 and over in the labor force has fallen from 45.8 percent in 1950 to 26.8 percent in 1970, and is expected to drop to 16.8 percent in 1990. An expanding retired population combined with a shrinking working population could make the maintenance of present levels of old-age benefits a heavy burden in the future. To reverse the trend toward early retirement, the author believes that a reduction in the incentives to retire under the Social Security System and private pension plans is necessary.

COLIN D. CAMPBELL
Dartmouth College
Hanover
New Hampshire

OTHER BOOKS

ADAM, ELAINE P., ed. *American Foreign Relations 1976: A Documentary Record.* Pp. xiv, 559. New York: New York University Press, 1978. $28.50.

ADORNO, THEODOR. *Minima Moralia: Reflections from Damaged Life.* Pp. 252. New York: Schocken Books, 1978. $11.95.

ANDORKA, RUDOLF. *Determinants of Fertility in Advanced Societies.* Pp. ix, 431. New York: Free Press, 1978. $19.95.

ANSCHEL, EUGENE, ed. *American Appraisals of Soviet Russia, 1917–1977.* Pp. 404. Metuchen, NJ: Scarecrow Press, 1978. $15.00.

AXINN, GEORGE H. *New Strategies for Rural Development.* Pp. 194. Dewitt, MI: Rural Life, 1978. $5.00.

BADEAU, JOHN S. et al., eds. *The Genius of Arab Civilization: Source of Renaissance.*

Pp. x, 231. Cambridge, MA: MIT Press, 1978. $15.00.

BAHL, ROY, ed. *The Fiscal Outlook for Cities: Implications of a National Urban Policy.* Pp. xvi, 136. Syracuse, NY: Syracuse University Press, 1978. $8.95. Paperbound, $3.50.

BARDACH, EUGENE. *The Implementation Game: What Happens After a Bill Becomes a Law.* Pp. x, 323. Cambridge, MA: MIT Press, 1977. $4.95. Paperbound.

BAUMONT, MAURICE. *The Origins of the Second World War.* Pp. viii, 327. New Haven, CT: Yale University Press, 1978. $22.00.

BAYLEY, DAVID H. *Forces of Order: Police Behavior in Japan and the United States.* Pp. 217. Berkeley, CA: University of California Press, 1978. $12.50. Paperbound, $3.95.

BECK, ROBERT C. *Motivation: Theories and Principles.* Pp. x, 470. Englewood Cliffs, NJ: Prentice-Hall, 1978. $12.95.

BEER, SAMUEL H., et al., eds. *The New American Political System.* Pp. 407. Washington, DC: American Enterprise Institute for Public Policy Research, 1978. $6.75. Paperbound.

BENNETT, GORDON. *China's Finance and Trade: A Policy Reader.* Pp. 256. White Plains, NY: M.E. Sharpe, 1978. $8.95. Paperbound.

BETTELHEIM, CHARLES and NEIL BURTON. *China Since Mao.* Pp. 130. New York: Monthly Review Press, 1978. $7.50.

BINGHAM, CAROLINE. *The Crowned Lions: The Early Plantagenet Kings.* Pp. 192. Totowa, NJ: Rowman and Littlefield, 1978. $13.50.

BOOTH, JOHN A, and MITCHELL A. SELIGSON, eds. *Political Participation in Latin America: Citizen and State, Vol. 1.* New York: Holmes & Meier, 1978. No price.

BRUGGER, BILL. ed. *China: The Impact of the Cultural Revolution.* Pp. 300. New York: Barnes & Noble, 1978. $19.50.

BRYM, ROBERT J. *The Jewish Intelligentsia and Russian Marxism.* Pp. viii, 157. New York: Schocken Books, 1978. $16.95.

BUTTON, JAMES W. *Black Violence: Political Impact of the 1960s Riots.* Pp. xii, 248. Princeton, NJ: Princeton University Press, 1978. $16.00.

CANETTI, ELIAS. *Crowds and Power.* Pp. 495. New York: Seabury Press, 1978. $8.95. Paperbound.

CIPOLLA, CARLO M. *The Economic History of World Population.* Pp. 155. New York: Barnes & Noble, 1978. No price.

CLASTRES, PIERRE. *Society Against the State.* Pp. 186. New York: Urizen Books, 1977. $12.95.

CLINE, WILLIAM R. and ENRIQUE DELGADO, eds. *Economic Integration in Central America.* Pp. xvi, 712. Washington, DC: The Brookings Institution, 1978. $19.95.

CLOUGH, RALPH N. *Island China.* Pp. vii, 264. Cambridge, Ma: Harvard University Press, 1978. $12.50.

COBB, EDITH. *The Ecology of Imagination in Childhood.* Pp. 139. New York: Columbia University Press, 1977. $10.00.

COHEN, STEPHEN P. and RICHARD L. PARK. *India: Emergent Power?* Pp. x, 95. New York: Crane, Russak, 1978. $7.50. Paperbound, $4.50.

COPLIN, WILLIAM D. *Teaching Policy Studies.* Pp. xvii, 204. Lexington, MA: Lexington Books, 1978. $17.00.

County and City Data Book 1977: A Statistical Abstract Supplement. Pp. lxi, 956. Washington, DC: U.S. Government Printing Office, 1978.

DAVIS, DAVID HOWARD. *Energy Politics.* 2d ed. Pp. 278. New York: St. Martin's Press, 1978. $12.95. Paperbound. $5.95.

DELBRÜCK, JOST. et al., eds. *German Yearbook of International Law, 1977.* Vol. 20. Pp. 569. Berlin, Germany: Duncker & Humblot, 1977. No price.

DEN TUINDER, BASTIAAN A. *Ivory Coast: The Challenge of Success.* Pp. xxi, 445. Baltimore, MD: Johns Hopkins University Press, 1978. $25.00. Paperbound, $7.95.

DIENER, EDWARD, and RICK CRANDALL. *Ethics in Social and Behavioral Research.* Pp. x, 266. Chicago, IL: University of Chicago Press, 1978. $17.00.

DOUGLAS, GEORGE H. *H. L. Mencken: Critic of American Life.* Pp. 248. Hamden, CT: Shoe String Press, 1978. $15.00.

DRAGNICH, ALEX N. *The Development of Parliamentary Government in Serbia.* Pp. 138. New York: Columbia University Press, 1978. $10.00.

DUNN, JOHN, ed. *West African States: Failure and Promise.* A Study in Comparative Politics. Pp. viii, 259. New York: Cambridge University Press, 1978. $27.50. Paperbound, $7.95.

ELLISON, WILLIAM HENRY. *A Self-Governing Dominion: California 1849–1860.* Pp. 346. Berkeley, CA: University of California Press, 1978. $16.00.

ELLWOOD, ROBERT S., JR. *Introducing Religion from Inside and Outside.* Pp. xi, 196. Englewood Cliffs, NJ: Prentice-Hall, 1978. $6.95. Paperbound.

ERICKSON, MARILYN T. *Child Psychopathology: Assessment, Etiology, and Treatment.* Pp. viii, 376. Prentice-Hall, 1978. $15.95.

ETZOLD, THOMAS H. and JOHN LEWIS GADDIS. *Containment: Documents on American Policy and Strategy, 1945–1950.* Pp. xii, 449. New York: Columbia University Press, 1978. $25.00. Paperbound. $7.95.

FARRAR, L. L., JR. *Divide and Conquer: German Efforts to Conclude a Separate Peace, 1914–1918.* New York: Columbia University Press, 1978. $12.00.

FEUERLICHT, IGNACE. *Alienation: From the Past to the Future.* Pp. ix, 273. Westport, CT: Greenwood Press, 1978. $19.95.

FOSS, DONALD J. and DAVID T. HAKES. *Psycholinguistics: An Introduction to the Psychology of Language.* Pp. xiv, 434. Englewood Cliffs, NJ: Prentice-Hall, 1978. $14.95.

FOWLER, ROBERT BOOTH. *Believing Skeptics: American Political Intellectuals, 1945–1964.* Pp. ix, 317. Westport, CT: Greenwood Press, 1978. $19.95.

GALAWAY, BURT, and JOE HUDSON. *Offender Restitution in Theory and Action.* Pp. vii, 212. Lexington, MA: Lexington Books, 1978. $16.00.

GOLDMAN, SHELDON, and AUSTIN SARAT, eds. *American Court Systems: Readings in Judicial Process and Behavior.* Pp. 600. San Francisco, CA: W. H. Freeman, 1978. $19.95. Paperbound, $9.95.

GOLEMBIEWSKI, ROBERT I. ed. *The Small Group in Political Science.* Pp. 519. Athens, GA: University of Georgia Press, 1978. $24.00.

GORDON, GEORGE, J. *Public Administration in America.* Pp. xii, 470. New York: St. Martin's Press, 1978. $13.95.

GUTTENTAG, MARCIA, ed. *Evaluation Studies Review Annual 1977. Vol. II.* Beverly Hills, CA: Sage, 1978. $25.00.

HEMINGWAY, JOHN. *Conflict and Democracy: Studies in Trade Union Government.* Pp. 184. New York: Oxford University Press, 1978. $15.50.

HINCKLEY, BARBARA. *Stability and Change in Congress.* 2d ed. Pp. viii, 213. New York: Harper & Row, 1978. $7.95. Paperbound.

HOGGART, RICHARD. *An Idea and its Servants: UNESCO from Within.* Pp. 220. New York: Oxford University Press, 1978. $13.95.

HOINVILLE, GERALD, et al. *Survey Research Practice.* Pp. vi, 228. Exeter, NH: Heinemann, 1978. $22.95. Paperbound, $6.95.

HOLLANDER, PAUL. *Soviet and American Society: A Comparison.* Pp. xxxiii, 476. Chicago, IL: University of Chicago Press, 1978. $7.95. Paperbound.

HOUSE, ARTHUR H. *The U.N. in the Congo: The Political and Civilian Efforts.* Pp. 435. Washington, DC: University Press of America, 1978. $13.50. Paperbound.

IPPOLITO, DENNIS S. *The Budget and National Politics.* Pp. 275. San Francisco, CA: W. H. Freeman, 1978. $12.00. Paperbound, $6.00.

JANCAR, BARBARA WOLFE. *Women Under Communism.* Pp. x, 291. Baltimore, MD: Johns Hopkins University Press, 1978. $16.00.

JONES, J. R. *Country and Court England, 1658–1714.* Pp. vi, 377. Cambridge, MA: Harvard University Press, 1978. $15.00.

KAGAN, DONALD, ed. *The End of the Roman Empire: Decline or Transformation?* 2d ed. Pp. xii, 188. Lexington, MA: D. C. Heath, 1978. No price.

KARSTEN, PETER. *Law, Soldiers, and Combat.* Pp. xviii, 204. Westport, CT: Greenwood Press, 1978. $15.95.

KASINSKY, RENÉE GOLDSMITH. *Refugees from Militarism: Draft-Age Americans in Canada.* Pp. 301. Totowa, NJ: Littlefield, Adams, 1978. $4.95. Paperbound.

KAY, DAVID A. ed. *The Changing United Nations: Options for the United States.* Pp. xii, 226. New York: Praeger, 1977. No price.

KEECH, WILLIAM R. *Winner Take All: Report of the Twentieth Century Fund Task Force on Reform of the Presidential Election Process.* Pp. xi, 82. New York: Holmes & Meir, 1978. $12.50. Paperbound, $5.75.

KELLERMANN, HENRY J. *Cultural Relations as an Instrument of U.S. Foreign Policy: The Educational Exchange Program Between the United States and Germany 1945–1954.* Pp. ix, 289. Washington, DC: U.S. Government Printing Office, 1978. No price.

KELLEY, ROBERT. *The shaping of the American Past.* 2d ed. Pp. xxvi, 846. Englewood Cliffs, NJ: Prentice-Hall, 1978. $15.95.

KETTERING, SHARON. *Judicial Politics and Urban Revolt in Seventeenth-Century France: The Parlement of Aix, 1629–1659.* Pp. xi, 370. Princeton, NJ: Princeton University Press, 1978. $22.50.

KIRALY, BELA K. and PAUL JONAS. *The Hungarian Revolution of 1956 in Retrospect.* Pp. x, 157. New York: Columbia University Press, 1978. $11.00.

KLASSEN, JOHN M. *The Nobility and the Making of the Hussite Revolution.* Pp. 180. New York: Columbia University Press, 1978. $12.00.

KRASNOW, ERWIN G. and LAWRENCE D. LONGLEY. *The Politics of Broadcast Regulation.* 2d ed. Pp. xiv, 213. New York: St. Martin's Press, 1978. $12.95. Paperbound, $5.95.

KUNICZAK, W. S. *My Name is Million: An Illustrated History of the Poles in America.* Pp. 181. New York: Doubleday, 1978. $12.95.

LADD, EVERETT CARLL, JR. *Where Have All the Voters Gone? The Fracturing of America's Political Parties.* Pp. 86. New York: W. W. Norton, 1978. $7.95.

LANE, DAVID. *Politics and Society in the USSR.* 2d ed. Pp. xvii, 622. New York: New York University Press, 1978. $25.00.

LANGTON, STUART. *Citizen Participation in America.* Pp. x, 125. Lexington, MA: Lexington Books, 1978. $8.95. Paperbound.

LEAKEY, RICHARD E. and ROGER LEWIN. *People of the Lake: Mankind and its Beginnings.* Pp. 298. New York: Doubleday, 1978. $10.95.

LEMERT, EDWIN M. and FORREST DILL. *Offenders in the Community.* Pp. xviii, 217. Lexington, MA: Lexington Books, 1978. $18.00.

LEVINE, STEPHEN. *Politics in New Zealand.* Pp. xi, 437. Winchester, MA: Allen & Unwin, 1978. $24.25. Paperbound, $13.50.

LEWIS, GORDON K. *Slavery, Imperialism, and Freedom: Essays in English Radical Thought.* Pp. 346. New York: Monthly Review Press, 1978. $15.00.

LIGHTFOOD, SARA LAWRENCE. *Worlds Apart: Relationships Between Families and Schools.* Pp. 257. New York: Basic Books, 1978. $12.95.

LYMAN, HOWARD B. *Test Scores and What They Mean.* 3d ed. Pp. xiii, 190. Englewood Cliffs, NJ: Prentice-Hall, 1978. $10.95. Paperbound. $6.50.

MACDONAGH, OLIVER. *Ireland: The Union and its Aftermath.* 2d ed. Pp. 176. Winchester, MA: Allen & Unwin, 1977. $16.25. Paperbound, $7.50.

MARSHALL, RAY, and VIRGIL L. CHRISTIAN, JR., eds. *Employment of Blacks in the South: A Perspective on the 1960s.* Pp. xiv, 247. Austin, TX: University of Texas Press, 1978. $17.95.

MASTERS, ROGER D. and JUDITH R. MASTERS, eds. *Jean-Jacques Rousseau: On the Social Contract with Geneva Manuscript and Political Economy.* Pp. viii, 245. New York: St. Martin's Press, 1978. $12.95. Paperbound, $4.95.

McCARTHY, THOMAS. *The Critical Theory of Jürgen Habermas.* Pp. xiii, 466. Cambridge, MA: MIT Press, 1978. $19.95.

McNEILL, WILLIAM H. and RUTH S. ADAMS, eds. *Human Migration: Patterns and Policies.* Pp. xviii, 442. Bloomington, IN: Indiana University Press, 1978. $22.50.

MILLETT, ALLAN R., ed. *A Short History of the Vietnam War.* Pp. xx, 169. Bloomington, IN: Indiana University Press, 1978. $12.50. Paperbound, $3.95.

MILNE, R. S. and DIANE K. MAUZY. *Politics and Government in Malaysia.* Pp. 415. Vancouver, CA: University of British Columbia Press, 1978. $15.00.

MORGAN, DAVID. *The Capitol Press Corps: Newsmen and the Governing of New York State.* Pp. xiv, 1977. Westport, CT: Greenwood Press, 1978. $14.95.

MURRAY, FRANCIS X. ed. *Where We Agree: Report of the National Coal Policy Project.* Pp. xii, 812. Vol. I, II. Boulder, CO: Westview Press, 1978. Two Volumes $37.50.

MUSGROVE, PHILIP. *Consumer Behavior in Latin America: Income and Spending of Families in Ten Andean Cities.* Pp. xxiii, 365. Washington, DC: Brookings Institution, 1978. $16.95.

NEWTON, GERALD. *The Netherlands: An Historical and Cultural Survey, 1795–1977.* Pp. xii, 300. Boulder, CO: Westview Press, 1978. $24.00.

OKUN, ARTHUR M. and GEORGE L. PERRY, eds. *Curing Chronic Inflation.* Pp. xiii, 297. Washington, DC: Brookings, Institution, $11.95. Paperbound, $4.95.

ORDESHOOK, PETER C. ed. *Game Theory and Political Science.* Pp. xii, 627. New York: New York University Press, 1978. $28.50.

PESKIN, ALLAN. *Garfield.* Pp. x, 716. Kent, OH: Kent State University Press, 1978. $20.00.

PRESCOTT, J. R. V. *Boundaries and Frontiers.* Pp. 210. Totowa, NJ: Rowman and Littlefield, 1978. $20.00.

PRESTHUS, ROBERT. *The Organizational Society.* rev. ed. Pp. 288. New York: St. Martin's Press, 1978. $12.95. Paperbound, $5.95.

PRESTON, ADRIAN, ed. *General Staffs and Diplomacy Before the Second World War.* Pp. 138. Totowa, NJ: Rowman and Littlefield, 1978. $13.50.

RANNEY, AUSTIN, and GIOVANNI SARTORI, eds. *Eurocommunism: The Italian Case.* Pp. 196. Washington, DC: American Enterprise Institute for Public Policy Research, 1978. $4.75. Paperbound.

ROBINS, PHILIP K. and SAMUEL WEINER. *Child Care and Public Policy.* Pp. ix, 234. Lexington, MA: Lexington Books, 1978. $19.00.

ROSE, R. B. *Gracchus Babeuf: The First Revolutionary Communist.* Pp. viii, 434. Stanford, CA: Stanford University Press, 1978. $18.50.

ROSSUM, RALPH A. *The Politics of the Criminal Justice System: An Organizational Analysis.* Pp. x, 287. New York: Marcel Dekker, 1978. $16.50.

RUBEN, BRENT D. ed. *Communication Yearbook 2.* Pp. xi, 587. New Brunswick, NJ: Transaction Books, 1978. $24.95.

RUSHMER, ROBERT F. *Humanizing Health Care: Alternative Futures for Medicine.* Pp. xii, 210. Cambridge, MA: MIT Press, $4.95. Paperbound.

SAID, ABDUL AZIZ, ed. *Ethnicity and U.S. Foreign Policy.* Pp. viii, 180. New York: Praeger, 1977. No price.

SCHICK, THOMAS. *The New York Constitutional Convention of 1915 and the Modern State Governor.* Pp. xv, 148. New York: National Municipal League, 1978. $9.00.

SHAPIRO, MARTIN, and DOUGLAS S. HOBBS. *American Constitutional Law: Cases and Analyses.* Pp. xvii, 766. Englewood Cliffs, NJ: Prentice-Hall, 1978. $15.95.

SHAW, G. K. *An Introduction to the Theory of Macro-Economic Policy.* 3d ed. Pp. x, 208. Totowa, NJ: Martin Robertson, 1978. $16.00.

SHERMAN, LAWRENCE W. *Scandal and Reform: Controlling Police Corruption.* Pp. 315. Berkeley, CA: University of California Press, 1978. $14.50.

SŁOMCZYŃSKI, KAZIMIERZ and TADEUSZ KRAUZE, eds. *Class Structure and Social Mobility in Poland.* Pp. ix, 211. White Plains, NY: M. E. Sharpe, 1978. $17.50.

STEVENSON, JOHN, ed. *London in the Age of Reform.* Pp. xxvi, 214. Totowa, NJ: Biblio, 1978. $17.50.

STOESSINGER, JOHN G. *Why Nations Go to War.* 2d ed. Pp. 246. New York: St. Martin's Press, 1978. $12.95. Paperbound, $4.95.

STOTLAND, EZRA, et al. *Empathy, Fantasy, and Helping.* Pp. 152. Beverly Hills, CA: Sage, 1978. $14.00. Paperbound, $6.95.

STREIB, VICTOR L. *Juvenile Justice in America.* Pp. 119. Port Washington, NY: Kennikat Press, 1978. $12.50.

SUMMERSON, JOHN. *Georgian London.* Pp. 348. Cambridge, MA: MIT Press, 1978. $17.50.

TAPINOS, GEORGES, and PHYLLIS T. PIOTROS. *Six Billion People: Demographic Dilemmas and World Politics.* Pp. xiii, 218. New York: McGraw-Hill, 1978. $5.95. Paperbound.

THURSZ, DANIEL and JOSEPH L. VIGILANTE, eds. *Reaching People: The Structure of Neighborhood Services.* Pp. 277. Beverly Hills, CA: Sage, 1978. $18.50. Paperbound, $7.95.

TOMASSON, RICHARD F. *Comparative Studies in Sociology,* Vol. 1. Greenwich, CT: JAI Press, 1978. $25.00.

TURNOCK, DAVID. *Eastern Europe.* Pp. xi, 273. Boulder, CO: Westview Press, 1978. $19.50.

VON WEIZSACKER, CARL FRIEDRICH. *The Politics of Peril: Economics, Society and the Prevention of War.* Pp. xi, 276. New York: Seabury Press, $12.95.

WEBER, GEORGE H. and GEORGE J. McCALL, eds. *Social Scientists As Advocates: Views from the Applied Disciplines.* Pp. 215. Beverly Hills, CA: Sage, 1978. No price.

WEEKS, KENT M. *Ombudsmen Around the World: A Comparative Chart.* 2d ed. Pp. xii, 163. Berkeley, CA: University of California, 1978. $7.00. Paperbound.

WEIL, GORDON L. *The Welfare Debate of 1978.* Pp. 134. White Plains, NY: Institute for Socioeconomic Studies, 1978. $8.00.

WINNER, LANGDON. *Autonomous Technology: Technics-out-of-Control as a Theme in Political Thought.* Pp. vii, 386. Cambridge, MA: MIT Press, 1978. $6.95, Paperbound.

WOOD, W. D. and PRADEEP KUMAR, eds. *The Current Industrial Relations Scene in Canada, 1978.* Pp. xiv, 693. Kingston, Ontario, CA: Industrial Relations Centre, 1978. $40.00.

WRIGHT, VINCENT. *The Government and Politics of France.* Pp. 280. New York: Holmes & Meier, 1978. $17.00. Paperbound, $8.50.

YATES, DOUGLAS. *The Ungovernable City: The Politics of Urban Problems and Policy Making.* Pp. xvi, 219. Cambridge, MA: MIT Press, $4.95. Paperbound.

ZWELL, MICHAEL. *How to Succeed at Love.* Pp. xxiv, 293. Englewood Cliffs, NJ: Prentice-Hall, 1978. $10.95.

INDEX

INDEX

RUSSIA AND THE UNITED STATES
Nikolai V. Sivachev
Nikolai N. Yakovlev
Translated by Olga Adler Titelbaum
Written by Soviet historians for an
American audience, this study traces
Soviet-American relations from be-
fore the American Revolution to the
human rights issues of the 1970s.
The United States in the World: Foreign
Perspectives series, edited by
Akira Iriye
Cloth   320 pages $12.95

THE CREATION OF A DEMOCRATIC MAJORITY, 1928–1936
Kristi Andersen
"This is the first study in the literature
which attempts to place mobilization
in the center of scientific analysis of
the New Deal realignment
sequence."
—Walter Dean Burnham, MIT
Cloth   176 pages $13.00

THE PASIEGOS
Spaniards in No Man's Land
Susan Tax Freeman
"This unique and fascinating study…
transcends the usual ethnographic
mode by dealing with local
ethnography, regional society and
culture, and national institutions and
ideology together."
—Davydd Greenwood,
Cornell University
Cloth   336 pages $25.00

chicago

F.D.R. AND THE PRESS
Graham J. White
"A good bit has been written
previously about Roosevelt and the
press, but never with such
thoroughness and perception….
Overall, White's [book] is sound,
innovative, and quite readable."
—Frank Freidel, Harvard University
Cloth   290 pages $13.95

MUSLIM NATIONAL COMMUNISM IN THE SOVIET UNION
A Revolutionary Strategy for the
Colonial World
Alexandre A. Bennigsen and S. Enders Wimbush
"This book goes far toward
explaining the seemingly irrational
attraction of many Muslims to
Marxism-Leninism, beginning in the
old Russian colonial empire in central
Asia. But it also has great
contemporary significance in today's
world where Muslim nationalism is a
powerful political force in the Mid-
east and has had, and continues to
have, a considerable ideological
impact in non-Muslim,
underdeveloped nations of the Far
East, Africa and Latin America.
Scholars and policy-makers will
obviously benefit from its research
and analysis, but so will anyone with
a serious interest in the appeal of
socialist doctrines to the third world."
—Robert Toth, *Los Angeles Times*
A Publication of the Center for Middle
Eastern Studies
Cloth   296 pages $20.00

THE UNIVERSITY OF CHICAGO PRESS
Chicago 60637

DEFENSE POLITICS
A Budgetary Perspective
Arnold Kanter

"*Defense Politics* shows how presidents and their civilian secretaries of defense attempt to control and work through existing military organizations to implement national security policy.... The normative implications of Kanter's work are important and obvious to anyone interested in civilian control of military organizations."
—John P. Crecine, Carnegie-Mellon University
Cloth   168 pages $12.50   May

FRANK MURPHY
The New Deal Years
Sidney Fine

"None need ever again attempt to set out the facts of Murphy's past in the prewar New Deal era; none need look anywhere for the relevant data except to the pages of this volume."—Philip B. Kurland
Cloth   720 pages   16 halftones $42.00   Available

LAW, LEGISLATION AND LIBERTY
Volume 3: The Political Order of a Free People
F. A. Hayek

This is the concluding volume of Hayek's comprehensive assessment and defense of the basic political principles which order and sustain free societies.
Cloth   224 pages $14.00   June

THE SUPREME COURT REVIEW, 1978
Edited by Philip B. Kurland and Gerhard Casper

"It is the repository of some of the best current critical commentary on some of the most important decisions of the Court."—John T. Flynn, *American Journal of Comparative Law*
Cloth   320 pages $30.00   Available

A SYSTEMS ANALYSIS OF POLITICAL LIFE
With a new Preface
David Easton
Paper   524 pages $8.95   Available

A FRAMEWORK FOR POLITICAL ANALYSIS
With a new Preface
David Easton
Paper   160 pages $4.50   Available

THE UNIVERSITY OF CHICAGO PRESS
Chicago 60637

Origin and Purpose. The Academy was organized December 14, 1889, to promote the progress of political and social science, especially through publications and meetings. The Academy does not take sides in controverted questions, but seeks to gather and present reliable information to assist the public in forming an intelligent and accurate judgment.

Meetings. The Academy holds an annual meeting in the spring extending over two days.

Publications. THE ANNALS is the bimonthly publication of The Academy. Each issue contains articles on some prominent social or political problem, written at the invitation of the editors. Also, monographs are published from time to time, numbers of which are distributed to pertinent professional organizations. These volumes constitute important reference works on the topics with which they deal, and they are extensively cited by authorities throughout the United States and abroad. The papers presented at the meetings of The Academy are included in THE ANNALS.

Membership. Each member of The Academy receives THE ANNALS and may attend the meetings of The Academy. Annual dues: Regular Membership—$18.00 (clothbound,

$23.00). Special Membership—contributing, $40.00; sustaining, $60.00; patron, $100. A life membership is $500. Add $2.00 to above rates for membership outside the U.S.A. Dues are payable in U.S. dollars in advance. Special members receive a certificate suitable for framing and may choose either paper or clothbound copies of THE ANNALS.

Single copies of THE ANNALS may be obtained by nonmembers of The Academy for $4.50 ($5.50 clothbound) and by members for $4.00 ($5.00 clothbound). A discount of 5 percent is allowed on orders for 10 to 24 copies of any one issue, and of 10 percent on orders for 25 or more copies. These discounts apply only when orders are placed directly with The Academy and not through agencies. The price to all bookstores and to all dealers is $4.50 per copy ($5.00, clothbound) less 20 percent, with no quantity discount. Orders for 5 books or less must be prepaid (add $1.00 for postage and handling). Orders for 6 books or more must be invoiced.

All correspondence concerning The Academy or THE ANNALS should be addressed to the Academy offices, 3937 Chestnut Street, Philadelphia. Pa. 19104.